# St Michael's School, Otford

Recollections, Observations, and Celebrations

# St Michael's School, Otford

Recollections, Observations, and Celebrations

The story of St Michael's School, Otford, since its foundation
in Hatcham, New Cross, in 1872

## Researched and written
by
Sally Maria Jones

AMHERST

ISBN 1 903637 22 8

Printed in Great Britain

First published in 2004 by

**Amherst Publishing Limited**
Longmore House, High Street, Otford, Sevenoaks, Kent TN14 5PQ

Dedicated to teachers, staff, parents, and students - past and present - and to everyone who has played a part in the rich history of St Michael's School

# Foreword

I am delighted to have the opportunity to write the foreword to this book.

St Michael's is a remarkable school. From its foundation by Father Tooth in 1872 through successive Wardens and Headmasters it has kept its ethos of a caring, moral, well mannered and happy environment where children can flourish in whatever field they wish. It also still continues its religious origins.

Over the last few years the Governors have committed very significant capital investment to the development of the school buildings and facilities; bringing the school from a 50 pupil, boys only boarding school, to a 400 plus coeducational day school.

I am sure, as you read the book you will be enthralled as Sally Jones guides you through an amazing story of kindness and dedication, told so well by many anecdotes of past pupils.

As a pupil in the 40s and 50s and now as Chairman of the Governors, St Michael's has a very special place in my life. I have said to many people during my life, that without St Michael's, Father Blofeld and Donald Cormack, I would never have achieved what I have. For that I give thanks.

I wish St Michael's all success and happiness in the future and thank Father Tooth for its foundation.

Gordon Owen CBE
Chairman of the Governors

# Preface

Taking over as Headmaster of St Michael's in September 2003 was an exciting challenge. With its superb site, an impressive new development nearly completed, happy pupils and a very caring, professional staff, the attractions of the school were evident immediately.

The £2 million development includes two new science laboratories, an art room and kiln room, two classrooms, a doubling in size of the existing dining room to enable a drama room to be created, and very large changing rooms. All areas of the main school will then be under one roof and able to be accessed internally. A further loft space is available to be completed at a later date.

Returning past pupils will see major changes made to the site over the last 10 years but I hope they will still recognise the ethos of St Michael's: a school where each pupil genuinely has every chance to flourish in a wide range of areas as well as making the best level of academic progress suited to their ability.

The last few years have seen changes in the leadership of the school and this current year has included a period of consolidation as we press ahead with the aim to make St Michael's the leading co-educational prep school in this area.

Keith Crombie
Headmaster 2003 -

# Contents

# Introduction

**"You must begin well – if you don't, you will not get very far. If you don't begin well – you will find when you get to the end what a howling mess you have made of the whole thing.**

**Let me risk it..."**

The words of Arthur Tooth, aged 87 in 1927.

With these wise words from the founder of St Michael's School, Otford, Father Arthur Tooth acting as a warning to me, I commenced the arduous task of sorting, logging and filing letters, pamphlets, newspaper cuttings, photos, newsletters and other evidence of the history of St Michael's. It was Dr Roots (Headmaster from 1996 to 2002) who launched the school archiving project with the help Old Michaelian Paul Barraclough [1935/38] who showed his deep commitment to the school by transcribing the handwritten logbooks covering the years 1916 to 1941 into 150 pages of typed text. Dr Roots was fascinated by what he read and selected pieces to include in the school's weekly newsletter. A logbook for 1982 to 1986 was also discovered covering some of Revd Paul Cox's Headship.

My involvement came as a result of a plea in one such newsletter asking for help with the archiving project. With three children at the school and a love of history, I marched into the Headmaster's office the next day and offered my services. Little did I know what I was letting myself in for.

On that first day I was handed a couple of boxes and bin liners (!) of papers that had not been looked at for fifty or more years and I was instantly entranced. I started to forage in drawers and boxes and the more I looked the more I found. There were photo albums belonging to past Headmasters (in a terrible state of repair caused by damp), admission records, newsletters, personal letters, minutes of Governors' meetings, architects' plans, invoices and accounts. All higgledy-piggledy. My home office was soon taken over by dusty books and boxes, as the 'great sort' got under way. Two years later, most of the historically interesting material has been filed carefully into fifteen or so extra-large ring-binders. Archiving is a never-ending project, so I cannot begin to guess how large the collection will grow to over the coming years.

It soon became obvious that the material I was unearthing would merit the writing of a book and with Dr Root's whole-hearted support I began to research into the beginnings of the school and its famous founder, Father Arthur Tooth. Material was to be found at Croydon Library, Asburton Library in Addiscombe (a former site of St Michael's) and of course, on the Internet! I made 'virtual' friends all over the globe – people who have a deep interest in Anglo-Catholic traditions who were delighted that Father Tooth was being 'resurrected'. Thus the first few chapters covering the early years of St Michael's were drafted.

The next job was to track down Old Michaelians. I had been convinced from the earliest stages of the project that the bulk of the book had to be written by the people who actually attended the school. I did not want the book to be a mere factual account of the school's history that would be loyally purchased by friends of St Michaels - but then left on the shelf. I wanted the book to *live* through the personal anecdotes of those who loved or loathed their time at the school and to be read by adults and children alike. I have been astounded by the intensity of emotions and the vividness of memories that have been flushed out.

The structure of the book: chronological chapters (focussing on portraits of the various Wardens and Headmasters) interspersed with themed chapters, is designed to take the reader on a colourful journey from the school's earliest beginnings in 1872 to the present day. Anecdotes from Old Michaelians are *italicised* and logbook entries have a rule above and below.

**"Very few of us (if any) quite outgrow the personal conditions of birth, early education and associations – they remain in the background more or less until the end of life"**

**Father Tooth in 1917**

The search for Old Michaelians was greatly helped by the existence of the Old Michaelian Association which was founded in 1948 and has held annual reunions ever since. After writing to all those on the OMA address list, I put adverts in local papers, a plea on Radio 2 and searched the internet. This last method proved to be the most fruitful and many OMs must have been surprised by contact out of the blue from me. One such surprise was for Eric Crabbe who attended St Michael's from 1934 to 1938. I tracked him down with the knowledge (from a 1947 school newsletter) that he had been in the British South African Police. I found a BSAP forum, asked if anybody knew of his whereabouts and 24 hours later I had his phone number. His astonishment at hearing a voice from Old Blighty, asking him for memories of his schooling 70 years ago, must have been great (especially as I got him out of bed – sorry Eric!) but he has been an enthusiastic contributor to the book since that day.

Many of the OMs contacted sent me wonderful descriptions of life at St Michael's and personal memorabilia, for which I am very grateful. The vast majority of anecdotes and memories came from people for whom nostalgia had 'kicked in' so I'm assuming there will be regular reprints of this book to include memories from students from the 1960s onwards.

I also managed to contact all living ex-Headmasters, all who have given enthusiastic support to the book and have made their own significant contributions, in their own words.

For the most part, I have tried to keep my voice out of the book and have shied away from passing judgement. The balance of the book comes from the contributions received and obviously those who remember their time at the school with fondness have waxed lyrical, whereas those with more negative thoughts have stayed quiet. As with any school, particularly with boarding schools in the days of corporal punishment, rigid adherence to religious ritual and dogma, and little parental influence, there have been some aspects of life at St Michael's which might shock parents in the 21$^{st}$ century.

Equally, there will be many OMs who will read this book and will mourn the loss of the identity of the school which Father Tooth had maintained during his lifetime and which was in existence for 60 years after his death. The 1990s was a turning point for the school. It could no longer survive as a tiny boarding school for boys, with a heavy high-church atmosphere and charging minimal fees. As was soon discovered by Simon Cummins (Headmaster from 1990 to 1996), the real educational need was for local, high quality day schooling with top-quality facilities – and parents were willing and able to pay top fees for the privilege. The school now has more than 400 pupils (girls and boys) and a long waiting list. As Tony Rumm [1946/49], Chairman of the Old Michaelian Association, wrote to an Old Michaelian who feared Father Tooth would be turning in his grave:

> *"I have to admit that going back to St Michael's now, I marvel that so many children can take advantage of a superb education and enjoy fabulous grounds and facilities albeit the cost is roughly £2500 per term instead of £45 in our day!"*

One thing I am absolutely sure of is that this book will provoke thought, laughter and even heated debate. I am also sure that now that it is in print wonderful stories will emerge which I would have loved to have included. There will certainly be further editions, so I encourage all OMs and friends of St Michael's to contribute to this on-going project.

Through the help and enthusiastic support of Old Michaelians, past and present staff and the Governors I hope I have avoided making a 'howling mess' of this school's fascinating history.

# Acknowledgements

There are many, many people to thank for their support in the production of this book. Too many to mention each individually. However, amongst Old Michaelians, the following stand out for special mention:

**Paul Barraclough** [1935/38] for his painstaking transcription of the lengthy Log Books from 1916 to 1941. This must have been an incredibly time-consuming and arduous task - the handwriting is almost indecipherable at times - but no doubt both fascinating and rewarding. No task better illustrates his tremendous loyalty towards the school. He has also donated an enormous amount of material for the archives and has helped me with the book, every step of the way.

**Douglas Keddie** [1923/31] for being the first 'archivist' of St Michael's material. He is the oldest Old Michaelian and luckily for the school (and for this book) he has been collecting memorabilia and photos since he started at the school in 1923!

**Tony Rumm** [1946/49] for having the memory of an elephant! Without his magnificent powers of recollection, many of the boys in the photos would remain unidentified. As Chairman of the Old Michaelian Association he has also provided continuous and unflinching support for the whole project.

**The Board of Governors** who have believed in this book from the start. Also grateful thanks to the current **Headmaster, Keith Crombie**, whose enthusiastic support gave a significant boost to my confidence just as my spirits were flagging.

Lastly, thanks to my family for putting up with me and especially to my Mother who proof-read the draft for me.

Wherever possible the book has been based on the memories of people who actually attended the school. Every effort has been taken to check the accuracy of facts but inevitably memory will colour some events or play tricks. Please accept this book in the spirit in which it has been compiled.

Every effort has also been made to trace authors of copyright material. Regpretably this has not always been possible and in these cases I offer my sincere apologies and ask for the author or photographer's understanding.

* * *

# Arthur Tooth

'A young slim clergyman with a thoughtful countenance, marked self-possession, and possessing great extemporaneous powers.'

# ~ 1 ~

# The Founder: Arthur Tooth

## The Early Years

The founder of St Michael's, Arthur Tooth, was born into a large family on 17 June 1839. He was the tenth child of Robert Tooth and Robert's first wife, Mary Ann Reader. The family lived at Swift's Park, a substantial mansion house in Cranbrook, Kent. Arthur's father had a large estate, was a Justice of the Peace and prosperous hop merchant. His uncle John was a successful brewer who emigrated to Australia and founded the Tooth's Kent Brewery in Sydney. Arthur's brothers Robert Jnr., Edwin and Frederick all went into the brewing business with interests in Australia and England.

At the age of eleven Arthur began his public education. He went to Tonbridge School (Judde House) under Dr Wheldon, and then on to Trinity College, Cambridge to read science where he obtained a BA in 1862 and an MA in 1865.

Soon after leaving university Arthur travelled round the world – twice! Whilst in the Far East he collected many beautiful and strange curiosities and he added to this collection with a large number of ecclesiastical artifacts from Europe. Not much else is known about these years though it can be assumed that his travels gave him a sense of adventure, independence and self-reliance.

One story from his travels illustrates these qualities in the young man. During one of his visits to Australia (presumably visiting his brothers) he joined a large party of people who were out on a shooting expedition in the bush of Queensland. He somehow became separated from the rest of the group and although a search party went out looking for him, they eventually had to call off the search and give up all hope of finding him alive. However, the young Arthur was very resourceful and used his knowledge of the stars to navigate his way across the plains to a river shelter and eventually to safety.

Arthur's brother Robert combined a career in commerce with religious and political responsibilities but Arthur rejected commercial life for a life within the Anglican Church. On returning from his travels he was ordained a Deacon by Charles Richard, Bishop of Winchester, in 1863, and his first curacy was at St Mary-the-less, Lambeth. In the following year he was appointed curate of St Michael's, Folkestone but did not stay there long either.

He spent the next three years as curate-in-charge of St Mary Magdalene Chapel at Chiswick where he is said to have lived very frugally and was able to make generous gifts of food to those in need even when it was intended for him.

Chiswick
5 May 1868.

Dear Sir
We beg to send you a Cross & a Pair of Candlesticks for the Altar, which we hope you will accept as a slight token of our high Esteem and affection for you.

We beg to assure you that it is with very deep regret on our part, that it is necessary that you should take your leave of us.

He was obviously well-respected and well-liked. This letter was signed on behalf of more than 60 of his grateful parishioners on his departure. Their gift of a pair of candlesticks and a cross would have been very gratefully received by Tooth.

## St James', Hatcham

Arthur's next move was a surprising one. His brother Robert had been Church Warden of St James' in Hatcham, New Cross, soon after the church was first built in 1845. By 1867 the unfinished church had fallen into a terrible state of disrepair after a period of four years without a Vicar.

St James' Church at the end of Church Road (now known as St James's)

There were building debts, a dilapidated vicarage and a congregation of 'moths, spiders, black beetles and kindred objects….whose time of excommunication had now arrived'.

This dubious gift was the advowson (the right in English law of presenting a nominee to a vacant ecclesiastical benefice) that the barrister Robert Tooth Junior bought for his brother in 1867 – presumably to preserve the high church tradition introduced by him as warden. Arthur took his place as Vicar there on 25 August 1868.

Father Arthur Tooth immediately set about renovating the church and reintroducing a congregation. As reported in a local newspaper several years later, he did this with the minimum of fuss:

> [Mr Tooth] came in without any blast of trumpet, without any introductory 'palaver',
> without any demonstration whatever. Any stranger visiting the church on the first
> Sunday or so of Mr Tooth's vicariate, would have heard sermons from a young
> slim clergyman with a thoughtful cast of countenance, marked self-possession,
> and possessing great extemporaneous powers.

The Irish Times was less complimentary, stating that 'his voice is squeaky' and that 'there is little in his appearance to attract anyone, for it is priestly rather than manly' and that 'he looks as though he had stepped out of a pre-Raphaelite painting.'

The inside of St James' Church during Arthur Tooth's time as Vicar

The new vicar added a sacristy and a baptistery, the sanctuary was furnished and decorated, and a second altar erected in the Lady Chapel - much of the work done at his own personal expense.

He also introduced a number of practices which at the time were thought by many to savour of Popery, although they were strictly in accordance with the provisions of the Book of Common Prayer rubrics. He introduced the daily Mass, daily Matins and Evensong, and a Sung Mass on Sunday, which was preceded by Matins.

Within five years all the 'Six Points of Ritual' that defined Anglo-Catholic practice were introduced: the Eastward Position (in which the celebrant faces the altar during the Consecration), Eucharistic Vestments, the Mixed Chalice, Altar Lights (candles on the altar), Unleavened Bread at the Eucharist, and Incense.

A journalist for the Croydon Reporter asked him, many years later in April 1912, when he had adopted such an affinity with Catholic practices. 'He said almost from childhood. Although brought up in a Protestant home, directly Catholic truth was presented he seemed instinctively to realise its beauty and to feel that a worship consisting of negations was insufficient'.

Father Tooth abolished pew rents so that the church was now open to rich and poor on equal terms, and the ability to pay for a seat no longer ensured precedence. He also abolished fees (except for bridegrooms at weddings) and refused to take collections at church services and baptisms – a move that won over parishioners to whom money was an ever-pressing problem. St James' Church soon attracted a large congregation from the parish and beyond its borders through his simple, straightforward teaching from the pulpit.

# St Michael's

It was during this time of great change that Arthur Tooth founded St Michael's. In 1872, at the age of thirty-three, he set up a convent in Laurie Grove, Hatcham, called the Community of Sisters of the Paraclete, which housed six nuns. He then rented three houses next to the church in the avenue of St James (or Church Road) in order to open two 'orphanages' - St Michael's for boys, and St Gabriel's for girls. He also opened a home for alcoholics known as St Raphael's.

St Michael's started with twenty-four fatherless boys from the age of eight to fourteen who needed a good education and it was run partly by the sisters. One of his objectives was to provide a disciplined and well-trained choir for the church as the one he had inherited at St James' lacked dedication and commitment.

# The Troubles Begin

Two years after the foundation of St Michael's (its official foundation date being 25 April 1872), Parliament introduced the Public Worship Regulation Act in order to put down 'Ritualism' and 'the Mass in masquerade'. It had the active support of Queen Victoria, Lord Shaftesbury, Disraeli the Prime Minister, and Dr Tait, the Archbishop of Canterbury. Under this act a new court was set up, presided over by ex-Divorce Court Judge, Lord Penzance. It was an entirely secular court, without any authority from the Church but it could deprive clergy of their living or even imprison them.

As the Croydon Reporter reported in 1912:

> The Act was passed at a time when the Oxford Movement was fresh in men's minds and Dr Pusey was in the ascendancy. A force to be reckoned with. Religious bitterness and prejudice, second to nothing in its intensity, was rife, and machinery was provided to put down ritualistic practices. Clergyman after clergyman was proceeded against, with but one result, to prove the utter impotence of an Act of Parliament which has long been a dead letter.

In March 1876, Father Tooth received notice from the Bishop of Rochester that legal proceedings under the new Act were impending. The charges were: the use of Eucharistic Vestments, Lighted Candles, Incense, Mixed Chalice, Eastward Position, Genuflexion, Elevation of the Host, the sign of the Cross at the Absolution and Blessing, the singing of the Agnus Dei, and various other things such as the wearing of birettas.

Arthur Tooth, in a series of letters addressed to the Bishop and published in the press, flatly denied the authority of the new Act of Parliament and he made it very clear that he would make a stand on the grounds of conscience. He also claimed to have a petition of 1452 signatures of parishioners who "are not distressed by the Services and teachings of this church, they pray that no difficulty may be placed in my way to limit or hinder my work in my parish" [The Church Review 11 March 1876]

In July 1876, Father Tooth's case was heard undefended and he was ordered to refrain from the various practices outlawed by the Act. The church ornaments were to be removed and he was ordered to pay the costs.

However, Father Tooth took no notice of the judgement and the services carried on just as before.

Again in December he was called in front of the judge, but refused to appear despite his name being called three times. This time he was formally 'inhibited' and suspended from performing Divine Service for three months – a penalty that would continue unless he intimated his intention to conform to the order of the Court. Father Tooth remained defiant and matters came to a head on Christmas Eve 1876 when he refused to allow the Bishop's Chaplain to conduct Mass at St James', turning the Chaplain away at the door of the church.

The situation turned very nasty after Christmas Day when a series or riots began which were organised and paid for by the 'Protestant underworld'. 'Men of the lowest type' were paid two shillings or more each Sunday to protest outside the church. However, Catholic supporters also came in their hundreds and Mass was conducted amid the hisses and blasphemous jeering of the rioters.

After the service, Arthur Tooth had to be escorted to the vicarage by a body of faithful followers whilst windows were smashed, the doors of the church broken open and members of the congregation assaulted. Despite large numbers of police, the riots continued and hastily erected barriers were broken down.

# Imprisonment

These riots continued every Sunday until 21 January 1877, but on 22 January Arthur Tooth was arrested and taken to Horsemonger Lane Gaol – the crime being contempt of court. It was the thick of winter and despite a small fire in his cell, the cold was intense and Tooth wore his muffler, heavy coat and even his hat in an attempt to keep warm. He had plenty of visitors but the routine was 'oppressively monotonous'. The sympathetic public longed to show their support, so when Father Tooth wrote to the newspapers appealing for funds for St Michael's orphanage, the money poured in.

Cartoon entitled 'The Christian Martyr' which appeared in Vanity Fair on 10th

The words of Father Tooth, fifty years after the event, as retold by Revd Desmond Morse-Boycott (author and founder of The St Mary of the Angels Choir School), give a picture of Arthur Tooth's life during the first part of 1877:

'He told me the story one day after I had walked through a swirling mist to his charming school for poor boys at Otford, Kent. The mist made me think of years which separated the old man from descendants like myself, of his contemporaries.

"Will you smoke?" said Father Tooth, beaming graciously, in his richly furnished study, hung with tapestries, pictures and relics collected over the world. "Have one of mine." I had one of his. It was dry with age and I should not have been surprised to know he had bought the packet when he came out of Horsemonger Lane Gaol. While the ancient weed crackled and blazed up he told me the story:

"I had a fine united congregation at St James', Hatcham," he said, "Sunday by Sunday I had to say Mass with booing and hooting for response. Hooligans were sent by the Church Association to disturb us, and, if possible, to break up the service. They were paid half-a-crown each, whilst boys received a shilling. They would keep their hats on throughout the service, and often there were fights between loyal members of the congregation and the toughs. Then a charge was brought against me and I wouldn't appear. They could find me nowhere, and thought I had slipped through their fingers."

His eyes twinkled and his mouth twitched.
"I went to Maidstone," he continued, "to await arrest, but nothing happened, so I came back to London, and there they took me. Horsemonger Lane Gaol doesn't exist now, and what do you think they have done with the bricks?" – I could not think – "built a church with them. The gaol was a shocking place for draughts". The old man shivered in remembrance, and then laughed merrily. "I didn't mind, and I was always obedient. I expected to be there for years, and I must say they

treated me fairly well. The warders did not know what to make of me. I felt uncomfortable only when I exercised in the yard. There I was seen by the women, who used to wonder what the "gay old dog in the clerical collar" had been up to. They let me keep my clothes."

However, the general public was shocked at the idea of a priest being sent to prison and even his enemies now applied for his release. After a total of twenty-eight days in prison, Father Tooth was released but his health had suffered terribly through his ordeal. On the express orders of his doctor he travelled to Italy for rest and recuperation.

When Father Tooth returned to the parish in May he found that his church was locked against him so he broke in through a window, and again celebrated Mass – to the joy of his parishioners and to the consternation of the Protestants.

Father Tooth in 1877, shortly after his release from prison.

The conversation between Father Tooth and Desmond Morse-Boycott continued thus:

'What happened when you came out of prison?' I queried.

"One day," he replied, "they told me to go, and being always obedient, I went. I got back to Hatcham and found my church bolted and barred. I broke in by a window, and said Mass in the usual way, as it is now said in thousands of churches, with altar lights and vestments. But it could not go on for long, and the congregation was broken up. My opponents bought the advowson, and put their own man in."

In fact, the reason that the advowson had passed into his opponents' hands was because Arthur's brother Robert had been made bankrupt and the advowson was one of his assets which had to be sold. Arthur offered £600 for it himself, but it was sold for £800. Why did he not use his proven fund-raising skills to secure the purchase so that he could put a Vicar in charge that he approved of? Perhaps he was tired of all that Hatcham signified in his life. He certainly took no time in moving away from the area which had given him such notoriety.

In 1878 Father Tooth appealed against the legal proceedings and won. It was found that the Judge, Lord Penzance, had held his court at Lambeth Palace, which was neither in London,

Westminster, nor in the Diocese of Rochester so the proceedings were 'Coram non judice' (before someone who is not a judge). However, Tooth wrote to the Archbishop that he had no desire to be vindictive - to take legal proceedings against those who had attacked him and falsely imprisoned him. He had made up his mind to resign and to spend more time with his orphanage work.

\* \* \*

The turning point in Arthur Tooth's life occurred after his imprisonment on his return to Hatcham. There were three paths open to him at this time. He could have fought for his church and so brought about a great deal more unpleasantness and bloodshed, possibly causing his own downfall through ill health.

An alternative would have been to have followed many of the great Tractarians into the Roman Catholic Church – an option that was unacceptable to him as a totally committed member of the Church of England who believed (and was correct in his belief) that the practices he held would become accepted by the church.

Father Tooth took the third path – and left the church at Hatcham to concentrate on helping others in more practical ways.

He was a priest without a church and until his death in 1931 he was never again allowed one. Towards the end of his life he wrote with sadness to a friend:

> It is a fact that the Church of England has been everything to me but there is a long record that I am nothing to it. No one can accuse me of self-seeking. I ask for nothing and I make no complaint. With a rebuff now and then from the authorities, I have unwillingly lived as an outsider, but this is no fault of mine and so most likely it will be to the end…

# THE TOOTH THAT WON'T COME OUT.

Punch cartoon

# ~ 2 ~

# The Woodside Years

Arthur Tooth was a wealthy man and in 1878 he purchased a large 18th century mansion called Stroud Green House in the Borough of Croydon.

There was farmland, a park with a small lake and a considerable number of outbuildings and stables. The mansion house was a classical Valentine Wright porticoed house, with lodge buildings and yards, which had been built in 1788.

*Stroud Green House (on the right) with the Woodside Extension (on the left)*

To this 20-acre estate he transferred the Sisterhood and St Michael's Orphanage from Hatcham, himself acting as Warden.

Despite its name, St Michael's was not strictly an orphanage. To qualify for admittance it was only necessary to have one parent deceased – and sometimes this was not even the criterion. There is an account of an Army Officer's three children being sent by the Court to 'Mr Tooth's School for the Sons of Destitute Gentlemen' following a matrimonial tangle.

The Croydon Reporter (1912) states:

At first he started with the poorest lads, until he became convinced that the need of the middle classes was still greater. Those now in the school, about 70 all told, are children of parents once of good social position, and nearly every case has a tragedy connected with it.

When the boys leave the school, every effort is made to give them a good start in life, and many are doing well. One of his old boys is now an actor of much promise. He is "going straight, an abstainer, and looked up to by all his company."

Unfortunately, the name of this promising actor remains a mystery.

In 1882-83 new buildings including a lodge, cloisters, a chapel and dormitories were added to the original mansion house and the complex now became known as Woodside.

Woodside (now Ashburton Library)

The beautiful chapel at Woodside was furnished with ornaments ejected from Father Tooth's old church at Hatcham and other items which he had collected on his travels. Indeed many of these ornaments, including the statue of Christ Crucified were transported to Otford in 1925 and some are still displayed to this day, though many others have been sold over the years.

Father Tooth had an even more ambitious plan for the Woodside complex: to build a hospital for 'Women Suffering From Intemperance', to be called 'St Raphael's Hospital'. Drawings exist from 1884 for a complex comprising nine houses, a chapel and a refectory surrounding a quadrangle - each house designed to accommodate twelve 'inmates'. In 1884, the red Gothic looking buildings were begun but only one wing of the quadrangle and the chapel were completed – presumably due to lack of funds.

One section of the complex is still in existence today serving as a lending library known as the Ashburton Library. The adult section is housed in the Chapel and the pulpit where Father Tooth addressed the boys can still be seen.

The Junior lending section of the library uses two rooms upstairs which previously had been the nuns' quarters. A small hole in the ceiling of one of the rooms held the pull for the chapel bell. There are several Delft blue tiles surrounding a fireplace and although most depict religious scenes, including a rather gory one of John the Baptist's head being served up on a platter, one tile depicts a scene from Alice in Wonderland. This is interesting as one of Tooth's nieces married a relative of Charles Lutwidge Dodgson, otherwise known as Lewis Carroll.

Whilst work on St Raphael's was progressing, Father Tooth welcomed alcoholic female 'patients' into the Woodside complex, whereas male patients remained in the village. In the 1881 census twelve girls, aged between seven and seventeen are recorded as resident. However, by 1891 there were no longer girls at Woodside. Perhaps Father Tooth's comments from his own publication of 1919 gives us a clue as to why:

> Now, once upon a time we had boys and also girls. It did not work quite well. Of course, someone said it was all the boys' fault; others said it was the girls to be blamed. There certainly was a harmless surprise now and then. I'll leave it to others to say who would deserve the scolding.

The convent gradually became an 'orphanage' solely for the 'sons of gentlemen': more specifically the sons of officers in the army and navy, clergymen and professional men.

The basis of the whole community during the forty-five years at Woodside was the role played by the Sisters. The Orphanage could not have run without them. There were four Sisters and two Lay Sisters who, on joining this independent community, gave up whatever wealth they might possess and put themselves under the rule of Arthur Tooth. It was they who cared for the boys and women, and did all the cooking including baking the bread. They also looked after the accounts, did odd jobs such as chopping wood and went begging for clothes for the 'orphans'.

# Life at Woodside

Although only 23 boys were moved from Hatcham to Woodside, the number of boys living in the orphanage and attending the school at any one time was usually between thirty and forty.

**Teaching**

When St Michael's moved from Hatcham to Woodside in 1878 the school was given a grant by the Board of Education. There was an agreement that the school would be conducted as a public elementary school within the meaning of the Elementary Education Act of 1870. The 'public' ideal of the school remained until 2nd July 1915 when Father Tooth wrote to the Board of Education asking for the school to be withdrawn from its present status as it was now to be continued as a private school. From that date the school received no government help, and it is as a private school with charitable status that it exists today.

Although Father Tooth did very little teaching himself, he had strong views on education:

> As an educationalist, he [Father Tooth] speaks rather sadly of our present system. It is unfitting the people for their walk in life. They are growing up with no notion of tolerating anything, and they want everything, and do not want to earn it. They are losing sense of the duties in life…
>
> …All the domestic work at the home is done by the sisters, except the rough work of the house, which they are not strong enough to do. The boys, also, although drawn from the ranks of the upper middle class, are taught domestic work. He [Father Tooth] tells them, most properly, that to gentlemen no service is menial. Only the spirit in which it is performed can be that.'
>
> **The Croydon Reporter 1912**

In his pamphlet written in 1919, Arthur Tooth writes with pride of the high standards his school attained:

> You must not suppose that when poverty and distress have had their share in home life that education has been thought of. It is never so. Schooling comes last. The education of the boys as they arrive is always deficient, even in those who have suffered the least. It is no great misfortune; boys who get their education rather late, develop much better than those who are clever and get overworked at first.
>
> We have an excellent standard of education. Music is excellent. The senior boys have sat for the Local Cambridge Examination. They all passed last year; and in our section at Croydon, of three successful candidates who obtained honours, one was a St Michael's boy with a mark of distinction for Algebra.

Perhaps the credit for this initial success should go to the Master at Woodside, Mr Frederick N. Wareham, who joined the school at Hatcham on 2 January 1873, aged 23. He completed forty-three years' service before his retirement in 1916 at the age of 66. He was succeeded by Charles Manning Jaggard.

Teaching within the school was formal, as was normal for the day. All the boys were in one large classroom and they were instructed in turn. Most of the teaching was based around the 'question and answering' sessions, and there was almost no practical work. Although Father Tooth had a fully equipped laboratory, the boys did not have science on their timetable. Mr Wareham took the boys for music lessons. Art consisted only of copying flat copies. Despite the fact that Father Tooth was himself a keen sportsman - fond of horse riding and a good shot - it was not until Mr Jaggard came to the school that an interest in sport was taken: then the boys played both cricket and football against surrounding schools.

In the period 1907 to 1913, the school inspectors visited Woodside three times. On each occasion a report was made and the judgement was always that there was a lack of practical application in the teaching. The Inspector in 1909 took into account in his report that the one teacher taught all standards, and most of the boys were at the orphanage for a short time so that organisation of classes was difficult. However, he said that he found the master 'discursive in his teaching', and the simultaneous answering by the boys which was prevalent was not a sign of good discipline. The teaching of arithmetic seems to have been a weak feature, with the boys having no grasp of underlying rules. The inspector also states that he found the boys 'not unintelligent'.

By 1913 Mr Wareham, the master for over forty years, was finding the task of teaching several groups of scholars difficult, but the boys in his care still made fair progress and were able to read fluently, gain information from their books and express themselves intelligently - both orally and in writing.

## Religion

Although there was no religious education within school hours, Woodside was recognised as being Church of England in denomination. Religious services were held out of school hours. Each morning there was a High Church service in the chapel, and on Sunday there were three - all services conducted by Father Tooth and conducted in English. Although incense was burnt, confession was not taken. The chapel was open to the public for special services throughout the year.

A journalist from The Croydon Reporter was given a guided tour of Woodside in 1912:

> We went into the little church, which is well furnished, and has an altar screen and organ. The lighted lamp before the altar suggests the reserved sacrament is there. Father Tooth says it is not a practice to keep this, but it is done at times to teach the boys, and he has been much struck by their appreciation. Last week, being Holy Week and the Presence there, they had asked as a special favour, which was granted, to perform their devotions in church.

> 'He [Father Tooth] told me of an instance which touched him much in regard to his boys. One of the lads' mothers had recently died. When the boy was told of it in the evening he was naturally very distressed, but later on Father Tooth was much impressed by finding all the boys round their schoolfellow that night praying for

that mother, and it seemed to comfort the lad very much. That was beautiful.

Mr Wareham was a very good organist and choirmaster so work by composers was taught and sung during the services.

## Food

*'Any misdemeanours would be punished with a period on bread and water. They baked their own bread, speckled with white lumps of uncooked dough, and often we used to exchange our possessions for slices of bread. We were always hungry.*

*They did have a vegetable called sea kale and it was so bad, we would watch out for the nuns - Mother Superior at the end of the refectory and one nun at the head of each table - and then scoop this stuff into the handkerchief on our lap and dump it over the playground fence.'*

**Duncan Jackson 1920/21**

The food provided for the boys was very plain. Bubble and squeak was always very popular and a favourite was gooseberry fool as one person was sure to find a sixpenny piece in his.

The food eaten by Father Tooth and the Sisters was of a higher quality, but as one old boy put it:

*'It was usual for the Lay Sisters to provide special fare for his evening meal and on innumerable occasions I have known him bring it over from his study and share it with the older boys, eating little or nothing himself.'*

Father Tooth would also bring in a bag of sweet chestnuts during the winter months, and all the boys would spend a pleasant evening round the fire eating roasted chestnuts.

## Outdoors

The boys were very lucky that at Woodside there was plenty of space, so they all led a healthy outdoor life. The older ones were expected to help in the grounds by doing such tasks as wood chopping and even, on various occasions, blasting trees. Father Tooth, a man who was born in the country and who had a love of outdoor life, believed very strongly that the boys should be taught farming skills as well as classroom skills. He also wanted to make the orphanage self-sufficient so the grounds at Woodside were laid out as a market garden with over four thousand fruit trees planted by the time of the First World War. Pigs were kept and even grapes were grown in numerous greenhouses. At times there were anything up to sixteen gardeners to tend the grounds.

You will want to know how we are getting on. Very well indeed, thank you, and the wonderful good health of the boys is still maintained. We have had no illness to make us at all anxious; but, then, we live in the country and have our own farmyard and garden for supplies.

**Father Tooth's Pamphlet 1919**

Extracts from the Senior Master's logbook of 1917, show that boys spent a good deal of time working outdoors, to the detriment of their studies:

---

**2 March 1917:** The boys have started to dig up some grass ground with a view of planting potatoes as recommended by the Government. They appear to take great interest in the work.

**9 March 1917:** The garden work is progressing satisfactorily. Some of the pupils too have done a good amount of tree felling and woodcutting.

**16 March 1917:** The weather has been very cold and hindered our gardening somewhat. Still we are making headway and hope to be able to plant potatoes early in April.

**3 April 1917:** On account of the heavy snowstorms gardening operations have been entirely suspended this week.

**11 May 1917:** Several boys are suffering from wounds on the hands which have somewhat hindered their progress.

**29 June 1917:** Haymaking and totally necessary outside work has to some extent dislocated routine

---

Edmund Thornton in an appreciation to Father Tooth in *The Times* in 1921 said:

*'I was at Woodside during the war from 1915 to 1918 and we boys had much to be thankful for during those years....The grounds at one time were stocked with over four thousand fruit trees, and during the scarce years of War, fruit and vegetables were available to us in abundance. We were encouraged to do things for ourselves and our hobbies included felling, sawing and chopping large trees in the grounds, grafting, pruning and tending the fruit trees and collecting and storing the fruit.'*

In 1924 the Woodside complex was compulsorily purchased by Croydon Council so Father Tooth, the nuns and the boys were forced to find a new home at Otford in Kent.

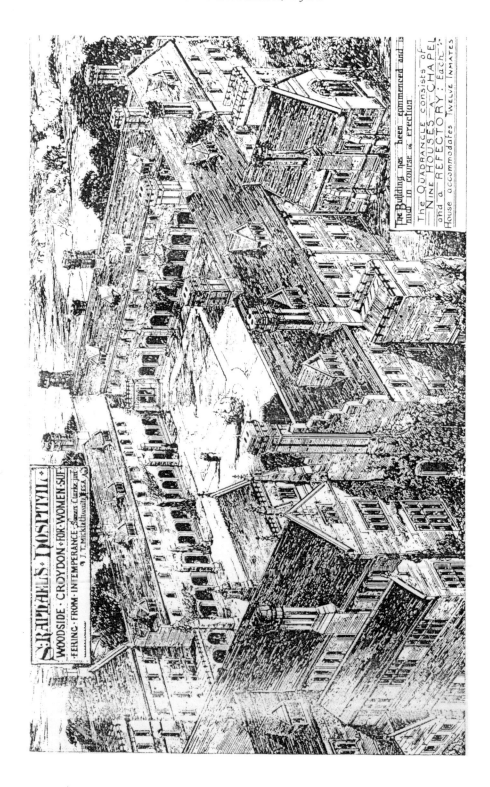

# Woodside 1878 - 1924

**1878** – Father Arthur Tooth purchases Stroud Green House and moves his convent and orphanage with 23 boys from Hatcham. Frederick Wareham (Master since 1873) moves with them.

**1878** – St Michael's is given a grant by the board of Education and 'the school is to be conducted as a public [state] elementary school.'

**1882 – 1884** – New buildings are added to the Stroud Green Estate and the complex becomes known as Woodside.

**1915** – Father Tooth informs the Board of Education that St Michael's will now be run as a Private school.

**1916** – Frederick Wareham retires as Master of St Michael's after 43 years service and Charles Manning Jaggard succeeds him.

**1916** – Mr Jaggard begins his daily logbook chronicling misbehaviour, sporting events, outbreaks of sickness and his 'private' opinions on all aspects of school life. The logbooks only become 'public' once Michael Cork takes over as Headmaster in 1932.

**1924** – Woodside is compulsorily purchased by Croydon Council and a move to Otford in Kent is planned.

Beechy Lees in the 1880s

# ~ 3 ~

## The Move to Otford

From as early as 1919, Father Tooth realised that the orphanage and school would have to move out of Croydon. His own fund-raising pamphlet states:

> The housing scheme is not to be overlooked. We are very comfortable here and our pleasant home leaves nothing to be desired. It is most convenient, and so the authorities of the Housing Scheme seem to think, for they have served us with this formal notice: that our reasons for not wishing to sell the land are not such as to restrain the corporation (of Croydon) from proceeding further.
>
> It has tended to unsettle us; but, after all, the country is the proper place for every Institution, and not a crowded suburb of London. This district will soon be part of London, and not one for young life; and so, sooner or later, we must be prepared to move and re-establish ourselves elsewhere – it is only a matter of time.

The *Croydon Reporter* had seen the writing on the wall even earlier in 1912:

> The estate at Woodside must be yearly increasing in value, and as there are about 36 acres of it I should never be surprised to hear it had been decided to sell it in the interests of the institution and rebuild the Orphanage farther from the lava tide of mortar and of brick.

However, it was not until the end of 1924 that the Woodside Estate was compulsorily purchased by Croydon Council for a sum of about twenty-one thousand pounds.

---

**2 December 1924:** No school today. Master away to see a prospective home of the new school. This estate has been sold to the Corporation of Croydon and the school will have to be removed by February next.

---

Mr Jaggard writes in his logbook at the time of the momentous move from Woodside:

---

**9 January 1925:** There are now 25 names in the Register of Upper School. All are in good health, apparently happy, and working well. Two boys went down to Otford during the week and were absent for three sessions each. Otford is our proposed new home to which we migrate some time in February.

**23 January 1925:** During the past week we have been occupied in collecting books useful *(sic)* and burning a lot of dilapidated books and material that are of no use whatever. On Monday next some twenty boys are going home for a fortnight and will not return here but to the new "Home" at Otford. The Registers are closed for the present school and will not be marked again until the boys reassemble at Otford.

---

Father Tooth, aged 86, Charles Jaggard, the Sisters and the boys all decamped to the Beechy Lees Estate in Otford, Kent. The house and grounds were larger than at Woodside, although there were no separate quarters for the sisters. Much of the eighty-eight acres of grounds were wooded – an ideal playground for the boys.

# Beechy Lees, Otford

In 1878 Barclay Field, a wealthy brewer who had once played cricket for Marylebone Cricket Club, bought several hundred acres of land in Kemsing from Earl Amherst, the owner of Dynes Farm. Barclay Field's monogram can be seen on several houses in Heaverham suggesting that he was a major property developer in the area.

On the 88 acres north of the Pilgrims Way he built a hunting lodge and called it Beechy Lees. The total cost was about £2870. James Pulham probably laid out the grounds and his artificial rocks of Pulhamite Stone form the large rockery at the entrance of the school. He also cleared the grounds of scrub and planted many specimen trees and bushes.

Since Barclay Field was childless, his brother George Hanbury Field inherited Beechy Lees on his death in 1892. George lived at Ashurst Park, Tunbridge Wells and, like his brother, also played cricket – this time for Kent County. He died in 1901, leaving the property to his son, C.A. Field. He rented the house to Mr. J. Murray MP from 1915 onwards. The last-named Field died in 1917.

Father Tooth eventually acquired the house and grounds in 1925.

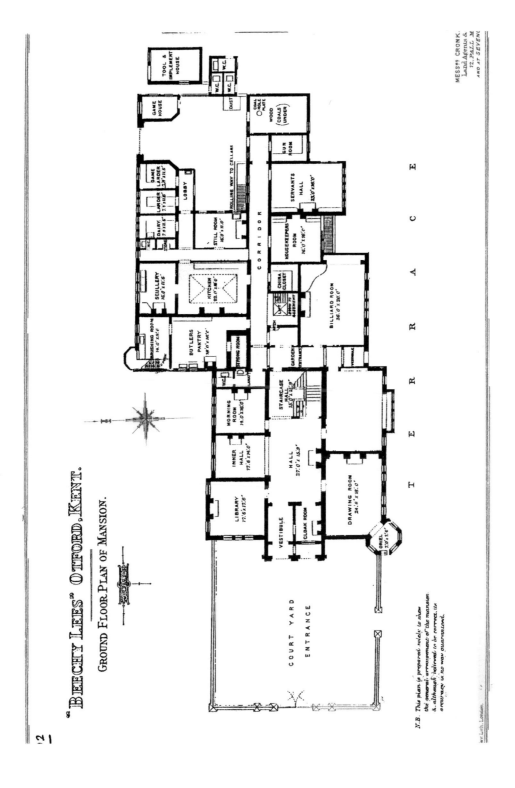

"BEECHY LEES" OTFORD, KENT.

GROUND FLOOR PLAN OF MANSION.

N.B. This plan is prepared solely to show the general arrangement of the mansion, & although believed to be correct, its accuracy is in no way guaranteed.

MESSRS CRONK,
Land Agents &
12, PALL M
AND AT SEVEN

# Life at Otford

Father Tooth describes in one of his own fund-raising pamphlets, written shortly after the move to Otford in 1925, how he perceives life in their new home:

> From St James' Hatcham, we moved to Woodside, Croydon to a comfortable house with 38 acres of land, altogether delightful – then it was Woodside, a country place, nothing more, until London claimed it as a suburb; evidently not the best place for young life: and so with much regret, after 47 years' residence at Woodside, we came to Otford in Kent, quite in the country, a place of great interest in the past: chiefly because S. Thomas of Canterbury held the benefice of Otford, and as Archbishop occupied the fine manor house of the Diocese, together in turn with S. Anselm: there is too, the well of S. Thomas and the Pilgrim's Road, full of devotion and romance in those days: it is pleasant to be living in the twilight of such history.
>
> There is real country life here for the boys, cricket and football, of course, with an excursion now and then to the woods (we have eighty acres of land), and what a romance a thick wood affords to the sporting instincts of the young, and to all who remain always young – the deep shadows, the silence – a presence you feel, but do not understand – there is no pathway: you go as you like: the trees seem to be whispering together: about this new intruder on their privilege.
>
> Not all romance: several snakes, one fled to a hole, it was not large enough, the tail was outside, it was only a little sportsman who would venture to take it by the tail and pull it out; so he did – perhaps he was thinking of what Moses did when he stood before Pharaoh.

---

**5 February 1925.** The present rooms used as classrooms, I believe are temporary. It is proposed to transform a building removed from the mansion into a school. A very pretty little chapel has been evolved from a large room and is to be used for services on Sunday next, but unfortunately as yet we can have no organ.

**23 February 1925:** This morning I had an extra classroom given to me. This has quite removed the congestion and I have now ample room. The only drawback to this most suitable acquisition is that there is no connection between the two rooms. I have to leave one to go to the other.

---

This log from the days shortly after the move to Otford implies that the original intention was to turn the stable block into the classrooms and to leave the rooms in the main house as the living quarters. The large room converted into the 'pretty little chapel' was originally the billiards room designed with a glass roof to let in as much light as possible directly above the table.

**2 April 1925.** Owing to weather, colds rather prevalent; still our new home judging by the bracing air & splendid position here is preferable to Woodside. Personally it is not so. There is no residence here & no house to be obtained in the village. Thus I have to live in apartments & walk upwards of two miles to & from school

It is perhaps surprising that there was no accommodation for Mr Jaggard but as well as the thirty or so boys who needed dormitories, rooms were needed for Father Tooth, the Sisters, various servants and other school staff.

Otford Court in the 1930s

Otford Court in the 1980s

# ~ 4 ~

## A Portrait of Arthur Tooth

Father Tooth's personality radiates out from his pamphlets and letters, written as if he is having a cosy chat with a group of good friends and sometimes a little meandering, fragmented and poorly punctuated as a result. More help to build up a picture of this man is gained from the stories of people who knew him and through the recollections of Old Michaelians, for whom the intensity of the memories have not diminished for over seventy years.

Father Tooth spent the last few years of his life at Otford - as much out of the gaze of the public as he had always been since his release from prison. Although he had very little to do with the care or education of the boys he was still held in very high esteem by them. He was a person to whom people were automatically attracted - very far from the 'stuffed-shirt' dour image of a serious clergyman.

As one Old Michaelian remembered in an obituary in The Times:

*'The boys were one and all much attached to Father Tooth. His appearance in the grounds was the signal for a rush in his direction, and it was considered an honour to be the first to arrive and link his arm.'*

Old Michaelian Douglas Keddie [1923/31] tells:

*'I well remember that on the occasions when Father Tooth appeared, we would run to meet him – not so much, perhaps, at the pleasure of seeing him, but from the fact that he usually had 'goodies' to dispense! On other occasions he would throw apples to us and seemed amused at our scrambling for possession of one.'*

---

**17 June 1920:** Holiday. Revd Father's Birthday. In the morning the Choir Boys sang a Birthday song beneath his bedroom window at 6.45am. He told us he much appreciated our small endeavour, an acknowledgment which gave us infinite pleasure.

---

*'Father Tooth was very much a recluse and other than at Chapel services we seldom saw or had contact with him. He had an endearing and rather mischievous side to him. On occasions you would see him slowly shuffling, not so much walking, in the grounds and you would join up with him. Little would be said when all of a sudden apples, oranges, sweets would come tumbling out from beneath his cassock and even his biretta (never saw him without it) and blithely go walking on but with a twinkle in his eye, half watching you and others with you scrambling around picking up as much as you could, by which time he had disappeared. Another favourite of his was to stick apples and oranges on the spikes of the front entrance gates so that when you came out of school to play in the fields they were there for the picking. I'm sure he would be watching you from somewhere.'*

**Gerry Winter 1924/30**

As Desmond Morse-Boycott affirms in his book *Lead, Kindly Light*, the fondness between Father Tooth and the children was mutual:

> 'It was my privilege to become the friend of this old saint, in later years, and to take my choirboys year by year to his orphanage, where he would feed them with pies full of sixpences, and then send them out to play cricket. Every few moments during dinner, which we took on the lawn, he would come strolling out from the kitchen with a hot pie under his arm. He loved little children, and they loved him. There was an intangible bond between them – the link of childhood, natural and supernatural.'

His writings reflect his light-hearted, cheerful nature.

'You need to have your wits about you if you live with children. They ask questions: very frank and surprising they sometimes are.

The day came round when King Alfred died: was to be commemorated. It stood in the calendar as Oct. 26. Hollingshed in his Chronicles says it was Oct. 28; but let that pass. Now, as long as English history lasts there will be the remembrance of the Danes. The King as a tramp, then as a labourer in the field, then as a harper, then, as a climax, in charge of cakes, which he forgot and they were burnt. It was after all this that the further history got interesting: How the good herdsman, Denulph by name, leaving his cows, became Bishop of Winchester. Now who would have thought it – it could only be a boy who would ask – but what became of Mrs Denulph!! For the life of me I don't know; I can't say. Someone will suggest that she was a dear old lady who was always making cakes and doing good to everyone, and unkind to no one, and that she passed away, lamented by everyone. What became of Mrs Denulph I don't know. Did she go to the Bishop's Palace? I can't say.'

**Father Tooth's Pamphlet 1919**

## Sense of fun
Father Tooth had a very good sense of humour and a mischievous spirit. One incident that illustrates this occurred at Woodside. Many dares were made and carried out at St Michael's as is natural with children at boarding school. On the eve of 1st April, two boys had been dared to spend the night in the schoolroom and settled down to sleep at the back behind the desks. Very early next morning they were woken by a noise and, peeping from under their covers, they saw Father Tooth enter the room. They kept very quiet and saw him creep over to the clock on the wall and turn it back by one hour. Apparently he had already done this to every other clock in the house. Next morning everyone was roused from their beds an hour later and even the Sisters were an hour late for matins!

'A bright-eyed, lithe, cheery man, from whose somewhat ascetic face, although long past the three score years and ten, the lines of youth and humour had not departed'.

**The Croydon Reporter 1912**

His humour emerges even in his exasperation with regard to the housing shortage (written in 1927):

What a fuss and fidget there is just now about getting a place to live in. To begin with I must live somewhere. Now people are getting crazy over small houses or even a flat. Is there not something to be said in favour of large buildings?

I remember a large building – a very large building, down the other side of the River in the Borough [Horsemonger Lane Gaol] the best built place in London, well arranged, very popular it was, always full, the company a little mixed I allow, but very interesting.

I stayed there for a time, we called it 'THE QUEEN'S HOTEL', the arrangements were orderly – I ask is there another Hotel in London where every resident goes to Chapel every morning? True the Chapel was unusual – it was like a circus with boxes too, for special residents – now and then (not often) the bell went gently, and there was one less poor fellow perhaps with no home and without a friend in the world.

'Don't be hard on any of these chaps, there is always some romance to be found in their lives – a little sympathy would go far to get them right'

He had a taste for absurdity as the following abstracts from his writings illustrate:

'It still lingers with me; last Sunday I read in chapel (it must be true) that Daniel found 'prosperity' in the lion's den. I should never have thought it: the other people didn't.'

**Father Tooth in a letter to a friend 1926**

'You must not scoff at the Socialists - some times they count - one. A delightful story reached me a few years ago - a triumph of their new standard of life - I did not make up this story, honour bright I did not. A bishop to encourage the working-man would always travel third-class - what silly stuff this sort of thing is - as though the working-man of today needs any encouragement - the look of a clergyman is enough for him. Ask him - he will reply, "'E ain't of our sort,"

However so it was, third-class carriage full, Bishop in one corner, a rough hard-working chap in corduroy and leathers in another corner - "I say, parson - do you know everything?" "Well, no," (the bishop's always kind and pleasant spoken) "I am always glad to learn."

"Well, then, my wife is your washerwoman. This week I am wearing your shirt."'

**Father Tooth in A Jubilee Retrospect 1927**

## Hobbies and Interests

Arthur Tooth's hobbies covered a very wide field. As a younger man he had been very keen on a variety of outdoor sports and was know to be fond of riding and a good shot. He maintained a healthy outdoor lifestyle, and one of the reasons he moved St Michael's from Woodside to Croydon was because he disliked the encroachment of urbanisation on the countryside. Even to the end of his life he grew prize pears, kept pigs and was a great lover of animals.

He loved to travel and to meet people from all walks of life. He was a keen motorist and continued to embark on vast tours of the country well after his eightieth birthday.

"I drive my own motor [aged over 70], and also do its repairs when needed. In fact, I have just returned from a 2,000 miles' drive".

While he says this he seems to become more youthful than ever.

**The Croydon Reporter 1912**

He was very fond of art and collected many types during his travels round the world. He was also a talented artist in his own right (he painted the wooden screens in the Chapel at Woodside) and loved photography. The 1912 article in *The Croydon Reporter* continues:

> [Father Tooth says] "I am fond of photography" and goes on to ask whether I know anything about it. I am glad I hesitate, because the next moment we are standing before two pictures about four feet in length, sacred subjects, and so beautifully soft, such perfect detail, such delicate tone that it is difficult to believe that they are photographs at all.

Father Tooth had taken a science degree at Cambridge and he retained an interest in this subject all his life. He had a fully equipped laboratory at Woodside and was known to 'mess about' with the wireless in his last years. Many of his friends were aware that during his last few years he suffered from the effects of an explosion which occurred while he was carrying out some experiments.

Hypnosis held a fascination for him and he used his skill at this to help drug addicts and alcoholics. He also used it for the painless extraction of teeth. He says in the *Croydon Reporter* 1912:

'I feel that we best approach this fascinating study from the fact (governing all our being) that we are spiritual - and not material. Thinking then (and at Easter time in particular) of this soul, as soul; and its power over matter, to govern it as a living thing. When this power is withdrawn into the soul, and it rests, the material body has no support and returns, losing form, to its primitive order: this (vegetative) power of the soul is, however, not lost, it is dormant and will one day find a response to the call to the resurrection life.

Meanwhile most of us feel that the soul does give evidence of better, higher things - inchoate [in an initial or early stage] it is true, but very true. I am now too much occupied to give this the time I would like to this research; it is very laborious, and the practical side of life is heavy on us all. For the recovery of inebriates, this action of mind on mind is quite real, these patients may be kept under control, and the restorative power of an invalid may be induced to re-assert itself - I have often seen it.'

## Financial Dealings

Arthur Tooth was able to buy the property at Woodside because he came from a wealthy family. His monetary problems in connection with such a large property and enormous undertakings were also greatly eased by the wealth which the women who joined his order of nuns brought with them.

However he still took out mortgages on his property and lent money for the interest it would bring, and in his last years at Woodside some of the land was sold.

He never missed a money making venture and although he may have been a very generous man, he never allowed an opportunity to make money slip through his fingers. He frequently wrote pamphlets to his friends and supporters where he made insistent and blatant demands on their charitable natures and their religious devotion:

'With a household of some sixty people, the daily requirements of life soon make themselves felt. There is food and clothing to be provided, and everyone must be made happy and contented. Won't you go to your draper or to your tailor and send us a nice piece of clothing? Don't trouble about sizes and measurements - we can fit the boys to the clothing; they are from 6 to 14 years of age.

You will ask: Don't the little chaps arrive provided with a good send-off of clothing and boots, farewell gifts of loving aunties and others? Not often; it was what they stand up in - not always clean and in best repair. We are expected to do all that. Sometimes they do bring a little luggage. Recently a new boy brought some - it was a pot of jam and a toothbrush: nothing more.

And then, with fog, frost and snow, to say nothing of the east wind, what a business it is to keep warm at night. Send us some blankets for 50 beds to keep the boys warm at night. Don't forget the sheets - we shall want them too - the Government linen, which has been much advertised of late, is just the very thing.'

**1919 Pamphlet**

He continued to beg for money at his Golden Jubilee celebrations on 17 February 1927:

'Send me, send me, I ask you to send me, for the love you have for the Catholic Faith, your most generous offerings for the Chapel Fund - marked Chapel Fund. I shall want £10,000, this I know. That the hearts of our people are worth more than this.'

## Love of Life

Not only could Arthur Tooth see the humour in his misfortune, but he loved life and all that could be gained from it. He was a natural optimist and his glass was always 'half full' rather than 'half empty':

'Don't you like the fogs – I love them: though they don't get a place of mention in the Benedicite. They are with us: full of romance telling us of things, which really are, although not seen. Life is like this.'

**Father Tooth in a letter to a friend 1926**

'When a priest is a good deal over eighty years of age and sees that ninety is not far off, he would like to say, once more, how grateful he is for the unbroken record of kindness he has received for very many years: truly it is pleasant to live.'

**1926 Pamphlet**

He also had time to look at the lives of those around him and have sympathy for them. In fact he felt a kinship with those who had the 'devil' in them. In Desmond Morse-Boycott's book *Lead, Kindly Light* the author recounts his conversation with Father Tooth:

'"I have trained fourteen hundred boys," he said a little sadly. "They're all over the world. Some are doctors, some are clergy, some are lawyers. Some have been very bad boys..." He said that as if he loved them more dearly than the good ones.'

In a passage called 'The Tramp!' Father Tooth wrote of his empathy and sympathy for those less fortunate than himself - tramps - and again showed signs of real affection. Once again, people are drawn to him and he makes them feel comfortable in his presence. The passage also illustrates his love of life and his love of motoring.

'I know these roads fairly well from Inverness to Land's End, from East to West Coasts; since the motor made us alert and happy, nothing could add more to a day's outing than the halt for tea, Gipsy fashion, at four o'clock, at some quiet spot on the road. Ah! Sure enough a Tramp, ragged and forlorn comes along, possibly a little party of them. It was always our custom to ask them to sit down and join us - a bit risky perhaps for a motorist carries some cash - anyhow no harm ever came for it - once I felt it prudent to get along; perhaps I was mistaken!

Yes, a Tramp would be a bit shy, then as he lost his very natural surprise, he would open out, and tell his simple tale of sorrow; the burden shifted to a passing friend for a moment, it could not be that the whole world, to a man, stood against the poor Tramp.

On one occasion I saw a Tramp sleeping under a hedge, my interest was aroused. We had finished our meal some time before, and were quite sober! So I took the remains of a duck and a nice apple pie and placed them under the poor fellow's coat! Was it very boisterous of an elderly priest? Anyhow it was very pleasant to be young once more, and to think of the dream the poor Tramp would have of some Good Fairy, who had brought him duck and apple tart that summer evening.'
[1927]


**Religious Views**
Father Tooth was a practising Christian all his life; from the time of his ordination and probably before, he was a follower of the Oxford Movement. This was an organisation set up by a group of Anglican theologians and philosophers at Oxford University in the 1830s. Their basic position was that the Church of England was becoming a protestant sect, and should be realigned, to become the national church again.

Although he was never a person to condemn another for his views, he strongly kept his own. An article which appeared in *Vanity Fair* on 10 February 1877 described his intransigence:

He is an ascetic, devoted, earnest, honest man, incapable of seeing two sides of a question, but a favourite of all who knew him, and endowed less with a great power of will than with an enormous power of won't.

The boys did not know Father Tooth's past history or the religious views he held. This, according to one of Father Tooth's fund-raising pamphlets written in 1925 when he was in his late eighties, was how he wanted it to be:

I am not going to say anything about St James', Hatcham, about the happiness of my life as it was to me then and now: or the interesting exchange of opinions which took place there in 1877. Few people remember those days: that is how it should be. I'll leave it to others to say who got the worst of it; other and more important matters have arisen since then.

As Douglas Keddie recounts:

*'Father Tooth was 84 years old when I joined St Michael's Home in 1923. I remember him as a white-haired but sprightly gentleman and, not then knowing his age, and as a seven year old lad, and without having had any experience or previous practice in the Catholic Faith, he soon impressed me as a kindly and saintly man. We really saw little of Father Tooth during the week; he was rarely to be seen in our 'quarters' and never, as far as I can remember, looked in on school classes...'*

In Father Tooth's obituary an unnamed Old Michaelian said:

*'Although Father Tooth had such advanced religious views, these were never enforced on his boys. Capable guidance, and encouragement to act always as gentlemen, were his main principles. Certain ritual was carried out in the school chapel, but it was only after I left his care that I learnt he had once been a public figure.'*

\* \* \*

A final description of Father Arthur Tooth:

'No one could have been in his company or heard him preach without realising his deep spirituality. The heavenly things were always present; he was at once a mystic and yet of practical mind. He was a holy man who lived in the constant companionship of the Angels and the Saints. Every material beauty reminded him of the beauty, the glory, and the peace of God. He was a lover of the poor and the outcast, and some day the Church of this country will recognise him as a saint.'

**Heroes of the Catholic Revival,**
**The Catholic Literature Association 1933**

# The Final Years of Arthur Tooth

It might comes as quite a surprise to Old Michaelians that in 1927, Father Arthur Tooth took the opportunity at the Golden Jubilee celebrations of his release from prison to announce his intention to change the very nature of St Michael's from a home for boys, to a training college for the clergy and a 'retreat'. In *A Jubilee Retrospect*, (a record of Tooth's speech to a group of churchmen at Church House, Westminster), Tooth says:

'Now then, would you like to hear the news?

Yes please.

For a long time we have been suffering from an insufficient supply of clergy…There are young men who would gladly come to our help and become Priests. We must help them and educate them for their work.

There is quite a charming house and grounds in the country not far from London – quite all that can be desired – at your disposal. At present it is owned and occupied by an old man. I know him very well – I have been on intimate terms with him for many years. I can now say – he is no good at all…There will be no difficulty in getting possession of this place, Otford Court.

What then?

Devote it to the clergy – provide for the best education of candidates for ordination – a resting place for hard-working clergy needing periods of rest and refreshment...

As an act of appreciation of his work for the Church it is proposed that this new venture be called The Halifax College. I say Give it. Give it all your sympathy and support.'

As Desmond Morse-Boycott tells in his book *Lead, Kindly Light*, his wishes were unfulfilled:

"If so sunny a saint could be said to have a shadow over his life it was cast, during his later years, by the unsuccess of his efforts to give away his magnificent mansion and grounds, first to the Anglo-Catholic Congress, and then to the Diocese of Southwark, to the S.P.G. and to the Archbishop of Canterbury, as a training centre or a rest house for the clergy, and to see erected in Canterbury Cathedral a worthy memorial to Thomas à Becket, his favourite saint. He had offered £10,000, and a committee was prepared to find a like sum, but negotiations were protracted, and the Chapter rejected the design by Mr Comper."

In 1930, at the age of ninety-one he attended the Anglo-Catholic Congress and received acknowledgement and acclaim from a vast crowd of supporters, as recounted by Desmond Morse-Boycott in *They Shine Like Stars*:

'No more dramatic event has occurred in the history of the Movement (Oxford) than when he walked out, bent with age, to take part in High Mass on Stamford Bridge Football Ground, during the Anglo-Catholic Congress of 1930. The shout of welcome was one of the great authentic shouts of church history.

In the midst of the green turf there stood a mighty altar glowing resplendently in the sun. Around was a tapestry of colour that made the scene very beautiful; many nuns in black and white kneeling on the greensward; monks in divers habits; massed choirs in cassock and surplice; a vast company of priests in robes; ranks of servers in scarlet and fine linen winding sinuous trails around the ground; and thousands of lay folk, men, women and little children looking down on the arena upon the sacred ministers in golden vestments, the bishops in copes and mitres - all combined to make such a scene as Arthur Tooth could never have imagined on the desolate day when he left the prison, broke into his locked church, and said mass with a handful of friends around him.'

Father Tooth died peacefully in his room at St Michael's on 5 March 1931 at the age of ninety-one whilst sitting in a chair.

---

**5 March 1931:** Grieved to record the Revd Father 'passed away' about 10.15 this morn quite suddenly. I was talking to him about 10 min before he died, when I did not notice any difference in him except he was very quiet.   R.I.P.

---

*'My final memory of Fr. Tooth was following his death. We were taken into his study to pay our last respects and to view his frail body, robed in white Eucharistic Vestments and looking peaceful and saintly – the first time I had ever seen a dead person. Myself and other boys attended the funeral as altar servers.'*

**Douglas Keddie 1923/31**

He was buried in Elmers End cemetery – just a few miles from Woodside – in a plot acquired by the convent. The High Mass of Requiem was held in St James's, Elmers End and was attended by friends, supporters, relatives and a by a number of people from St Michael's including the three Sisters, Mr Anderson (the gardener) and his daughter, other staff and several boys acting as altar servers.

A ceremony is still held every year at the side of his grave by representatives from three parish churches in the Beckenham area. The grave can clearly be seen to the right of the main pathway – almost opposite the chapel. There is also a cenotaph with Tooth's effigy and the words Confessor of Faith in the chapel of St Thomas of Canterbury at Walsingham.

Although Father Tooth had purchased Otford Court in 1925 using his own personal wealth, he was determined to ensure that what remained of the 'Community of the Paraclete' – the two Sisters Grace and Christine – would continue to run St Michael's Home after his death. This desire, however, kept solicitors very busy during the months following Father Tooth's death. Firstly, there was the question of who legally owned Otford Court. Was it a private property belonging exclusively to Father Tooth – and therefore his to dispose of how he wished, or had he handed it over to the Community in 1925 when he signed a document stating, 'Now I hereby acknowledge and declare that I am a Trustee only of the said estate upon the trusts following…'?

Father Tooth's will, dated 1926, was a very simple one: 'I give devise and bequeath all my personal estate whatsoever and wheresoever unto and between Grace Evelyn Cowper *[Sister Grace]* and Ida Miles *[Sister Christine]* of the Convent of Otford aforesaid in equal shares or to such one of them as may be living at my decease.'

But the main problem was not that the Sisters would ignore Father Tooth's obvious wishes that the school should be maintained through his legacy – but the question of who would inherit the property on their deaths. Thus it was decided that Otford Court and St Michael's Home should be taken over by a body of Trustees, and the Sisters duly had wills drawn up leaving their legacies to this newly created body.

Father Tooth left £38,000 in his will to Sisters Grace and Christine so that they would be able to continue the work that he had begun in Hatcham in 1872.

# Father Tooth 1872/1931

**1839** – Arthur Tooth is born in Cranbrook in Kent.

**1862** – He graduates from Trinity College, Cambridge with a BA and is awarded an MA in 1865.

**1863** – Arthur Tooth is ordained.

**1868** – Father Tooth becomes Vicar of St James' in Hatcham, New Cross.

**1872** – St Michael's Home for Boys and the Community of Sisters of the Holy Paraclete are founded in Hatcham.

**1877** – Father Tooth is imprisoned for contempt of court in defying the Public Worship Regulation Act of 1874. He is released after 28 days.

**1878** – Father Tooth moves his orphanage and convent to Croydon.

**1925** – St Michael's Home for Boys is moved from Woodside in Croydon to an 88 acre site in Otford, Kent.

**1927** – Golden Jubilee Celebrations to commemorate fifty years since the release of Arthur Tooth from Horsemonger Lane Gaol.

**1930** – Father Tooth attends the Anglo-Catholic Congress at Stamford Bridge Football Ground.

**1931** – Father Tooth dies peacefully at Otford Court, aged ninety-one.

# ~ 5 ~

## Charles Manning Jaggard

### Headmaster from 1916 to 1932

The logbooks, which exist from 1916 when Charles Manning Jaggard was appointed Master, give many insights into the life of the boys at Woodside and later at Otford.

---

**2 May 1916:** Charles Manning Jaggard commenced duty as master of this school. There were 31 boys present and I found all in excellent order. The Revd Father visited, also the Mother Superior. In the afternoon the former gave a holiday to enable the Master to assist in the unpacking of furniture at his home.

---

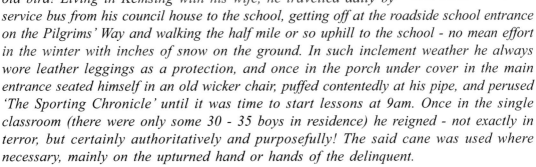

*'Jaggy, as we boys called him (behind his back of course!) was a strict disciplinarian who taught us in all subjects, including music (he was an accomplished pianist), except French, which was taught by Sister Grace, one of the three nuns in residence in Otford Court in my time, with the Linguaphone Method on gramophone records and text books, a very trendy resource in those days!*

*Jaggy, in spite of advancing age, was really quite a tough old bird! Living in Kemsing with his wife, he travelled daily by service bus from his council house to the school, getting off at the roadside school entrance on the Pilgrims' Way and walking the half mile or so uphill to the school - no mean effort in the winter with inches of snow on the ground. In such inclement weather he always wore leather leggings as a protection, and once in the porch under cover in the main entrance seated himself in an old wicker chair, puffed contentedly at his pipe, and perused 'The Sporting Chronicle' until it was time to start lessons at 9am. Once in the single classroom (there were only some 30 - 35 boys in residence) he reigned - not exactly in terror, but certainly authoritatively and purposefully! The said cane was used where necessary, mainly on the upturned hand or hands of the delinquent.*

*Sports Day, usually at the end of Summer Term, was arranged and supervised by Mr Jaggard, who for the occasion and for some unknown reason presided either at the start or the finishing posts in a frocked coat and striped trousers but wearing his usual trilby hat!*

*We only went home once a year, for the summer holidays, remaining at the*

*school for Christmas and Easter with only short breaks from lessons during these festivals. I don't think half-term holidays and such like were invented in those days - they were certainly never observed, nor the iniquitous so-called Baker Days so prevalent now. One could say with confidence therefore that Mr Jaggard earned his salary for the enormous amount of time spent in the classroom teaching us.*

*Jaggy's wife also took an important part in the life of the school on the occasions she acted as Matron while the real one was absent or indisposed (the Jaggards had no children of their own). A buxom lady and equally authoritative and purposeful as her husband (the Lord must have paired them!) she supervised our non-scholastic activities in a somewhat fierce and bossy manner, and to tell the truth we were always glad when the real Matron returned to duty; though (bless her!) Mrs Jaggard must have been sorely tried by us at times. When on duty she always wore a white veil like the real Matron, no doubt to impress on us her 'acting Matron' status!'*

**Douglas Keddie 1923/31**

...and here's 'Jaggy's' view of Douglas Keddie as recorded in the register in 1931: 'An excellent boy. Began with us to learn figures and letters. Left fit for matriculation.' A rare tribute to a pupil.

## Teaching and Academic Work

A visitor to Woodside in 1924 seems to have been impressed with Charles Jaggard's teaching methods:

> Perhaps the most interesting part of the Home is the schoolroom, where all the boys receive a sound education at the hands of an elderly master [Jaggard], who is evidently a personality. Such a school raises many considerable points in the mind of a visitor. It recalls the best type of old-fashioned seminary, where the child received guidance in the search for knowledge and in the free development of character, instead of having knowledge thrust upon him and his character forced as nearly as possible into an accepted mould, which is the apparent aim of many modern schools.

*Jaggard (on the right) with Father Tooth and some boys.*
*Douglas Keddie is pictured second from the right, lying on the ground.*

But a pupil of Jaggard's has a different point of view. Gerry Winter [1924/30] recalls:

*'Education was a very hit and miss affair. Mr Jaggard being our only teacher did his best with coping with Reading, Writing, Arithmetic, Geography, Latin and Art. When he wasn't too busy going from one classroom to the other (there were only two classrooms) he would be down at the kitchen and would come back with a handful of cold boiled potatoes with skins on, or a sausage roll or two or anything else that was going. He would then sit at his desk with penknife out, oblivious to all else.*

*When I left Otford I had to start my education all over again from scratch. Some boys got the benefit of his wisdom but I wasn't one of them. My interests lay in planning the next cricket match or the next model aeroplane to build, exploring the woods (out of bounds) and similar non-academic pursuits. Mr Jaggard had the foresight to see I was a non-starter from self-preference and thereby treated me accordingly.*

*He was a very fit man – he had to be when he would walk from his home at Kemsing to the school and back everyday, rain or shine. When the snows came he also came, much to our disappointment and expectations that he wouldn't.'*

Philip Morgan [1929/30] was more impressed with Jaggard's teaching skills:

*'I have to say the teaching must have been very good because when I left I went for a year (before going to school in England) to the old Grammar School in Carmarthen where I was streets ahead of my class, particularly, I remember, in Latin. It didn't last of course.*

*Jaggard was a fearsome Dickensian character, smelling always, it seems now, of whisky, tobacco and leather – the latter, though this may be fantasy, from his highly polished leggings. He wielded a mighty cane as befitted a Cambridge Blue who had bowled out the great WG Grace: but that might be a myth too.'*

Mr Jaggard had a few staff problems…

---

**10 January 1923:** This morning at 11am I had occasion to point out to Sister Dominica her boys did not know their tables. To my absolute astonishment she replied "Take them over yourself" and walked out of school. Comment unnecessary.

**11 October 1923:** Miss Searle commenced duty as an Assistant Mistress. She was not satisfied with her surroundings and did not return in the afternoon.

---

…but some notable teaching successes:

---

**16 March 1928:** Today Maurice Lewis left. He came to us in October of last year - a rough uncouth and backward boy. For the first two or three weeks I could do nothing with him & had to be rather severe. After a little time I thought I would try another method. I walked and talked with him. He gradually thawed and for the past weeks he has been everything one could wish for in conduct and attention to his studies. I am very sorry he has left.

---

**4 May 1928:** 3 times a week we have French lessons by a novel method. It is called Linguaphone French Course. The exercises are read through some three or four times by a gramophone - the voice evidently that of a Frenchman. By this plan the boys are able to hear the true pronunciation. They repeat the exercises as nearly as they can. Some of them are acquiring the accents quite well.

However, the overwhelming tone of Jaggard's log entries is one of despair and feelings of inadequacy. They make it clear that he found it very difficult to teach such a mixed group of children in terms of age and ability:

**14 September 1917:** We have three little boys who scarcely know their alphabet. All I can do with them is to spare one boy each session to look after them.

**3 May 1918:** There are now some seven or eight small boys here who know next to nothing and require individual attention, which of course I cannot give them.

**6 June 1919:** At the present time we have a preponderance of small boys that require a lot of attention. I have used one of the upper boys (Leslie Lorton) rather frequently as a monitor. Still having so many small boys is detrimental to the progress of the upper school as I am not able to give them so much attention as I should wish.

**14 October 1921:** I find the spelling & writing of the new boys very poor - in fact the crass ignorance of the majority of new entries is simply incredulous especially when the boys tell you they have been to certain schools.

**6 October 1925:** A fair amount of work has been got thro:- the very young boys are a source of great trouble and they are very slow in making a start. This week another little boy of 6 who knows absolutely nothing has been admitted. This policy must prove very detrimental to the place as a school. The upper boys very much resent the coming of these tiny boys.

**24 September 1926:** 25 boys have been present during the week. Of these 3 know absolutely nothing & can make neither a letter or figure. They are too young & most certainly should not have been admitted to a school of this class. At present I can do nothing for them.

**9 May 1930:** I have been specially working with the junior boys. Those who have been here some time are quite satisfactory, but the new arrivals are so totally ignorant that they are a complete drag and hindrance to the work of the classroom as a whole.

In 1932, with 16 years' service as Warden of St Michael's, Mr Charles Manning Jaggard retired. He died in 1940.

**27 January 1940:** I regret to record that Mr C. M. Jaggard has died. He was schoolmaster here for 16 years, resigning in May 1932. He will be remembered by many old boys for his long service devoted to them. All I have ever met spoke of him with great affection. He is the last but one of the old regime - Sister Christine alone remaining. His work in forming the school deserves grateful thanks from all of us. May he rest in peace. [Written by Mr Cork, Headmaster in 1940]

# Extracts from Charles Jaggard's last logbook entries in 1932

**11 January:** School reopened after the Xmas vacation. Three new boys have been admitted which makes 34 on Register. Of these the doctor has ordered 16 to bed owing to an epidemic of severe colds - leaving 18 present at school this morning. A new teacher (Miss Bentley) has taken charge of the smaller classroom.

**15 January:** Numbers are gradually going up so that there were 32 present today. The average for the week is 24. Hope to have things normal next week.

**29 January:** One of the hospital patients came home on Monday & we have one (Ernest Dipple) still there. Av. for week 32.5. The cough epidemic has now almost disappeared and all the boys are able to attend school.

**2 February:** School did not begin till 9.40. A Service (Purification) being held in the Chapel.

**12 February:** This week the two upper divisions have done some good work in mensuration - chiefly "triangles". There has been no absentees, 35 on Reg. Av. 35.

**19 February:** 15 boys were found "out of bounds" after being several times warned. These boys were punished by having to attend a morning session of school on Saturday.

**4 March:** Work proceeding smoothly and satisfactorily. Two boys have left but three new boys have been admitted. No. on Reg. 34. This Thursday we won an important football match. I had promised boys a half holiday if they were successful. This the Revd Father has sanctioned for them to have next week. We have an evening service during Lent on Thursdays. Prep. excused that evening.

**11 March:** On Thursday our football team went to Seal. I gave the whole school a half holiday to celebrate a very successful season.

**18 March:** Boys of both divisions have this week devoted extra time to "mensuration". A good week's work has been got thro'.

**8 April:** Broke up this morn for the transferred Easter Holiday. Yesterday we had our X Country run for a Silver Cup presented by T. Wellbeloved, Esq., the Revd Father also kindly added 10/- in money. Result 1. F. Corp (Cup & 5/-), 2. R. Fitzgerald 3/-, and 3. P. Jones 2/-.

**29 April:** I, (C. Manning Jaggard) resigned Mastership of this School.

# Charles M Jaggard 1916/32

**1916** – Charles Manning Jaggard commences at St Michael's as Master on the retirement of Frederick Wareham. He starts writing a daily logbook.

**1918** – The pandemic of Spanish 'Flu hits St Michael's but miraculously passes through within 2 weeks.

**1918** – 5 boys are entered for the Cambridge University Local Examinations. All pass and a day's holiday is given to the whole school.

**1919** – 4 boys enter the Cambridge University Local Examinations and once again, all pass. An afternoon's holiday is given.

**1920** – 6 boys enter the Cambridge University Local Examinations but this time 2 fail. No further students are entered.

**1925** – St Michael's School is moved to Otford Court.

**1926** – Jaggard introduces a system of prefects: 3 boys to take turns, one day each.

**1926** – The Reverend Mother, Sister Agnes dies.

**1930** – St Michael's welcomes over 1000 visitors for the Annual Corpus Christi event.

**1931** – The Founder of St Michael's, Father Arthur Tooth dies.

**1932** – Charles Jaggard retires from St Michael's.

# ~ 6 ~

## Father Charles Blofeld

### Warden from 1931 to 1938

Charles Harcourt Blofeld was born in St Pancras, London, in 1882. His parents were Thomas Blofeld and his Australian wife Ellen. He had a younger brother, Thomas Guest Blofeld (his successor as Warden at St Michael's) as well as other siblings.

Interestingly, on the 1901 census (aged 19) he is described as a Brewer's Clerk. Perhaps there was a connection through Australia and the brewing business that linked the Tooth and the Blofeld families?

At the age of twenty-seven Charles Blofeld was appointed Chaplain of the training ship Mercury. T.S. Mercury was one of over thirty pre-sea training establishments founded during

the Victorian period to give training to boys to meet the requirements of the Royal and Merchant Navies. At the start of the 20th century Britain needed at least 10,000 boys.

These training establishments ranged from fee-paying training ships for prospective officers in the Merchant Navy to reformatory ships for juvenile delinquents who mostly joined the navy as seamen or stokers. 'Mercury', however, was the only privately owned establishment training boys for both the Royal and Merchant Navies.

Some background history of 'Mercury' and the extraordinary people who ran the ship gives a fascinating insight into the environment in which Charles Blofeld found himself.

The 'Mercury' was founded in 1885 by a wealthy banker called Charles Hoare and his mistress (and mother of his illegitimate children) Beatrice Sumner. These two people had created a great scandal in the 1870s when their relationship hit the headlines. Not only was Beatrice a mere fifteen-year-old girl, just half the age of her lover, but Charles was a married man with several children of his own. Beatie's family tried to prevent them from seeing each other but despite a court injunction, their relationship continued. Hoare was taken to court and was threatened with imprisonment but was let off with a fine, which hardly affected his deep pockets.

Following the scandal Charles and Beatie needed to get out of the limelight. Their love of the outdoors was a factor is the establishment of their joint business located on the Isle of Wight. Beatie threw herself with great relish into the training of the boys and became an expert sailor herself.

The training ship put very little emphasis on education – not surprising since neither Charles nor Beatrice had received formal education themselves – so physical exercise and nautical skills filled the boys' time. Beatie's love of music also had an impact and the trainees frequently gave concerts.

After moving the training establishment to Hamble in Hampshire, Hoare and Beatie's relationship started to flounder and Hoare even moved out to a separate house, twenty miles away. However, their public standing started to improve and Hoare began to see the benefits of his public display of philanthropy. In particular, he was able to attract visits from famous sportsmen to the 'Mercury', including W.G. Grace, and in the 1890s, a young all-rounder called C.B. Fry.

# CB Fry

Charles Burgess Fry was to become a significant figure not only in the running of the 'Mercury' but subsequently in the life of St Michael's. He was probably responsible (along with Headmaster Michael Cork) for the school's strong tradition of cricket.

He was born on 25 April 1872, a truly significant date in the history of St Michael's as this is the school's foundation date.

'CB', as he liked to be called, was an extraordinary person and the list of his achievements is breath-taking. He won 12 blues at Oxford, captained England at cricket - scoring 94 first-class centuries, was a world-class sprinter, played rugby for Blackheath and the Barbarians, and played in an FA Cup final for Southampton. He was academically outstanding, an accomplished writer and one of the handsomest men in England. He was also invited to be King of Albania!

His first involvement in T.S. Mercury was noted with ten fateful words in Beatrice's diary: 'Charles Fry came to play cricket today. I like Fry.' In 1898, when CB was twenty-six and one of the most eligible bachelors in Britain, he married the long-term lover of Charles Hoare who was ten years his senior and mother of two illegitimate children.

Surprisingly, Hoare forgave CB and Beatie, and they all remained friends. Whilst CB forged ahead with his cricketing career, Hoare spent his time running the training centre and watched as its reputation increased and his social standing improved.

A year after Charles Harcourt Blofeld was taken on as Chaplain to the Mercury, Charles Hoare died and although he left a very large estate, he provided very poorly for the training centre. Lawyers estimated that with the provisions from Hoare's will, the centre would only be able to last for a few months.

CB Fry resolved to save the Mercury from the risk of closure and set about securing its future by raising funds from a number of sources. His motive was straightforward: he was simply annoyed by the 'sheer stupidity of allowing such a work to die.'

Although CB took an immediate interest in the running of the ship, he also enjoyed teaching, albeit on an irregular basis. In December 1908, when he became the Mercury's Captain Superintendent, his subjects were listed as 'Greek, Latin, Moral Philosophy, Ancient History, French, German, Spanish, Mathematics, Physics and Naval History'.

Fry's method of selecting from applicants for the Mercury was an unusual one – and will provide amusement for mothers of St Michael's pupils today. In the 1940s CB told readers of *The Sunday Graphic*:

> 'The main trouble was that parents applied from all over the United Kingdom... Distance and expense more often than not precluded interview... What did I do? I simply insisted that with application papers should be sent the mother's photograph. And if I liked the look of the mother I decided in favour of the son.'

By the time that CB took the helm, Charles Harcourt Blofeld had been Chaplain at TS Mercury for a year. CB's friendship with the future Warden of St Michael's, Charles Blofeld resulted in him being invited to be a patron of the school, an arrangement which continued long after his friend Charles's death - although without the official title of 'Patron'.

This photo of CB Fry handing out Sports Day prizes in the 1950s illustrates this enduring relationship.

## Warden at St Michael's

In 1917, after 10 years as Chaplain on T.S. Mercury, Fr Charles Blofeld was appointed Warden of All Saints Orphanage in Lewisham and then, on the death of Father Arthur Tooth in 1931, Father Charles Blofeld was immediately appointed as Warden of St Michael's.

*'Charles Harcourt Blofeld was fairly portly, with a twinkle in his eye. He was generous financially, and enjoyed the good things in life. He ran an SS Jaguar car, and in the 1930s this was quite eye catching.*

*He smoked cigarettes quite heavily, which probably killed him at the early age of 58. The boys loved him and I cried when I heard of his death.'*

*'One of many happy memories: a trip by steam train to Hastings. Father Charles took all the senior boys for a day by the seaside. We loved it, but unfortunately on the way back the train was pretty crowded, so Fr Charles herded us into a First Class compartment. I'll always remember the inflexion in the ticket inspector's voice when he opened the door*

*and looked hard at Fr Charles, "FIRST Class, Sir!?? We ended up scattered in various seats throughout the train.'*

**Paul Barraclough 1935/38**

CH Blofeld's car

*'There were two great celebrations during my stay at St Michael's (1934/38).*

*The first was the Silver Jubilee of King George V which fell in 1936. The King had, during his reign become perhaps more respected than beloved. He had managed somehow to become less Germanic, more British. Nothing endeared him more to his subjects than his oft-quoted remark: "Abroad is bloody. I know; I've been there!"*

*Queen Mary was regarded as governessy - people were a little frightened of her, while yet admiring her dignity and her upright and beautiful carriage. It was not until the outbreak of war that she softened, seemed to become more human, and attracted genuine affection.*

*To us schoolboys the Jubilee was a disappointment in one way. Avid stamp collectors all, we had expected a plethora of commemorative issues from all over the Empire. Instead there was a standard design for all countries, from the greatest Dominion to the smallest Crown Colony. All printed in Britain and on sale in Britain. Dullsville!*

*St Michael's celebrated nonetheless. We all went up into the woods, collected kindling, brushwood, broken branches and old logs; dragged them out to the pre-selected spot on the hillside, and there built our great bonfire. It was not to be a bonfire so much as a "beacon", one of a line of beacons across England reminiscent of the signal beacons that once had heralded the approach of the Spanish Armada. And true enough, on the night, when our great fire got going, we were able to see some of the others, some quite distant.*

*The following year the King died. Michael Cork [Headmaster] - very true-blue Brit for an Irishman - strode into class (he took large paces for a not-very-tall man), declaiming. "The King is dead. Long live the King!" So it became both duty and pleasure to celebrate the accession of King Edward VIII. Up into the woods again, more brushwood, more logs, but slightly less enthusiasm this time. And once again our beacon shone out across the Garden of England.*

*It was about this time (but I have no knowledge of the actual date) [30th November 1936] that the greatest beacon of all lit up our night skies. That was the night the Crystal Palace burned to the ground. The sky was as ruddy as I never saw it again until the Blitz. What a conflagration! We boys, of course didn't know what was happening, until Michael Cork announced it melodramatically the following morning.*

*I had seen the Crystal Palace, briefly through the trees, from a train on the way to London. At the end of term, when I went on holiday, it just wasn't there. I'm glad I had seen it once.'*

**Eric Crabbe 1934/38**


# Trustees and Governors of St Michael's

Following the death of Father Arthur Tooth in 1931, the future security of the school was in a precarious situation, as St Michael's was now owned by two elderly nuns. To ensure that Father Tooth's legacy would continue after their deaths a trust was set up with the school as the sole beneficiary. The St Michael's Trust Association Limited was incorporated in April 1937 and the Trustees had their work cut out handling the portfolios of investments which Sister Grace and Sister Christine had put together during their lifetimes (The Cowper-Miles Trust). Their first transactions involved selling diamond, tea and rubber shares to invest in London Transport and the Southern Railway Company.

The first meeting of the combined Trustees and Governors of St Michael's was held on 14 June 1937 at St Ermins, Westminster. It was chaired by Father Fynes-Clinton who started the meeting by making a statement on the objects and value of the school and by giving details of the formation of the Trust Association. The school had as Patrons the Right Revd Bishop O'Rorke, His Grace the Duke of Argyll and Sir George Arthur, Bart. The Trustees were Father Fynes-Clinton, Father C.H. Blofeld (Warden) and T.G. Blofeld, (Chaplain of the Gordon Boys Home). In addition to these three, others were listed as Governors: the Reverend Dudley Symon, (Headmaster of Woodbridge school); the Revd. A. Hope-Patten (Vicar of Walsingham); Revd. R.W. Pilkington; Revd J.W. Mills; Major Bowker; Mr R.W. Hodgkinson (of the firm of Messrs. Raphael, Stockbrokers); and Mr Philip Hale.

According to the minutes, the Chairman explained that:

'The property of the late Rev. Arthur Tooth consisted of the house and land of about 80 acres known as Otford Court and investments totalling about forty thousand pounds worth at the present time. The house and land had been put into trust by him, himself as sole trustee and the investments he had bequeathed to the surviving members of the community, Sisters Grace and Christine. They had been led to make it over to a trust in the names of Mr Fuller and Mr Darrell under misunderstanding. These however, under pressure had now made over the property to the three Trustees above mentioned. In addition there was a residue of the late Sister Grace's estate bequeathed to the Trust Association for the benefit of the school.

Mr Hale then gave the meeting detailed account of the financial position, explaining that, should securities maintain their present value, the school should just about be able to pay its way; but there would be nothing left with which to meet any extraordinary expenditure that might arise...

The Revd. C.H. Blofeld then gave an account of the school, explaining that its capacity was forty boys. There was now a Headmaster, Mr Cork, an assistant Master, and a Mistress for the Juniors, together with a Matron, under Matron and servants. He outlined the purpose of the school which should be, in order to carry out the intention of Father Tooth, to provide a home and a school of preparatory standard for boys of the professional class, who normally would have received such as education but through some death or calamity were financially unable to do so.

This was made possible by taking boys at present at the fee of forty pounds per year. Further, the aim was to give the boys a sound Catholic upbringing, to avoid the 'institution' atmosphere and prepare for scholarship those able to proceed to a Public School.'

The work of the Governors continues to this day. These 6 individuals have full responsibility for governing the school but delegate the day-to-day running to the Headmaster. They have responsibility (with the help of the Bursar) for managing the fixed assets of the school and for all capital investments. They also oversee all policies and make sure that the school meets all the statutory and governmental regulations.

\* \* \*

Charles Blofeld died suddenly on 8 October 1938. He had suffered a heart attack brought on by heart disease.

*'Following the death of Father Charles Blofeld, we were all wheeled into the study and then through to his bedroom to view the body robed in white vestments. It was the first dead person I had ever seen.'*

**Jeffries Stratton 1937-41**

---

**8 October 1938:** On this day our beloved Warden Fr. C. H. Blofeld passed away very suddenly at 10.15 in the morning. He suffered very little & had only been in bed one day. The Doctor was in attendance. All his life here was one of service - at the altar - in his study - on the fields - his prayers and thoughts were always with his boys. His wisdom, his patience, his kindness, made him Father, Councillor and Friend to us all. What he did for this school many, many, boys past and present and his many gifts can testify.

**12 October 1938**: We buried Fr. Blofeld today. A Mass of Requiem was said at 11.15, the celebrant being Fr. T. G. Blofeld. After the Absolutions of the Dead - he was taken to Kemsing where Fr. H. J. Fynes-Clinton committed his body to the earth. There were many mourners and some 40 wreaths. There is an empty place at St. Michael's.

---

In 1939, the Patrons and Trustees of St Michael's decided to 'procure a worthy memorial of the Founder Father Arthur Tooth and of Father Charles H. Blofeld'. They requested money from parents and friends so that the school would be able to provide leaving Exhibitions for deserving boys entering public school from St Michael's. A valedictory statement from CB Fry features in the document:

'Charles Blofeld was Chaplain of the Mercury for many years. He was intensely fond of boys and they were devoted to him, so he helped to establish in the Mercury a high standard of Church influence which still endures. He is well worthy of a memorial in the form proposed.

He played games fiercely. He was never wanting at a crisis.'

Above:
Boys at school in the 1930s. Sitting in the chair is a young teacher, and standing at the back is Old Michaelian Douglas Keddie on one of his many visits to St Michael's.

Right:
Two ruffians! Patrick Shipp & Roy Haines.

# Charles H Blofeld 1931/38

**1931** – Father Charles Blofeld becomes Warden of St Michael's on the death of the Founder Father Arthur Tooth.

**1936** – The Three Sisters: Grace, Christine and Hilda (lay Sister) retire and Miss Whitling takes the place of the 'Lady of the House'.

**1936** – It was announced that holidays at Christmas and Easter would now be of three weeks duration. Boys would not be kept at school for either Christmas or summer, but could remain for the Easter vacation if it is was particularly requested.

**1936** – The running of St Michael's is taken over by St Michael's Trust Association.

**1937** – The first meeting of the Trustees & Governors of St Michael's is held at St Ermins, Westminster. Father Fynes-Clinton is appointed Chairman.

**1937** – Donald Cormack takes the post of Second Master at St Michael's.

**1938** – The news of the possible sale of Otford Court is seen in the press. Parents are subsequently assured that they would have a year's notice of a move to a new school at Walsingham – partly owing to 'war scare' and partly with a view to providing a choir school for the shrine.

**1938** – Father Charles Blofeld dies of heart disease aged just 58.

# ~ 7 ~

## 'Corky' – Michael Cork

### Headmaster from 1932 to 1941

Michael Cork took up the position of Headmaster of St Michael's on the resignation of Charles Manning Jaggard in May 1932. He reported to Father Charles Blofeld who continued as Warden.

Not much is known about Mr Cork's life prior to St Michael's except that he was born in Cork, Ireland and was a graduate of Sidney Sussex College, Cambridge.

Old Michaelian Paul Barraclough [1935/38] believes he was about 40 years old when he took office and was married to Margaret, who initially took over the junior form in the afternoons. They lived in a rented bungalow on the other side of Pilgrims Way, though their main residence was in Larkfield.

At the school's first ever Prize Day, in December 1932, Mr Cork spoke of his plans to improve the standards of the teaching in the school. This is how the local newspaper recorded his speech on that occasion:

> Mr Cork said that he much wanted to explain what the St Michael's system of education was, and what it was going to be. Their general standard was not high, but a syllabus was drawn up which at the end of four or five years would enable a boy to qualify for any public school in England. In the first place, Latin was placed foremost, for it was a fact that civilization derived from Rome and the Continent, and it was up to every man to learn the history of his derivation… For those who were able, and for those who would need it, after Christmas they would be taught Greek.

Careful attention had also been given to mathematics, and algebra, subjects which of course would be essential for public school entrance.

Their method was that education was not 'stuffing' a boy, but drawing out of the pupil that which was most stressed in him, as the boy enjoyed his best subject, and gradually gained and developed his interest therein.

Father Blofield (left) and Mr Cork at Sports Day Prizes

As well as overseeing the introduction of school prizes, Mr Cork also produced the first ever school play and, alongside Father Charles Blofeld, instilled a strong enthusiasm in team sports amongst the boys. His teaching methods were strict - sometimes harsh - but to many he was an inspirational teacher.

*'The fear? That was every Monday morning when Mr Cork strode in, sometimes brandishing his cane. What had we done during the weekend? What had he found out? But let's give him his due. He was also an imaginative teacher in many ways. I still have an illustrated "The Coronation Scot" which I laboriously produced as what would now be called a "project", not to mention my Coronation booklet, complete with cigarette card pictures. Then there was stamp collecting, with approvals from Stanley Gibbons to be chosen in strict pecking order. That's how I learned my basic geography, that and our games of "capitals", "rivers", "mountains" etc. A pity so many names have changed today!'*

**Roy Haines 1932/38**

## Corky - Michael Cork

*'On my first morning I made the acquaintance of Mr Cork, who was to be my pedagogue and mentor for the next four years. Some 30 of us sat in his classroom, aged from 9 to 13, and he taught us all. He taught us English and French and History and Geography and Arithmetic and Algebra and Geometry and Latin and even a smattering of Ancient Greek.*

*He presided from a rostrum mounted on a platform. He had a cane which he brought with him each morning and placed on his desk pointing towards him. I never saw him use it on the flesh of one of his pupils but he would sometimes (if we were extraordinarily stupid) thwack a desk with it, and we all cowered.*

*A huge man was Mr Cork, an Irishman from Cork (which he spelled 'Cobh'), with pebble glasses and sandy hair, a straggly moustache and a very large red nose. He wore baggy Oxford trousers and a moth-eaten green sports jacket with leather patches on the elbows over a machine-knitted button-fronted cardigan in black and red wool.*

*Mr Cork ruled us with a rod of iron. We were terrified of him, but for him we would always put forth the best we had – not out of fear but out of the pride he called forth in us. I would say we loved him. No man in my life has motivated me more than he. This was the archetypal educator, a man born to teach, dedicated to the art (and of course it is an art) of drawing out the best from the young minds placed in his charge. Cork set us **thinking,** set us asking questions of the world around us, querying the platitudes that were being thrown at us from all sides. To me, that's what education is all about.*

*I remember the day he strode in, thwacked the desk with his cane, brandished the* Daily Express *and asked us: "So what do you think of this?" The front-page headline announced that Britain (under Stanley Baldwin) had opted for re-armament at a cost of £365 million a year, "That's a million pounds every day." he reminded us. As a taxpayer, he didn't offer us his views on this expenditure but left us to think it out.*

*We knew about Hitler,* 'Mein Kampf' *was on secret circulation, as was* 'No Orchids for Miss Blandish'. *We preferred Miss Blandish to Herr Hitler, I might mention, but I think most of us realised it was necessary to arm for a forthcoming war.*

*As a human being Michael Cork may not have been unflawed. I would say, and I thought this even then, that he was a man not unfamiliar with the jug and bottle. We boys sometimes had the feeling that all was not well between himself and his wife (whom we never saw).'*

**Eric Crabbe 1934/38**

'I am most grateful to Michael Cork who gave us so much general knowledge, be it mythology, history or geography that have served me so well in my life as an inveterate traveller.'

**Ivan Green 1934/38**

'Education, due largely to 'Corky' was of a very high order. 'Corky' taught Latin, History – English, Roman, Economic History and his very own Potted History, also English Literature and he introduced Greek. I think back now and believe 'Corky' had a brilliant mind. He was no less than a walking Encyclopedia. But there was one snag: he was a bully. He had a bamboo cane bound at one end with red wire and I am sorry to say he rather delighted in using it.

The severest thrashing I recall was given to Peter Scarland [1930/38] for cribbing in a French exam. He was given 12 of the best and I seem to remember he never cried, let out a yell – not a murmur! Michael Waite [1934/38] was always getting the stick. One night he was changing into his pyjamas when Matron came in and noticed the marks on his backside. Matron immediately went down to tell Father Guest Blofeld (who was then the Warden) and Father came up to the dormitory, examined Waite and turned to Matron saying, "I'll have a word with Cork in the morning." Corky was not so liberal with the cane after that.'

**Peter Bull 1935/40**

'Fortunately I have purged most of my memories of 'Corky' away, except that I do remember that he usually went home to lunch and came back suffering from rather too much 'falling down water', which did nothing to improve his temper.'

**Jeffries Stratton 1937/41**

'After a week or two, I spilled some ink all over the rickety old desk and proceeded to mop it up with a flimsy textbook. There followed a summons before the senior school and the tyrant Mr Cork who was the big, somewhat red-headed, and certainly red-faced Headmaster. After a few well-chosen words, he slapped me very hard across the face, which certainly cured as well as stunning me. After this experience I realised that 'Corky' was someone to be avoided at all costs – and I for one, was glad when he left.'

**Paul Rose 1940/44**

The logbook entry, entered in Fr. T.G. Blofeld's hand after the summer 1941 term had ended states:

---

At the beginning of the term we lost the services of Mr. D. Cormack, who had been called up for Military duties. His enforced departure is an enormous loss to the school, but we look forward to the time, not far distant we hope, when he will be able to return to us.

Then, in the course of the term, it became known that Mr Cork felt the time had come for him to seek a new sphere of work & he has been offered and accepted a Mastership at Nevill Holt School, near Market Harborough, Leics., taking up his new duties in September.

The Warden, in his review of the term's activities on "Breaking Up" Day, paid tribute to the devoted work of Mr Cork throughout the nine years and one term he had held the post of Headmaster. Not only had he raised the standard of education at St. Michael's to a high level of excellence, but he had helped the school to attain considerable success in Cricket and Football, & had produced plays each year at Christmas, which had become a marked feature of the School Year.

As a small mark of appreciation of all his labours Parents and Friends contributed towards a Testimonial which took the form of a cheque, the names of the contributors being inscribed in a book handed to Mr Cork.

Goodbye, Mr Cork, we shall miss you much, but we wish you all success and happiness in your new sphere of work.

---

One description of Mr Cork comes from the words of Rev T Guest Blofeld, presumably acting as a referee for him:

> When he (Michael Cork) took up his duties in 1931 the standard of education at the school was at a low ebb, but by his outstanding organising and teaching abilities, and his unbounded enthusiasm, he raised the standard to a high state of efficiency. He prepared a number of boys for various Public School Scholarships, and the Schools Honours List shows many notable successes.
>
> He was a very firm, but kindly, disciplinarian, and gained the respect and affection of all who passed through his hands.

Mr Cork is also a keen sportsman. He had charge of the School Cricket and Rugby Football, and the achievements of the various Teams, under his able coaching, were most gratifying. He also organised the Annual Athletic Sports with great success.

In addition Mr Cork is an enthusiastic believer in the educational value of Acting, and the Annual Plays, of Shakespeare or other great Dramatists, produced by him, were always an outstanding feature of the Christmas Term.

St Michael's owes a great debt of gratitude to Mr Cork, and his name will always be remembered with great affection and respect. [14th September 1944]

The whole school during Mr Cork's Headship (seen sitting to the left of Warden Charles Blofeld).

However, Paul Barraclough [1935/38] is not too happy with the 'reference' above:

*'This descriptive 'reference' is rather generous! I do not feel happy with the words 'kindly' and 'affection' as Corky could be rather rough with boys who were slow at learning, or broke rules, or misbehaved in some way. I shall never forget seeing a boy a little younger than me receive six vicious strokes of the cane on his backside whilst bent over a table, or the canings on the hands, even on one boy whose fingers were swollen with chilblains. At one time I calculated that every boy in the senior classroom had been caned at least once.*

*Apart from his Victorian attitude to discipline he could be an entertaining and amusing host. He would invite senior boys to tea at his home where we could play sedentary games and discuss the books we were currently reading.'*

# School Poem
### (as remembered by Peter Bull 1935-1940)

This time next week where shall I be?
Not in this academy
If I am I'll curse and swear
And knock old Corky off his chair.
If the matron interferes
Knock her down and box her ears
If she interferes again, knock her down and do the same!

When the train goes Puff! Puff! Puff!
I'll be in it sure enough
No more porridge stirred with sticks
No more cakes as hard as bricks.
When we arrive at Mother's door
Out comes Mother and a few more.
"What would you like, dear,
What will you take?"
A glass of milk and a slice of fruitcake.

After 7 weeks of jolly good fun
Back to the workhouse we do run.
When we arrive at Father's door
Out comes Father and a few more.
"What would you like, dear,
What will you take?"
A mug of ditch water
And a slice of bread and scrape!

# Michael Cork 1932/41

**1932** – Michael Cork becomes Headmaster at St Michael's on the resignation of Charles Jaggard.

**1932** – First 'Prize Giving' event and School Plays.

**1933** – Forms are re-organised into: VIth (Scholarship term), Vth, IVth, IIIa, IIIb.

**1935** – Silver Jubilee of His Majesty George V - the school is given a whole holiday.

**1936** – Sisters Grace and Christine and Lay Sister Hilda retire from St Michael's. The St Michael's Association is formed to continue the running of the school.

**1937** – The Coronation of Edward VIII is celebrated with war games in the grounds.

**1937** – Donald Cormack is appointed Second Master.

**1938** – Two Houses are established: Greeks & Trojans, and a 'Stars & Stripes' points system is introduced.

**1938** – The Warden Father Charles Blofeld dies age 58 and his brother Thomas Guest Blofeld succeeds him.

**1940** – 'Barbarians' join the other two houses.

**1941** – Donald Cormack is called up to serve in the army.

**1941** – Michael Cork resigns from St Michael's.

# ~ 8 ~

# Life at St Michael's

## My first day at St Michael's

### "When thou crossest a frontier enquire what is forbidden within"

Eric Crabbe who started at St Michael's in 1934 has contributed a fascinating account of a pupil's first day at St Michael's:

*'The first thing I saw as we arrived in the village of Otford was an oasthouse. It proved we were really in Kent. We wound out of the village in my uncle's Ford 8 up a gentle hill and through a handsome pair of gates. We were now in the grounds of Otford Court once the seat of a local manorial seigneur.*

*The drive meandered by a group of stately copper beeches. To the right the ground fell away to a distant view of the little town of Sevenoaks. My heart rose into my throat; I had not known that the English countryside had this much to offer.*

*Orphanages, by definition, are grim and forbidding. St Michael's, Otford Court, an orphanage bidding to be regarded as a Preparatory School, was (at first glance anyway) precisely the opposite – warm and inviting.*

*I must have been the luckiest orphan ever. There was this lovely building, three storeys, with a turret extending to a fourth storey and topped by a green copper cupola.*

*The double front doors were grand and opened into what was known as 'the refectory' – long oak tables, with benches either side.*

*A grand staircase extended up to the first floor landing, a gracious enclosure, lined with bookcases, its centrepiece a handsome billiard table. Once again a staircase, less grand this time, corner-placed and presuming to be inconspicuous, extended upwards to the second floor. The second floor landing accommodated a long deal table. The rooms off, there were several of them, had plainly been in manorial times servants' quarters. In modern days they constituted the orphanage dormitories.*

*Each dormitory accommodated a few single iron beds, from eight in the larger rooms to four in the smaller. The smallest room constituted the matron's quarters, sub-divided into her office and an alcove for her sleeping quarters. A matron – she is faceless in my memory for matrons came and went with bewildering frequency, some of them hard-faced middle-aged battle-axes, others nubile dewy-eyed nineteen year olds. You may guess which the boys preferred, even very little nine-year old boys like myself – though we were sometimes cruel and teasing, as befits (we thought) the male of the species. A faceless matron, as I remarked, politely dismissed my father and my uncle and bade me sit at the deal table until such time as I could be dealt with.*

*I sat there throughout a long afternoon as the sun slanted lower through the landing skylights wondering once or twice whether I actually existed or was only a shadow through which the regard of actual flesh-and-blood members of the human race could pass unhindered. Boys arrived from time to time with little bags and suitcases and filtered into this dormitory or that. Some glanced without interest in my direction before greeting friends; others ignored me completely. Matron's starched gown swished wordlessly by me so often that I despaired sometimes of ever re-joining society.*

*This, I believe is the universal experience of a first day at boarding school – particularly for one who is only nine years old.*

*Eventually I was noticed, asked my name and allocated a bed in one of the larger and most junior dormitories. I slept soundly and when morning came I found myself part of a community, as if I had been there always.'*

\* \* \*

Other boys who were pupils in the 1930s and 1940s add their memories:

*'My mother put me in the care of the guard on the train in Victoria station. I was being sent to my first boarding school at the age of 11 and arrangements had been made for me to be met at Otford station.*

*I stood on the platform at Otford feeling lost and nervous, when an authoritive voice from the other platform called "Are you Barraclough?" I crossed the footbridge and faced for the first time Father Charles H Blofeld, Warden of St Michael's School [1932/38]. He led me to an impressive car (later I discovered it was an SS Jaguar) and he chatted to me about my elder brother whom he knew when he was chaplain to the T.S. Mercury, and Michael was a naval cadet.*

**Paul Barraclough 1935/38**

*'There could have been few more impressive sights to a youngster than walking up the drive passed those beautiful copper beeches to come face to face with the 'White Nuns' – the gate posts to the school. To the left, the slope up to 'Creeper Castle' on the boundary of Row Dow (where we used to try and smoke creepers) and to the right, the railings down to the junior school playing field behind which lay the two flower beds at the bottom of the terraces which provided flowers for the Chapel.'*

**J. Martin Beech 1943/47**

*'I was introduced to the school at an interview with the Warden Father Thomas Guest Blofeld [1939/64] in the early summer of 1947. Father Blofeld was in a cassock and biretta, his foot upon a foot-stool. "Now, my dear," (this to me) "what is one over two?".*
*"Don't know sir". (Winchester House where I was currently at school was strong on fatuous girlie books, short on basic academic attainment). The interview continued amicably enough. My father asked what sports were practised. "Rugby, Association Football and Athletics in the Summer Term" replied Father Blofeld – who continued, "We encourage table tennis, but as a result of shortages in manufacture we have problems securing supplies of table tennis balls". "Let me find some for you", said my generous papa. He was as good as his promise. The two boxes arrived. My mother thought it would be appropriate if I sent them to the school as an ingratiating pupil-to-be gift. Mother proposed that I should write an accompanying note. "Dear Father Blofeld, I am sending this note and balls to you. Love John Underwood", I wrote. My mother collapsed into helpless giggles; I was deeply offended. "You can't say 'Love' to someone you don't know very well", she said to assuage my indignation. The letter was not sent; I have it still!*

*I arrived in September 1947. My mother left me with Matron Stockwell. I stood immersed in grief as the car disappeared. Matron (old school, King's College SRN, standard apron and cap) clutched me comfortingly to her starched bosom and crushed my forehead against her enamel SRN badge. Pain very effectively assuages grief.'*

**John Underwood 1947/53**

Later entrants to the school also record their first impressions:

*'Jon Goodinson was the first boy I got to know at St. Michael's. We were buddies from the first night in dorm three. "Thirty years from now this will be a class room," I thought, as I first set eyes on the place.*

**"No I didn't**!*" I protested at the posted notice that dorm three had a bedtime of 6.30pm and tuck was administered by Matron once a day after lunch...*

*I can vividly recall the fist time I set eyes on St. Michael's. As my father drove through the tiny village of Otford, a right turn onto Pilgrims Way and then a hesitant 'half left' approach to the tricky entrance to the grounds of St Michael's. A 'do or death dive' for the corner of the junction.*

*An old wooden sign nailed to a tree, distressed presumably through age alone, announced your arrival through fading gold paint. That board must have been there for decades, the sign itself suggesting a school with a rich history and pedigree. Winding down the private driveway, passing Father Eyden's house on the left, over a few speed bumps and through the white topped steel gates. I loved the sound the gravel made as it was crunched beneath the wheels of the car. Then the red brick building with dozens of oversized sash windows and the green copper tower.*

*When you first laid eyes on the grounds of St Michael's, any nine-year-old boy's imagination would run wild dreaming up the adventures that undoubtedly lay ahead. Weekends? Yeah! We loved and cherished them.*

*I hid my tears as my parents drove their Hillman Avenger Estate away from the school for the first time, down the gravel path towards Otford and onward towards Osnabrück, West Germany. They had a long drive ahead of them. I, in the meantime, looked forward to seeing them again.*

*The first morning away from our parents, Jon and I awoke early at around 6am. It was a strange feeling waking up in an unfamiliar place. I fished out my Monopoly game from under the bed and we began to play as if it was just a normal day.'*

**David Humphreys 1974/79**


# The Dormitory

New boarders found ways of coming to terms with the mass sleeping arrangements:

### At Woodside

*'The Jack Dempsey v Georges Carpentier fight was held on 2 July 1921 at Jersey City, New York, and coloured rockets were sent up from Crystal Palace according to whose round it was: red-Dempsey and green - Carpentier I think. We could see, surreptitiously I may add, the Crystal Palace from our dormitory window and we took turns to watch. On such occasions I had to stuff my clothes down the bed to make a hump, as it was in the corner by the door through which one of the nuns would pop at inconveniently odd times.*

*Our washing facilities were a line of tin bowls in the bay window behind which was a 3-water jug stand and 3 chamber pots beneath. That is something else I do remember as my next bedmate suffered badly from chilblains, and we were all ordered to use one chamber pot...another old belief.'*

**Duncan Jackson 1920/21**

## At Otford

*'Once or twice in the night I felt my bedclothes being tugged from my bed. There was no one there, yet the sheets would be pulled and I had to hold on to them. One awful night I woke to feel hot breath on my face and a paralysing weight on my chest; it pulsated with a low-pitched moaning sound. Terrified, I lay still, hoping I had not been noticed, as children do. I would have pulled the bedclothes over my head, but they were pinned down just as I was. Had I been a girl I would have screamed; but boys don't do that – at least not among other boys. In terror I jerked at last and the big black cat that had strayed in through the dormitory window jumped off my bed to the floor and strolled away.'*

**Eric Crabbe 1934/38**

*'There were 4 dormitories leading off the top floor landing and we were segregated according to age group and averaged about 8 boys to a dorm with the eldest being nominated to take over the duties of monitor. There was no luxury here and all was rather primitive and basic. There were only two toilets on this floor so the chamber pots usually found under each bed became an attractive alternative. These were known in schoolboys' vernacular as 'gerries' – probably because they looked somewhat like the steel helmets that the Germans wore in the First World War and I came in for a great deal of banter with my name being Gerald.*

*We had to abide by very strict rules. Lights out at 8pm, no talking thereafter, prayers to be said, no eating. I, like a few others, was a firm believer that rules were meant to be broken, or bent, and consequently these do's and don'ts were not strictly adhered to. Electric torches were frowned upon but one would often see my batteries on top of the radiator receiving a boost along with a few others.*

*Midnight feasts too were not uncommon when one, more hungry than brave, or both, would sneak down to the refectory and relieve the large wooden trays, stacked with slices of bread and marg ready for the morning breakfast, of some of their contents. This is where the ownership of a torch was paramount. The tell-tale grease stains under the nightshirt were dealt with swiftly and expertly.*

*Bath nights were noisy, steamy affairs. The two bath tubs were enormous and to save hot water it was often 3 to a bath. On these occasions it was considered necessary to have the Matron, or if not her, one of the Sisters, present to monitor the proceedings. It never seemed to worry us very much as they always looked very pious. Whether it worried them we weren't to know, what with the clouds of steam billowing out, I doubt they would see anything at all anyway.'*

**Gerry Winter 1924/30**

*'As far as I can recall the events in the following story took place in the summer term before the war. We were all borders at the time, I think about 46-48 all told. Father Charles Blofeld was the Warden and Mr Cork ('Corky') was Headmaster [1932-1941].*

*My great buddy at the time was Brian Henharen [1937/40], a stocky thickset chap. We were both in Dormitory Seven (hard left at the top of the staircase). Dorm 7 had a lovely view out over the terrace and many miles beyond, one of the nicest views of the Weald of Kent anywhere. Because Brian and I were the biggest boys in the dorm we bagged the best beds, which were both nearest the window.*

*During this time we would often play 'Dare', so one evening, shortly after Matron came round and said goodnight, I whispered to Henharen, 'Brian, I dare you to stand on the parapet near your bed, walk along the parapet – outside on the window ledge, a distance of about 20 feet, then jump down on to my bed." Like a flash, Henharen, clad only in pyjamas was on the windowsill, carried out the dare and hopped back into bed, much to the amusement and admiration of all the occupants of Dorm 7.*

*Five minutes later we heard the familiar crunch of footsteps on the pebbled pathway beneath us. It was Father Blofeld taking his nightly stroll. I shudder to think what he would have thought had he looked up five minutes earlier!*

*If anyone had told me that Henharen had gone on to earn his living jumping over busses or through hoops of flames, I should not have been in the least surprised. In fact he took up Holy Orders!'*

**Peter Bull 1935/40**

*'The first night I just survived the dormitory slipper treatment as new boys were made to stand in the corner, while all the other boys threw their slippers at the poor wretch. In my case, the nameless prefect had perfect aim and when the others had sent their soft slippers aimed at my body, he directed his two 'Cambridge Leather' shoes with deadly accuracy at my head.'*

**Tony Rumm 1946/49**

*'Each dormitory had an enamelled bucket, and a chamber pot. Urine from the pot was poured by the user into the bucket. By morning there was a considerable quantity of 'slops' in the 'slop pail'. At the whim of some senior or larger member of the dorm, a victim was chosen. I don't recall if any misdemeanour was necessary. It just seems to my jaded recollection that the smaller and more defenceless turned out to be the victims. This unfortunate would be grabbed and carried over to the pail. Then his head would be lowered into it until his nose just*

*touched the collected urine. He was held there for however long was necessary to satisfy whatever criteria were in the mind (for want of a better word) of the instigator. A great start to another wonderful day!'*

**John Wood 1947/53**

*'John Hurt [1948/54] was not only a good actor but also a good dormitory captain. I certainly enjoyed the times he was on duty as he was always chatty and interested in what was going on with the rest of the dorm. You could have a great laugh with him. He had lots of freckles in those days!'*

**David Sharpless 1951/57**

*'The sound which instantly recalls St Michael's to me is not a godly bell, but the sound of someone peeing into an enamel chamber pot before tipping the contents into a large bucket in the dormitory.'*

**Stephen Winkley 1954/57**

*'The dormitories were completely unheated and it was not unusual to wake to your face flannel frozen to the wash stand. The first to get up was the dormitory member whose turn it was to fetch a jug of hot water to fill the basins. "Slopping Out" in the mornings was then as it is to this day in some prisons. By today's standards, beds and bedding were fit only for a skip!*

*The heating system was erratic although I do remember a dapper wee Scotsman by the name of Bell Thomson who had the knack of getting real heat out of the boiler. I also remember teacher Kathleen Wagg arriving for morning classes wearing overcoat and scarf, carrying a single bar electric fire. Meanwhile, Michael Hatton would be going round the staff rooms with a bucket of coal, newspaper and kindling, lighting the open fires which lost more heat up the chimney than they gave out to the room. The only rooms always warm were the kitchen with its big coal fired range and Father Blofeld's study which had a proper closed combustion type Courtier stove.'*

**Alec Stevenson 1954/60**

*'During my time there as a trainee teacher at St Michael's I slept on the stage which I think is where the present dining hall was. Due to my extreme untidiness I kept the curtains of the stage drawn and was only evicted during school plays when I occupied the sick bay! I was also charged with looking after a beautiful golden labrador called Ben who belonged to one*

*of the boys whose parents were working in pre-Gaddafi Libya. I walked or ran with him, every morning and evening and like every lab he had an insatiable appetite. One day I was teaching, leaving him lying on the stage asleep. I returned at lunchtime to find him in the yard outside polishing off an outsize ham, which was the bulk of the school meal that day!'*

**John Wright 1954-1960**

*'On the top floor of the school were several dormitories off a central, very worn wooden floor-boarded area. As you climbed the final flight of the central wooden staircase (having used the stone staircase winding around the manual lift to get this far - not the main staircase which was exclusively reserved for staff), dorm three was over in the far left corner of the floor. Inside, two rows of beds - headboards lined up neatly against the wall, the foot of the beds facing each other.*

*As you entered the dorm, at nine o'clock in the morning, under the windows, stood the wooden wash stand with five large Victorian style enamel wash basins. Standing to one side of the basins was an enormous water jug. For a nine year old, to carry a full one required all the strength you could muster. Those trips to get the water at THAT time of the morning? Boy! The water was cold and as I recall, not at all welcome.*

*Off in the far right corner of the room, two beds were wedged into an alcove. This tiny circular room was directly under the distinctive green dome I was so taken by on my arrival at the school.*

*That was where Jon Goodinson and I slept. I can remember thinking how cool it was that we had our own little space in the dorm. Jon and I would peer out of our 'private' windows, mine overlooking the main entrance of the school, Jon's with a view of the Terrace.'*

**David Humphreys 1974/79**

*'One amusing occasion at school was when the fire officer visited and said that it wasn't safe for the boys to sleep upstairs, as there were not enough fire doors in the building at the time. Rather than send the children home in the middle of term, we asked 'Where would it be safe for them to sleep?" The answer was – the only safe place would be the Chapel! So....for 28 nights we all slept together in the Chapel. I was on the dais and the children were scattered all over the floor in their sleeping bags. It was rather spooky to say the least, and we were all glad when the experience came to an end.'*

**John Jennings – Housemaster and Head of History 1990/93**

In the 1990s, the number of parents wanting to board their children at St Michael's dwindled and in 1996, the school decided to no longer offer boarding as an option.

A dorm in the 1980s

# Ghosts!

No account of a school housed in a Gothic mansion – even if Victorian Gothic – would be complete without its ghost stories. Even Father Tooth believed that the building had its share of supernatural visitors:

> In making a purchase of this property consisting of a fine country house and many acres of land, I was reminded that early and late, it played a praiseworthy part in history; names are still current in these parts responsible for great deeds, some good, some very evil. Now these ancestors: there they are; you can't get rid of them, they go with the property, you buy the lot – only to think of it, it is appalling!! Most people are discreet in speaking of their ancestors, but here is a whole crowd of them all at once: here and there among them a great rascal, and so they say this place is haunted – very likely: I love a good ghost story, don't you? This ghost has played merry pranks I am told – now I have given instructions that when he comes again I am to be called, the ghost is to be asked to wait a moment, to take a chair; and that I will be there directly.

**Fund-raising Pamphlet 1925**

\* \* \*

### *The Ghost of Dorm Five by Richard 'Fatty' Buehrlen [1943/47]*

*'It was Sunday, the year 1943, or perhaps 1944, a Sunday evening like every other Sunday evening – culminating in Evensong and Benediction. For the juniors this meant the most cursory of ablutions, hardly more than the Asperges of that morning's mass, so that we should not go to bed very much later than our normal bedtime. There was no changing into pyjamas before washing or bathing, just a dash to the dorm to pick up one's things, followed by the descent to the washrooms for teeth and the briefest of cat's licks, then back again to the dorm – all at high speed. More free time to be enjoyed before Benediction, the quicker one got it over with.*

*The only hitch, a major one, was passing the duty prefect's inspection – yes, he of the 'jaundiced eye' and 'Byzantine sense of humour'. Such a hazard was he, that the whole thing became more of a steeplechase than a race over the flat; much honour was to be won by overcoming every let and hindrance and being the first back into the dormitory.*

*This particular Sunday, Gerard and I rushed up the back staircase well ahead of the field and barged into Dorm Five in that state of triumphant excitement which is known only to a boy of seven or eight. Yet we sensed that something was not right. We fell silent. We were somehow not alone! We were sure we were the first back; confirmed by the lack of towel, or flannel on the washstand; but the feeling of another presence persisted. Perhaps there was someone, who had not yet gone down to the washrooms, hiding under a bed, ready to play some sort of trick? We looked, searching high and low – nobody! And still, and still – palpably some other presence! The tension heightened.*

*In an explosion of fear and childish jest Gerard ran out of the dorm and on to the landing, shouting "Spooks! Spooks!" I followed him and would have cried the same, when the words were struck from my lips. To my horror, there, at the other end of the landing, near the stairs, I saw a skull suspended in the air, traversing slowly and deliberately from one side of the landing to the other and disappeared. Terrified I pointed, mouthing gibberish.*

*Also on the landing was Miss Richards, the Under-Matron, bandaging a boy's knee. She made me sit down on the bench and explain myself. She managed to get out of me what I had seen. Miss Richards was not one to encourage the wilder flights of fancy. She thrust a thermometer into my mouth and took my pulse; "You are over excited," she said kindly. "You need not go to Benediction. Better go to bed and rest."*

*Whatever her diagnosis, her proposed therapy was totally unacceptable. There was no way that I was going to stay alone facing the phantoms of the night, whilst everyone else was far off in the chapel. "I'm going down to Benediction with everyone else," I insisted, and off to Benediction I went.*

*Afterwards with us all tucked up in bed with the lights out, I narrated my experience to the other inmates of Dorm Five, much to their delight. A frisson of fright passed round, not unaccompanied perhaps, with a willing suspension of disbelief; after all, 'Fatty' Buerhrlen was the dorm storyteller. This particular story might have ended here, were it not for the next morning.*

*Just before breakfast, whilst we were all at call-over, the unmistakeable, slow, ponderous thud of Father Blofeld's footstep approached the junior classroom. He flung open the door in his inimitable way and marched in. We stood up. "I have a very sad announcement to make. You, of course, all know Miss Whittling – for many years the school's most loyal lady housekeeper. Last night about the hour of Benediction, Miss Whittling died.....Requiem.....Prayers.....'*

\* \* \*

Many years later, Greg McKeague [1980/84] also experienced supernatural happenings at Otford Court.

*'In 1983 I saw a 'Ghost' in my dorm. Of course I had heard rumours of Christ getting down from the cross on the main stairwell and floating heads outside matron's room, but I saw a 'Ghost'!*

*It was in 1982-83 and I was asleep in my dorm (room-mates I remember: Helmsley and Perry) when I suddenly woke up for no reason. I clearly remember opening my eyes and looking towards the sinks in the gloom whereby I noticed someone just standing there facing away from me. I could tell that the figure was indeed an old man. He was hunched over the sink dressed in white and holding on to the basin, but strangely I was not afraid.*

*I must have stared at the figure for a good 30 seconds trying to comprehend what I was seeing and it did seem to shimmer/fade in and out. The figure seemed to tense up and recognise that it was being observed and it started to slowly turn around.*

*All I remember is leaping out of my bunk (I was closest to the light and door) and switching the light on waking my dorm. As for my Ghost, it disappeared! It was truly the most wonderful and yet terrifying thing I have ever encountered and 20 years on still sends a chill down my spine and I have never seen 'The Friendly Ghost' or anything alike since.*

*My gut feeling and instinct at the time told me he was a religious man, possibly a priest. Also the 'vibe' I felt was that he needed to help the injured and had to wash his hands before commencing these duties.'*

**Greg McKeague 1980/84**

# Uniform

There were more humdrum aspects of life at St Michael's to which a small boy must accustom himself. In the early years of St Michael's there was no specific uniform but by 1915 it was usual for them to wear blue roll necked jumpers, and for dinner on Sundays they wore dress suits.

*'Our clothing consisted of grey flannel shorts and a scratchy grey high-necked jersey worn over a vest. The garments were hand-me-downs; but occasionally the stock was replenished and one might be lucky from time to time to be issued with something new. I considered myself very fortunate for a year to have a jersey that had a gap in its welt, providing me with a place of concealment for a miniature catapult I had fashioned.'*

**Eric Crabbe 1934/38**

From left: (wearing Sunday Best)
John Williams [1932/38]
Francis Johns [1932/37]
Eric Crabbe [1934/38]

*'When we went to St Michael's in 1980 the uniform was grey shirts, grey pullovers, cord short trousers and grey socks for everyday wear and grey suits with white shirts and*

*green/red ties for Sundays and for teams playing away from Otford. We abandoned wearing of school caps when out from Otford from about 1984. I think that we allowed boys moving up from the Pre-Prep to wear green blazers but they were not universally worn in the senior part of school until after we left.*

*We introduced tracksuits together with the school sports holdall – green with St. Michael's Otford Court printed on them in silver. I still have one! Jenny [Cox] chose the girls' uniform when they started in the pre-prep in 1986.'*

**Paul Cox – Headmaster from 1980/86**

In 1998 sweatshirts were introduced for the children in Kindergarten and years 7 and 8 were allowed to wear dark green jerseys with a white shirt – with Lindsay kilts for the girls. Then in 2000, a summer uniform was introduced for the boys which consisted of burgundy or green polo shirts in main school, and white polo shirts in the pre-prep.

# Food

Until recently the poor quality of the food was an absorbing topic and has elicited vivid memories.

*'The other Sisters always had their meals with us [not Sister Hilda as she did the cooking] but at a separate table in the refectory alcove on the left. We would watch them enviously as they were served their hot, delicious looking food in china plates and bowls and then back to our chipped enamel plates and mugs. The food was notable for its simplicity and monotony. Boiled cabbage, boiled potatoes with their skins on, rabbit stew including the lead shot, and maybe with luck, cold beef.*

*Breakfast was no less exciting except that often the porridge, non-sweetened, had the consistency of wallpaper glue.*

*Little or no talking was allowed at meal times – just as well as the noise made from 40 odd boys eating off tin plates had to be heard to be believed. We did our own washing up in a very large stone sink in the locker room. The noise made at meal times was a murmur compared to what was being made here. Lifebuoy soap was the cleaning agent here, rinsing was very important as it's not known for its delicate fragrance.'*

**Gerry Winter 1924/30**

*'Of course, the food that went to high table was different from the food that was served at the refectory tables. Breakfast, for us, was a tin bowl of porridge oats, sugared in advance (we were not to be trusted with sugar basins), without milk but with a thin veneer of warm water – perhaps from the porridge itself – floating on the surface. Sometimes it was possible to come by a second bowl. I became very fond of oatmeal porridge in my four years at St Michael's; it was the staff of life. But, to be fair, there was also bread and butter (I think it was butter), both brown and white, sliced and spread; and of this there was an abundance. I would describe our provisions as monastic fare.*

Father Tooth's Dining Room in about 1926

*Boys who had some financial backing were permitted to be served a boiled egg no more than three times a week. This was by arrangement between a parent or guardian and the village general store. No boy was permitted to go to the store, or indeed go down into Otford village at all. Boys who had eggs were regarded rather as 'King rats' – lesser boys would be willing to provide services for them such as shoe-cleaning in return for an egg-top, sliced off with a knife and passed across at breakfast. After a year of being service-provider I explained the system to my father, who gamely stumped up sixpence a week for my three eggs, as well as sixpence-ha'penny twice a term for a jar of Robertson's Golden Shred marmalade, and in my last year an unknown sum for a miniature jar of marmite per term.*

*We were not permitted money in our pockets (for good reason); pocket money for the term was deposited in advance with Father Blofeld, who operated a sort of 'company store'.*

*Once a week (Saturdays after lunch I think) we queued up outside his study in order of seniority and were able to select an ounce of winegums or suchlike from a row of large jars placed seductively on his table. The cost was marked down against the sum deposited. The profits, small if any, accrued to Father Blofeld; but the system enabled him to ensure that no boy was able to exercise excessive power over his fellows.*

*Of course a black market existed, as in any community. Many of us, returning from school holidays, were able to sneak in a shilling or two we had conned out of those who loved and cared for us back in our home surroundings. Adoring aunts were usually good for a bob or two! We had our hiding places and often these were not in the school buildings at all but under a special stump up in the woods. It was with these secret slush funds that we were able to indulge our boyish vices.'*

**Eric Crabbe 1934/38**

*'Sister Hilda and Mary attended to the cooking in the kitchen, such as it was! Lunch was invariably a stew of some kind or rabbit caught in the grounds. In my early days breakfast and tea consisted of bread and a mug of tea. After a year, parents were allowed to arrange for 1lb jar of marmalade and 1lb jar of jam to be sent up weekly from Lowry's in Otford. This 'tuck' as we called it, was locked away during lent. I used to put salt and pepper or mustard on my bread to relieve the monotony until one day Matron saw me and stopped the practice. My brother John used to cut the crusts off his bread and make a sandwich of that and we often laugh now, 67 years later and recall that he actually invented the crust sandwich!*

*Reverting for a moment to the refectory, if Father and the nuns had boiled eggs for breakfast, Sister Christine would ring a small bell on her table and summon the smallest boy forward, who with outstretched hands, would receive her egg top rather like receiving communion. This was quite a ritual performed in absolute silence.'*

**Peter Bull 1935/40**

*'When the Sisters left, Mary Fargher took over the cooking. Mary was an angel. She worked 18 hours a day but always remembered boys names and allowed them to watch her working. I'll never forget the mounds of bread and butter that she had to prepare every day for the boys' breakfasts and teas. She cooked for everybody in the school and her roast potatoes were a dream made in the old coke fired ovens of the time.'*

**Paul Barraclough 1935/38**

*'Considering it was wartime I think the food was pretty good. We had a treat on Sunday evening of bread and dripping after a lunchtime joint. However, the walled kitchen garden*

*near the entrance which had been productive in 1938, and provided amongst other things Jerusalem artichokes, had gone, due to the call up of manpower I suppose.*

*In spite of the quite adequate diet, like most young people we liked to kick over the traces, and one of the 'dares' was an expedition down to the village grocery shop in Otford where we purchased packets of dry biscuits, dog biscuit quality I think. We consumed these at night by torchlight under the blankets in 'dorm' feasts. Once somebody was caught breaking the bounds. I think the punishment given by Father Blofeld was somewhat draconian by today's standards in that the offender was confined to his desk in free time for a whole term.'*

**David George 1938/48**

*'Sunday evenings meant bread and dripping – presumably after the weekend joint. That was a treat: we were fed but some of it I'd rather not recall. I do seem to remember milk – it was about the time it became pasteurised, and it had something of a taste to it. Mary's roast potatoes were occasionally 'remaindered' to the top table and treated as a delicacy. I've already mentioned the atrocious greens ["abominable over-stewed"], another horror was pink rock cakes, as hard as their name applied.'*

**Paul Rose 1940/44**

*'Food must have been a nightmare for Matron Stockwell and Mary the cook in the kitchen but we boys seemed to eat anything that was given to us with the possible exception of Sunday afternoon rock cakes. These rock cakes were pale pink and hard, very hard, and made dangerous weapons when threaded with a piece of string or bootlace.*

*Each table had a table boy appointed who laid the table, collected the meals from the service table, and at the end of the meal cleared the table and cleaned/washed it down. On Sundays the tables were scrubbed and then inspected: they looked like leached bones. The perk for being a table boy was seconds.*

*It was always a treat to go to 'Aplines' in Sevenoaks for lunch or tea on the day of an exeat for there you could get a cream cake which was almost certainly synthetic but tasted good.'*

**J Martin Beech 1943/47**

*'The cruelest blow, after my first week with no meat, few vegetables, no fruit, no cheese or butter, one egg and a little ghastly margarine, was to laugh at an attempt to make me an "apple pie bed". Desperate for something to eat, and having just heard the words apple pie, before getting into bed, I thought I was in for a clandestine midnight feast! Once again the butt of my new mates.*

*I also remember the day Dicky Buehrlen ate all his herring: bones, skin and head and being so hungry he finished all the other leftovers, heads included, on our dinner table.*

*'Tuck' was almost the most important part of the day. After a meagre lunch, all 48 of us, if we had any, had to queue for one sweet, or piece of chocolate that was locked away by the assistant matron, her instruction being to make tuck last all term.'*

**Tony Rumm 1946/49**

*'The food, which for obvious reasons of shortages after the war, volume, old equipment and budgetary constraints, was not great. Matron made up the menus and tried to make the meals nutritious but I don't recall anyone talking about the four food groups. Fruit was obviously only available in season, and we did have some splendid apple pies, but generally the food was at best boring and at worst not very healthy. For example, dripping sandwiches were a staple part of the diet!*

*The kitchen staff were, however, always very friendly to us and undoubtedly did the best they could with the available resources. The day that sweet rationing was eliminated (1952?) was an occasion for much rejoicing and a tuck shop was opened in the closet to the left of the Chapel entrance. It wasn't really a tuck shop in the sense that one could buy sweets but rather a depository for the sweets our parents sent us, which the school administered.'*

**Kendall Carey 1949/56**

*'Mary was a dear! She could also be quite stern. Her cooking was great. The smells that came from the kitchen sometimes made your mouth water. The best occasions were when you were able to go to the kitchen late evening in the senior school to ask Mary for a "dripping" sandwich. It's been a favourite ever since.'*

**David Sharpless 1951/57**

*'Father Blofeld used to drive his Austin 7 into Sevenoaks once a week and bought supplies. We would order goodies: Horlicks tablets (ugh) were my favourite. Sweets were given out each day from large jars on the top landing after lunch. Assistant Matron Jessica Johnson used to hand them out. I hated her because she used to force-feed me with various milk puddings, holding my nose to force me to open my mouth.'*

**Stephen Winkley 1954/57**

*'Meals were eaten in the refectory just inside the main door. Each boy had to take a turn as a table boy for a term; this included laying up the tables and clearing away the dishes.*

*I remember one member of staff who was matron called Matron Stockwell who* insisted the boys ate everything in front of them, "you never know if you don't like it, till you've tried it' was her motto. Staff had better meals than the boys and while we put up with fatty lamb and lumpy spuds, they had roast beef and Yorkshire pud. One Saturday she was digging into her roast beef when she found a slug in her cabbage. Her expression was a picture and one boy piped up "Eat up Matron you never know whether you like it till you try it". He was dispatched to a corner in disgrace and we had to stay behind for laughing at him after the others had finished dinner.'

**John Wright 1954/60**

'We all loved Mary, but except for her bread and dripping and spotted dick and custard, I don't think we loved her food too much. It was very hard eating bread, margarine, and whatever was left of our jar of marmalade from last leave day at breakfast time, while the staff tucked into toast and real butter and a generous helping of marmalade.

Just as it was hard contenting ourselves with whatever pudding was served, while watching staff tucking into lemon meringue pie. There were two ways round this. One was to be a server at late Mass. This allowed you to share the priest/teacher's toast and marmalade (I'm thinking of Fr Parkes who died of cancer, and Fr Finch who 'went to Rome'). The other was to serve the staff. Then, if there was any lemon meringue pie left over, Father gave you a piece. I enjoyed this privilege so much that I continued to serve even when I became a prefect.'

**John Crowther-Alwyn 1957/62**

'I remember the cook - ancient wizened skin and bone who turned out the same cycle of meals for 60 three times a day, day after day from an intact Victorian kitchen. The slops and leftovers were carefully stored in large drums collected by a farmer and returned to us as remarkably tasty sausages.'

**Colin Emmett 1960/65**

'I can recall eating cream crackers by candle-light for weeks during the bread strike and the electricity strike...can't recall the exact year but it was great fun at the time as I recall. When they started delivering bread again we still had to eat crackers for weeks because we had such a huge supply of the damn things. And sugar puffs every breakfast time for five years. Still can't look one in the eye...the best five years of my life though.'

**Simon Maurice 1974/79**

'In 1982-83 amongst the vast grounds of the school a group of us stumbled across this old rotting storage hut. 'The Shed' was locked but in true St Michael's fashion and being twenty miles from school (or so it felt) we managed to get in. I remember Myself, Coki Manella,

*Henry Rogers and a couple of other "nameless phantoms" thinking we had struck gold... It was full of sweets especially Space Dust.*

*We loaded up our shorts with kilos of the stuff. If I remember correctly I think we did about three runs (at unexplainable times) to 'The Shed' in the first week before we made a dent in the stock.*

*The following week was incredible. Everyone was putting this stuff on their tongues listening to it explode as it mixed with saliva and turned your mouth red/green/yellow etc. The only downside being that it was two years out of date! But that didn't stop us. It was like a Columbian drug cartel dealing in packets of Space Dust (10 packs for 20p rings a bell). Then 'The Cartel' invested the illegal funds into The Tuck Shop to change their diet.'*

**Greg McKeague 1980/84**

*'How on earth can a place which served up the worst food ever tasted in Victorian surroundings under concentration camp rules give fond memories? But for some reason it does. It is a shame they have changed it, I can't show my kids what purgatory we had to go through!!'*

**Rory Brennand 1980/83**

## St. Michael's School Menu

| Week 3 | MONDAY | TUESDAY | WEDNESDAY | THURSDAY | FRIDAY |
|---|---|---|---|---|---|
| The Main Event | Sizzling Pork Sausages with Gravy | Lamb Rogan Josh | "Your Favourite" Roast Dinner | Crunchy Macaroni Cheese | "Friday's Treat" Tempting Turkey Twizzlers |
| And to go with... | Creamy Mashed Potato<br><br>Spring Greens | Turmeric Rice<br><br>Carrot Batons | Roast Potatoes<br><br>Freshly Steamed Broccoli | Mixed Vegetables | Crispy Chips<br><br>Baked Beans |
| Scrummy Puds! | Summer Strawberry Dessert | Homemade Apple and Sultana Scone | Fruity Jelly and Cream | Freshly made Chocolate Chip Shortbread | Creamy Vanilla Ice Cream Tubs |

The food provided for the children by Wendy Halford and her team nowadays offers healthy variety and international dishes. The canteen even holds regular themed days.

# Missing Home and Running Away

Duncan Jackson was at St Michael's between 1920 and 1921 when the school was at Woodside. He achieves notoriety in the admissions register with the entry: 'Seconded. A bad boy' and in the logbook:

---

**30 Sept 1921:** Duncan Jackson ran away twice. The Revd Father has refused to have him back after the second crime. He was always a very troublesome boy.

---

Here is his story:

*'The one and only master [Charles Jaggard] sent my friends and I out to the farmyard to gather acorns for his pigs. It was a fine day and we ate more acorns than we gathered, but we did discuss the possibility of escape and came to the agreement that 'tomorrow morning at 6 o'clock would be the time.*

*I awoke all right, called my friend but he flunked it, so I dressed and with my boots between my teeth crawled, for some reason, past matron's door, down the stairs and into the schoolroom. I put my boots on, collected my magic lantern from my locker and heard matron about, so I was off.*

*Out to the playground, across the farmyard to the wicket gate to the footpath, magic lantern under gate (glass might break in dropping) and over the gate into the lane and away.*

*I enquired the way to Crystal Palace from a man going to work who asked me if I had just run away from school. Learning that I had, he took me along Blackhorse Lane and away I went to Woodside Green, Portland Road, South Norwood Hill, Anerley Hill and there I was at the Crystal Palace. All I had to do then was to follow the no. 3 bus route which would take me to Westminster Bridge and from there to Parliament Square, Birdcage Walk, across Green Park to Piccadilly, up Bond Street to Oxford Street, Marble Arch and Edgeware Road and home to Mother... and she took me back to my nightmare. I was sent to the dormitory to sweep out and sprinkle water – it was a hot summer.*

*This time I had a 'friend'. I'd taken my 2 inch high teddy bear that my uncle had brought from Paris when I was 2 years old. I still have it...a bit worn. I used to confide in him, and on a suitable quiet occasion we were 'off' again. But as I cautiously peered round the corner of the front, the nuns were sitting on the porch balcony and I was spotted, so I shot back to the dorm to await the arrival of Matron who carted me, in nightshirt, off to her room and got the birch (like a witch's broom without the handle). Outside the nuns were waiting to hear me scream. That did it, I didn't scream and she chased me round the room holding the tail of my nightshirt up and whacking me with the birch. After this I was sent to bed and my clothes were taken away.*

*Teddy consoled me and a little later an evening church service took everybody off to church dressed in their best. I whipped somebody's shorts and stockings and my own nightshirt and Teddy and I was off again 'doing a Bannister' across the frontage and west towards Croydon again – only this time the idea was to sleep in Hyde Park (I knew it was done) and then on to my Grandmother in Ilford.*

*But at 2 o'clock in the morning I was approached by a 15-foot high policeman who carted me down the Edgeware Road to my Mother's in Harrowby Street. This was the address in the book I had with me 'The Boy's Life of Nelson'.*

*He rang all the bells and banged the knocker and the house guessed it was me again. This time for good. The penny dropped and Mother concluded that I did not appreciate St Michael's Convent and I went to school round the corner for a while.'*

The logbook makes it clear that his non-return to St Michael's was not his mother's choice. He was expelled!

Duncan was not the only would-be runaway nor the only unhappy pupil:

*'My first night I was so unhappy I went out back towards the outside 'bogs' but I was so frightened by the darkness and woods that I abandoned my wish to run away.'*

**Ivan Green 1934/38**

*'The first Christmas was at school. Before the festival we made a trip by car to Maidstone, I think it was, and I bought some vanishing cream for my mother. I wasn't sure what it was, but I certainly hoped she wouldn't vanish. It was hard to be away from home, but I can remember the presents and I had a large box full of books. My mother was keen on education!'*

**Roy Haines 1932/38**

This is an extract from a letter which was found hidden behind a fireplace at the School when renovations were carried out recently:

*Dear Gordon* [Boland – 1936/38]

*Thank you for writing. I feel lonely too – and it cheered me up to hear from you. I wish you were here to tease me even!!! ...*

*I am so sorry you find the work so hard this term. There is nothing else to do but stick it and never leave off trying. I am quite sure masters do always see if a boy is trying – even if things don't come right they allow for it – much more than if a person gives it up and slacks...I never forget all the schools you have been to and that has made it much harder for you...I saw your dad yesterday, he has not been well – he was thinking of coming to see you next Saturday but he does not know if he will be well enough. Write to me soon again. I am sorry the work seems so hard but Gordon, you see, unless you can master it a little you will feel it so much harder later on. All boys feel like that except the very clever ones...*

*Love from Gran*

'*Saturday morning letter writing from 9.30am to about 10.30am was held in the main classroom and was supervised by a junior teacher – almost always an Old Michaelian. For that hour we had to write home to our parents telling them truthfully how much we had enjoyed our lessons, our games and anything else which occasionally came to mind. It was probably the most difficult session of the week as we all tried to convey to those at home how good things were and to disguise any unhappiness we felt. I cannot think of anything more difficult in my life – trying to write down 13 different and interesting letters (usually packed with lies) to two parents who never replied. I often wondered if the letters were censored at all – no evidence – just a canny feeling.*

*The master in charge would sometimes try to help us by reminding us of events of the week, but in most cases he was only there to help correct the spelling and to help create the impression at home that the parent's school fees were not being wasted.*

*My parents rebuked me at the end of term for not writing the address of the school properly; like all the other boys I used SMOKE [St Michael's Otford Kent England] and always began "Dear Mum and Dad, How are you?" and then giving them a breakdown of the past week's weather.*'

**Tony Rumm 1946/49**

*'We had a close contemporary who was so desperately homesick that he fantasized a flying chair his mother had constructed for his rescue. It was equipped, we were told, with a model airplane diesel engine on each leg! She was going to fly in and scoop him from his misery!'*

**John Wood 1947/53**

*'I'm not sure of her name, but I think it was Stockwell, Matron Stockwell. She was matron when I first went to Otford Court in 1957. We drove up that long drive, parked the Standard Vanguard, and I went up to matron and said, Matron, I've come at last. This was because my elder brother was at the school, and matron knew me well. So the impression might be that I was longing, at the age of eight, to leave home and parents, whom I wouldn't see until the first leave day a month later. Far from it in fact. I was miserable, but too much of a 'man' to show it. For the first three nights I went under the blankets and cried my heart out. Then I thought to myself "This is pointless", and stopped.'*

**John Crowther-Alwyn 1957/62**

*'My own claim to fame is when I ran away from St Michael's and actually made it home to Croydon much to the dismay (and I suppose the relief) of Donald Cormack, my parents and the police who were checking the trains into London looking for me. Although I made it back home I seem to recall setting off a mini-craze of 'escape attempts' although none as successful as my own as I recall.*

**Simon Maurice 1974/79**

---

**13 November 1982:** Three boys went out of school to Otford. Two boys, with money from other boys, went to Bromley by train. Eventually they went back to the station where the ticket-issuing clerk questioned them, put them back on the train to Otford where the police returned them to school.

**29 January 1984:** From 11.30am until 7pm four boys were out of school…Parents were not informed until 2.30pm/4pm after [a parent] had heard from his son and was very angry at not being informed earlier; the other parents were grateful to be informed but were not particularly anxious at the timing. The police had been informed at 2pm after the Headmaster had searched for the boys for 1 ½ hours. They finally were handed over to the police by a farmer at Ryarsh and were collected from West Malling police station. As punishment the four lose the Leave Day next Saturday. None could give any real reason, although they gave excuses. None was readily ashamed when first met at the police station.

---

# Health and Well-being

In 1918 over 20 million people died in a pandemic of 'Spanish' flu, many of them healthy young adults. St Michael's was not unaffected, though it seems to have got off very lightly:

---

**2 October 1918:** An epidemic of influenza is running through the school. Today there are fifteen boys in bed. Six more boys have gone sick this afternoon. By the Revd Father's permission I have closed the school for tomorrow.

**7 October 1918:** Majority of boys are still in bed with influenza. Have closed the school until Monday 14th inst.

**18 October 1918:** Am glad to note that the epidemic has apparently left us. Judging by what is happening around us we have been most fortunate to have escaped so lightly. The boys must have been tended most diligently during their convalescence. A fair week's work has been got through, though the sickness has thrown things a little out of gear.

---

*'Returning to the school after the holidays we were supposed to have had a medical examination. However, probably whitsun 1921, one of the boys did not have it, and the result was we all got ringworm and had to go up to London to have x-ray treatment at hospital. This resulted in our hair coming out and all having to wear linen caps. We were like watching a cricket match on the green.'*

**Duncan Jackson 1920/21**

---

**14 March 1922**: I am deeply sorry to report that ringworm has again broken out among the boys. Already we have 10 isolated cases.

**21 March 1922:** There are some 18 boys away, some with ringworm others (the smaller ones) with chicken pox. This of course has considerably upset the work of the school and coming so soon after my own illness makes it worse. We had just got into full swing and were working might and main to make up for lost time

---

**24 March 1922:** Nearly half the boys are absent either from ringworm or chicken pox. The remainder are working well but this epidemic is very serious from the point of view of the boys' education.

**4 February 1926:** I am sorry Eric Merrin leaves tomorrow. Mother made some foolish complaint re chilblains & domestic work. The boy has just begun to show marked improvement in his schoolwork.

*'Matron Stockwell was a pious virgin who believed the rays of the moon provoked cancer. In Upper Vestry dormitory which I shared with James Leonard (whose father Graham [later to become Lord Bishop of London] had persuaded my parent to send me and Roger to St Michael's, far from home) we had to keep the curtain closed for that reason. Matron Stockwell used to paint our tonsils with a vile substance if we complained of sore throats.'*

**Stephen Winkley 1954/57**

Today, there is no longer any need for a school nurse and the only niggling 'health' issue for the children is the ubiquitous nit!

# Growing Up

*'Becoming adult, to our way of thinking, was two-pronged. The first and most important prong was to become (and to be seen by one's peers to become) a smoker. The second was to have a girlfriend. There was a little village that could be reached surreptitiously on foot from the school grounds (Kemsing?), and while not bubbling over with eligible little girls the village did have a corner newsagent not averse to making a profit of a farthing a packet by selling cigarettes to little boys. My first sinful indulgence was in a threepenny packet of five Park Drive. Woodbines were the same price but we considered them somewhat down-market – only smoked by sailors (and besides, they were rather strong).*

*An occasional indulgence was a single Churchman's No.1. This might be obtained by inserting one penny in a vending machine on Otford Station while the stationmaster wasn't looking. It came out in its own dinky little green cardboard packet, individually wrapped in its own silver paper. It was rather fatter than a Park Drive so perhaps it was lucky that I was only able to purchase one of these at the end of each term while waiting for the London train.*

*So at the age of eleven I had become a smoker. It was several more years before I became a swain, so I cannot claim to have reached adulthood while at St Michael's.*

*Boyhood is such a joyous condition that had we known then what we know now (si jeunesse savait...) we might never have wished to leave it. Yet Father Charles Blofeld was sincere in his duty to prepare us for the adult world. He taught us billiards, for instance; that is to say, on his table elder boys taught younger boys the art of the cannon, the in-off and the pot, and once we had passed our apprenticeship we were permitted to test our skills against those of the reverend father himself – and they were considerable.'*

**Eric Crabbe 1934/38**

*'Headmaster Donald Cormack was against gender mixing. Julian Somerville and I formed an attachment to a pretty girl called Diana Warren. She had a brother at the school and she used to come to Evensong on Sunday. One evening Julian and I were caught talking to this girl in the Junior Classroom normally occupied by Mrs Wagg. The roof fell in. I was Captain of school on probation: no more of that. Father Blofeld was so upset he cancelled the usual Sunday barley-water reception for prefects. The whole school was told that I had been caught 'poodle-faking', a word I have never encountered since then.'*

**Stephen Winkley 1954/57**

[Poodle-faker: A man who cultivates female society for the purposes of promotion or social advancement, otherwise a 'ladies' man or socialite. The term is also used for a young, newly commissioned officer. It implies that the person so designated is a 'fake poodle', impersonating the actions of a fawning lap-dog. Source: Brewer's Dictionary of Phrase and Fable]

*'We had a very sexy assistant matron at the school one term and once when Michael Bond [Second Master] was meant to be away, boys would be naughty on purpose so as to be sent out on the landing just to be smacked by her. Oh the look on their faces when Michael arrived back earlier than expected... "Thank you Miss Jones, I'll take over from here..."'*

**Rashid Chinchanwala 1972/77**

# Discipline

Corporal punishment was used at St Michael's, as it was in many schools until the 1980s, though other forms of punishment were administered for lesser offences.

In the early 1900s George Cribb's [1905/06] remembers being punished by being forced to take cold baths by the Sisters for having run away with one of his friends. Mr Wareham (the Headmaster at the time) was obviously not inclined to use the cane very often. On his retirement from the school in 1916 he apparently broke the cane and gave a piece to each boy who had received a caning from him. This could not have been a high number! Numa Bardet [1915/18] is recorded as saying that there were very few occasions when corporal punishment was given.

---

**21 September 1917**: By the Revd Father's order, or suggestion rather, the following boys were punished for pilfering fruit & breaking out of bounds: Numa Bardet, Richard Bardet, Laban Jenner, Richard Kingston, Thomas Imray, John Lovell.

---

It is not clear what the punishment was for this misdemeanour, as Numa Bardet says that the only time he was caned was after he had reflected a mirror through the classroom window, so distracting the boys within. Perhaps a case of selective memory?

Duncan Jackson [1920/21] remembers a 'red-headed and sadistic' assistant matron:

*'One night I remember, a bean feast or a pillow fight I'm not sure, but she was brandishing her cane. Nightshirts up and the first beds got it until she came to me and the cane broke. Whether it was my bones or because of an old schoolboy belief that orange peel rubbed into the posterior was an effective deterrent, I do not know but she was quite vexed and stormed back to her room for another cane and the same thing happened. Her face was so red that she did not return and the rest of the dorm got away with it.'*

---

**8 June 1917**: Usual routine. Had occasion to severely punish Graham Amos for dishonesty. He stole a quantity of pen nibs from my desk at a time when I was called away into the Playground.

**1 February 1918**: Petty thefts of food etc. have taken place of late. Aubrey Allen after telling many falsehoods at last confessed to having stolen a large pot of preserved fruit from a shelf just outside the refectory. I have dismissed him from the choir and otherwise punished him.

**11 October 1920**: I am sorry to record that the following boys were found guilty of Fruit Stealing. Taking into consideration the amount of fruit so kindly given to them I consider such thefts very blameworthy. I thoroughly investigated each case and awarded:- J Coldwells: 4 cuts, Eric Bird: 6 cuts, C Pridavin: 2 cuts, Eric Valantine: 2 cuts, C Westrope: 2 cuts, G Gardner: 2 cuts, J McDonald: 2 cuts, L Waterfall: 3 cuts, G Smith: 3 cuts, M Reynolds: 2 cuts. The punishment was really less than deserved but I trust will prove sufficient.

---

**5 November 1920:** I notice the boys are eating far too many sweets. I have also heard (and corroborated) one boy has spent 12/6 in sweets since the beginning of term. I have spoken to the "Superior" about it and endeavoured to point out how a matter of this kind tends to promote bad discipline. As a matter of fact I am sorry to record the discipline is going back. There does not appear to be any restraint on the boys after I have left them.

**15 December 1922:** A boy named Douglas Johnson has left. He made a complaint of being punished by me. The boy was a simple milksop & lazy boy & we are well rid of him.

**4 December 1929:** Revd Father had to speak very seriously to the boys re 'disobedience'. Many times they had been cautioned not to kick the football about in any of the rooms of the house. Two boys broke one of the electric lights in the boot room last night by kicking the empty case of a football. By direction of the Revd Father I gave the two boys a severe caning at Play Time today.

During Father Thomas Blofeld's Wardenship, the termly newsletter always 'welcomed' new boys with the words: "When thou crossest a frontier enquire what is forbidden within". These words acted as a friendly warning to the boys – that if they stuck to the rules, they would avoid punishment.

*'The sentiment is typical of his strict disciplinary character. He was very keen on written rules governing many aspects of school life, which I think he hoped would instil in his boys respect for authority and for one another.'*

**Paul Barraclough 1935/38**

For many years from 1938 a system of 'stripes' was used to log the number of offences carried out by each boy. A board was kept in the senior classroom on which was written the boys' names by House (Greeks, Trojans and Barbarians). On a monthly basis the stripes (black ink marks against each name) were counted up and if a boy had three stripes he was sent to the Warden, to the Headmaster or to another staff member (depending on the boy's House) for punishment. All staff, except for matron, were allowed to use corporal punishment and prefects were authorised to give out lines: usually 50 lines to be copied from the bible or some other worthy book.

Sometimes the crime was serious enough for the boy to be sent straight to the Warden. This was "like being sent to the Tower for execution" but Father Thomas Blofeld rarely used the cane, and only if he thought it appropriate after he had listened to the offender's side of the story. The shame of the boy was usually enough to prevent a repeat offence.

Headmaster Donald Cormack used a 'tawse' to administer corporal punishment. This was a thick leather strap with a split end, commonly used in Scottish schools. According to Old Michaelian Tony Rumm, he nicknamed his tawse 'lahoostan' (spelling and origin unknown!) and some Old Michaelians say that he sometimes used it indiscriminately and unfairly.

*'My memory of Cormack is his leather strap. He used it on me so often that when I went on to Bloxham my hands were so insensitive that I could take almost any hit on my palms without pain. This child was certainly not spoiled. He did however teach me a lot and gave me some confidence in my own abilities.'*

**Bob Horrobin 1951/57**

*'Cormack's Friday morning "belt tests" - simple, ten-question tests on every subject taught during the preceding week. I forget the exact pass standard but it was high. For every mark below the standard the boy would receive one whack of the belt. As an incentive to learn it was moderately efficient.*

*Michael Bond [Senior Master] had a monogram signature which took the form of a simple two or three stroke line drawing of a bird. He'd chalk this onto the backside of a wayward boy's trousers and beat with a plimsoll until the autograph had disappeared!*

*More serious offences were dealt with by the Headmaster: the summonses would be issued together with notices and announcements that invariably followed meals in the refectory. A small queue of trembling errants would form on the middle landing. This was particularly humiliating as there was, at the same time, a queue leading to the top landing of boys collecting daily sweet rations from their sweet jars. Their expectation were somewhat more joyful than those who were awaiting the punishment by cane or strap or detention or lines that would inevitably follow.'*

**Roger Harding 1954/60**

*'The first homework I received back from Michael Bond simply had the initials "G.S." in red ink at the bottom. Thinking this might stand for "Good show" or "Great Story" I proudly went to the front of class when called. Imagine my dismay when he pulled out a "Gym Shoe" from his desk and whacked me on the backside. I think it was because I wrote in biro, but I can't really remember.'*

**Peter Hardy 1971/73**

*'Discipline was everything at St. Michael's. No running down the corridors, making your bed after breakfast, silence after lights out. The most "innocent" of crimes was punished by the cane or the belt. We feared it at the time but few of us probably harbour any grudges - it was all part of growing up.*

*Being a school monitor in the final year empowered one with a lot of authority. Besides having the privilege of a ridiculously tiny monitor's locker in the changing rooms you became part of Donald Cormack's inner circle. You had the power to send boys to the back of the post lunch sweets queue for not standing still and to send them out on the landing for talking after lights out. Being sent out on the landing was the height of humility at St. Michael's. You would stand still facing the wall in the semi darkness until the end of master's supper, approximately 9:00pm. Then one of the masters, usually someone like Michael Bond, a Cambridge blue, would ascend the stairs and deliver the belt or slipper or whatever the flavour of the day was and then it was back to bed.'*

**Rashid Chinchanwala 1972/77**

Some see Donald Cormack as a 'Jekyll and Hyde' character: sometimes vicious, sometimes kind. When he was in a good mood, signalled by his 'singing' of the Radetsky March (diddle dee diddle dee diddle dee dee dee) or the William Tell Overture, he could be exceptionally kind and generous, especially to his favourites.

Punishment in the 2000s consists of a series of warning cards and detentions with the policy that:

'Wherever possible correction should be used without punishment; sanctions must be constructive and purposeful, never demeaning or humiliating; no valuable task should be associated with punishment (e.g. copying out a poem); and avoid punishing a group for the crimes of an individual.'

The first girls' tour (Netball) to Battle Abbey, Sussex in 1991.
Bottom right is Alison McLaren who was the first Main School girl.

# ~ 9 ~

# Religion

## The Chapel

The chapel was the first thing to be created at Beechy Lees following the school's move from Woodside to Otford. The former Billiards room with its glass ceiling was chosen for the purpose.

---

**9 February 1925:** A very pretty little chapel has been evolved from a large room and is to be used for services on Sunday next, but unfortunately as yet we can have no organ.

---

Father Tooth, however, wanted something grander and therefore sent out a begging letter to all his friends and supporters in 1927:

> Now my good friends I have asked you to come and see this place – one thing is needed to make it quite perfect – we want a chapel.
>
> I would like to build one, a beautiful, a very beautiful chapel – the best we can build, before I finally ask you to take over as your own and keep it going, doing good work. I must have £10,000 – the chapel must be worthy, exceedingly good – or nothing at all – now do help me: it is a large sum, I know – there are people with bigger hearts than this.
>
> Meanwhile there is a much simpler matter, it will not cost so much, we need a Mary bell, to ring the Angelus: it has been silent here in this neighbourhood for many years: in honour of the Incarnation we would revive the devotion of our good ancestors and ring it three times a day. I could quite well provide for it if some devout Catholic would send me £5000, don't delay, send it one day this week: and as soon as it is ready, come and ring the Angelus for the first time and break a silence which has been maintained for over 300 years.

It is not known how much of this exorbitant target Father Tooth managed to raise through this begging letter but he certainly created a lovely chapel and established the Angelus bell.

*'Chapel was a prominent feature. Servers galore, boat boy, thurifer, acolytes, were all in demand (I acted as boat boy to Pat Shipp's thurifer) while the choir secluded itself in the alcove to the left of the altar accompanied by the harmonium. A late addition was the statue to Our Lady.'*

**Roy Haines 1932/38**

The statue of Our Lady, as mentioned by Roy Haines, was commissioned in 1947 as a memorial to "our late beloved friend, Miss Margaret Whittling" (the Housekeeper at St Michael's from 1936 until her death in 1943). Unfortunately, the statue was not completed until 1949 and as *The Michaelian* magazine reported in the *Summer 1950* edition:

> All who have seen the new Shrine of Our Lady in the Chapel have expressed themselves as deeply disappointed with the expression on Our Lady's face. The criticism is fully justified. The statue has now been taken back to the studio, and both the Architect and the Carver assure us that the defect can be remedied. We devoutly hope so.

*'Services were formal; Blofeld resplendent in his cope, attended by his acolytes and a pretty boy swinging a censer, would advance ceremonially down the aisle to the swelling of organ music played by Miss Anderson.*

*Miss Anderson, a maiden lady of middle years, was the school's honorary organist and choir mistress. She occupied, 'honoris causa', quarters adjacent to the old stables. She was homely, and no one believed that her association with the school and its chapel was to be attributed to anything other than her musical ability.*

*The choir stalls, accommodating eight choristers, were offset at right angles to the congregation to the left of the chancel. Four of us were placed each side of the organist, facing inwards. Yes, I was a choirboy. Realising early that this positioned me out of sight of the congregation, I had offered my dulcet tones to the service of my God and they were accepted. In truth I enjoyed singing as a boy. I had no religious persuasions, but the music and song was infectious, and the services were colourful. Eventually I was promoted soloist and performed my Kyrie Eleisons soulfully and with the best of them.*

**Eric Crabbe 1934/38**

The Chapel St. Michael's School

'The beauty of our Chapel is often commented upon by visitors, and during the times of the Great Festivals this term it has looked quite magnificent. In this connection few know outside the School how much we owe to the devoted labours of our faithful Mary [the cook], and Michael Hatton, our joint Sacristans, and to the Matron for her work in connection with the floral decoration of the Chapel.

**The Michaelian – Summer 1950**

*Leading up to Christmas we would have a nativity service. The school owned no less than four beautifully embroidered and illuminated copes.*

*Blofeld would preside and senior boys, each wearing one of these copes would represent the three oriental kings bearing gifts – a wonderful sight, with all the candles ablaze and the smoke from the censers wreathing up to the ceiling. I saw it as a theatrical performance – exciting and stimulating but far from any sort of reality.*

*'The chapel was delightfully appointed; in the heart of the building – no excrescence this, built on to placate a demanding God, but the very pulse of the community. Its stained glass windows represented I know not what, but they were pretty.*

**Eric Crabbe 1934/38**

The Chapel at St Michael's is still an important part of the school. The current Chaplain, Father Richard Freeman, took on the duties in 1997, at the same time maintaining his role as Rector for Eynsford, Farningham and Lullingstone. A move to the role of Priest-in-Charge of the Church of St Peter and St Paul at Shoreham allowed Father Richard more time to dedicate to the school.

*"I relished the opportunity to spend more time teaching – and to have a greater involvement with school life on a regular basis"*

Eucharist is held every week for the upper classes in the main school and Father Richard takes assembly for the younger classes as well as for the children in Pre-Prep. The Eucharist is complete with three pupils acting as servers; full vestments being worn; and bells and genuflexion being used. Time, however, does not allow for the use of incense. The Angelus Bell is no longer rung and it is in need of repair.

In 2000 confirmation classes were introduced for all Year 6 pupils and in 2002, seventeen children were confirmed – their picture reaching the local newspaper. A Captain for Chapel is now appointed annually.

The school is licensed to hold weddings and Father Richard was privileged to bless the marriage of a member of staff in the Chapel – the reception being held in a marquee in the grounds.

A stained glass window depicting St Michael - once at Woodside, now in the room used as the library. You can see that an upper section of the window has been fitted in reverse so that the top of St Michael's lance is disconnected!

# Corpus Christi

*'During my time as St Michael's, the Anglo-Catholic Society of London used to come down to the school on the first Thursday in July for the Feast of Corpus Christi. No doubt this had been the case for many years previous and probably went on for a good few years after I left.*

*The celebration consisted of a sung mass in the chapel, during which a procession carrying the Holy Sacrament was made round the immediate school grounds, within the boundary defined by the iron fence.*

*On leaving the chapel it turned right along the path at the top of the terrace past the school, turned left down the steps, and followed the path round the face of the school overlooking the valley. Keeping to the path until turning left on the badminton court at the far end from the school between two spinneys, it then returned to the path and processed on to the fishpond (hit by a German bomb in 1940/41), and turned left along the path above the badminton court, moving towards the school, up the steps to the terrace, and returning to the chapel.*

*During the course of the procession, stops were made at three or four shrines, for a short service of hymns and prayers. At least two of these shrines were 'permanent' structures, one made of wood at the end of the badminton court, furthest from the school; the other was constructed from stone or concrete and situated at the top of the badminton court. The other two shrines were temporary installations erected on the day; one at the bottom of the terrace, set in the end of the trees, on the right looking down from the school, the other was at the top of the terrace, directly outside the chapel.*

*I have one abiding memory of this event. The floor of the shrine on the badminton court was made of wood and in a poor state of repair. So Donald Cormack pulled Peter*

*Arden [1942/46] and myself out of class for two or three afternoons prior to the event and set us to work repairing and making good the flooring with anything we could lay our hands on. We had to use logs and odd pieces of timber that were scavenged from the wood shed and the surrounding woods. There was definitely no money available to buy new materials even if they had been available so soon after the war.*

*We spent the whole afternoon of the ceremony with our hearts in our mouths, hoping the floor would remain intact when subjected to the combined weight of the celebrant and the attendants. I had a particular cause for concern as I was the Thurifer that year [the person who looks after the incense], and so, in close attendance to the celebrant.'*

**John Allart 1942/46**

*'The procession in my day was quite fantastic. The celebrant shrouded in a cope and with a humeral veil round his shoulders, carried the monstrance containing the Sacrament and was surrounded by assisting clergy and servers including the four who carried the wooden staves attached to the corners of an ombrellino covering him.*

*There was a clutch of quite comely young girls walking backwards in front scattering rose petals before the Sacrament. Behind them, also walking backwards, were three thurifers with censers also saluting the Sacrament. Thus each sacred place in the grounds was visited with hymns and prayers – both the permanent shrines as well as the temporary ones.*

*It was this sort of occasion when we would see Fr. Fynes-Clinton who was Vicar of St Magnus the Martyr in the City of London and Chairman, I think, of the school Governors. He was a lovely man who at the time I always felt was too heavenly minded to be of any earthly use.'*

**Jeffries Stratton 1937/41**

*'I remember the 'Strawberry Race', also known as 'Corpus Christi'. I don't recall it ever raining, and I do recall the wild strawberries available to the not too attentive procession members.'*

**John Wood 1947/53**

The Corpus Christi pilgrimages ended in the 1970s. The current Secretary General of The Catholic League, Chris Stephenson tells that:

'From the Catholic League minutes (from 1936) the League appeared to attend/ hold a Corpus Christi festival every year at Otford, including through the war years. The minutes are brief but refer each time to a mass, a procession, music supplied by a band and numerous references to the 'canteen' which was organised with varying degrees of success. The minutes of 1976 record that the 'pilgrimage' to Otford would not be held this year....and there is no further mention of Otford. I think the Corpus Christi event moved to Lavenham in subsequent years.'

## Memories of religion at St Michael's

*'When I mention that I was an angelic incense-bearer a look of total disbelief takes over; well, understandable I guess! I'm not deeply religious – a surfeit of church morning and evening, three times on Sunday – all day Good Friday – probably accounts for that and a total disenchantment with mankind in general later on, but I did have a good grounding in the Scriptures and developed an understanding for the needs and tolerances for all religions worldwide. The Ten Commandments and the Sermon on the Mount suit me as a way of life...*

*I remember that three red lamps hung over the Chancel and on special occasions the big one in the middle was pulled down lower than the other two and we had to make the sign of the cross (the Ace, King, Queen, Jack as I learned in later nautical days). Other times we just bent the head and knees.'*

**John or Frank Borton 1918/22 [at Woodside]**

*'You will no doubt have guessed that Sunday was no day of hilarious merrymaking with no schooling to do. You'd be right. Church before breakfast and then the morning was spent under the eagle eye of a nun, letter writing which had to be delivered to her unsealed for censoring. I never learned whether there were any obliterations. Silence was the order of the day.*

*Morning service, then dinner, then Sunday School with a nun, followed by tea and evening service, and so to bed. Sunday dealt with. Joyous devotion.'*

**Philip Jackson 1920/21[at Wooodside]**

*'We very rarely saw Father Tooth, but on Sundays and other holy days of obligation, it was of course, Fr Tooth who celebrated Mass in the school chapel and presided over Vespers and Benediction. Our religious observances, in keeping with Anglo-catholic teaching and tradition, were strict and most of the boys (there were 30 of us) had spells of either singing in the choir or serving at mass.'*

**Douglas Keddie 1923/31**

*'We were required to attend services in the school chapel on a daily basis. I learned that the Prayer Book lays down devotions for virtually every hour of the day. I knew them then. I have forgotten them (thank goodness) now. Best I can remember the daily service we children were required to attend was Vespers. On a daily basis also the chapel bell was rung to celebrate the Angelus. Wherever we might be about the school premises when this was tolled (three-pause-three-pause-nine) we were required to still ourselves and bow our heads. But no way to still our young turbulent thoughts; whether of the last over one had bowled at the nets, a butterfly one had captured, or the anticipation of supper.'*

**Eric Crabbe 1934/38**

*'Father Phyall was visiting the school to take confirmed boys' confessions. Something we dreaded (How can I possibly put THAT in words to a priest??) However with professional coaching and encouragement we managed to describe our "sin" as carefully as possible! I always remember Mr Cork's aside to another adult; "He's going to get an earful this afternoon!" He did!'*

**Paul Barraclough 1935/38**

*'The chapel featured prominently in our lives. The angelus was rung at 6am, noon and 6pm, and generally said in Latin. On Sunday there was Communion at 8am, the main service at 10.30am and Benediction in the evening.*

*Often a visiting priest would give a sermon. I remember once Father Mills, who was a guest raconteur, starting his sermon: "Tonight, I am going to tell you a story about Edgar Vernon Christian."* [Nephew of Jack Hornby, a legendary British explorer of Canada. The two men made a fateful trip to the Northwest Territories in 1927 but starved to death. Edgar Christian's diaries were found hidden in the ashes of the stove in the cabin where they died]. *He held us spellbound for about 40 minutes. On one occasion he visited the school with Wing Commander Axtell who was at the wheel of a most beautiful Bentley motorcar. Alas, Axtell was completely bogus!'*

**Peter Bull 1935/40**

*'The chapel meant a lot to me, and probably fostered my vocation which was to blossom many years later. I can still remember the great Corpus Christi processions round the grounds with Benediction at two shrines by the badminton court – the one a stone altar, the other a wooden shed that I think has now completely perished. They were organised by the Catholic League, which had its headquarters in Beckenham or thereabouts.*

*Many – perhaps most of us – were confirmed and mostly by the famous evangelical Bishop of Rochester, Christopher Chavasse. He had, I think, a false leg, and must have found St Michael's a difficult undertaking – he had forbidden the reservation of the Blessed Sacrament in his diocese of Rochester, where we were. I suppose we got away with it as a private chapel. However in 1943 I was confirmed by a Bishop Dalgliesh, who had I think been Bishop in the Bahamas; he had a very red neck and was definitely plenty High Church!*

*We had a choir of eight, several servers at every service, and chapel daily – and twice on Sundays. Mass was celebrated early every morning, and some few of us were pretty regular attendees. Long after I left, in I suspect the early seventies, Fr Harold Buckley was the Chaplain for a while, and I used to go and preach. He and I had been teachers at the C.R. Fathers St Augustine's Penhalonga (in what is now Zimbabwe) - he was head of the central primary school for years after RAF service in Gwelo (or Gweru as it now is). I distinctly remember having to divide my time at Otford between Donald Cormack and Harold to avoid any unfairness between the two.'*

**Paul Rose 1940/44**

*'I remember being confirmed aged 10 because that is what one did. I asked at confession before this confirmation if I had committed adultery. A bit tricky this confession business, I thought, since the priest was also the Headmaster.'*

**John Wood 1947/53**

*'Religion was, of course, the focal point of school life and it was always a great honour to ring the Angelus bell. The service that I remember as being particularly evocative was Compline, with its overtones of nostalgic reflection on the day and the powerful sense of frightening away the demons of the night. I loved singing in the choir and I loved the pageantry and theatre of it all. To this day, the smell of incense triggers an instant flashback in my mind to services in the St Michael's School Chapel.'*

**John Hutchison 1949/50**

'Mentioning the chapel inevitably reminds me of the many hours we spent in it amidst clouds of incense. We were all made very aware of the importance of religion and the time spent in Chapel. We were duly confirmed at a very early age (eight in my case), and were given our catechisms as a present on the great day. This of course meant that we could take communion, which in turn required that we be in the appropriate spiritual shape to receive it. This in turn necessitated that we make our confessions and the school brought in a visiting priest, so that we could do so.

The first time this was very awkward, because at that age, as I recall, I didn't feel very guilty about anything in particular, while at the same time knowing that I was a sinner in God's eyes, and did not know what to say. The priest suggested that I consult the section in the catechism, which gives a long (several pages) list of all the sins the Church can think of as an 'aide memoire', prior to my next confession. I did this and selected all the sins that I felt I had committed. At that particular time, I was always being told that I did not show sufficient respect for adults and therefore included in my list of sins that I had committed adultery! It was some time later that I learned what adultery really was because the priest was not about to touch that one with a ten foot pole!'

**Kendall Carey 1949/56**

'On her first visit to the school, my mother, who was by instinct not an Anglo-Catholic but a Methodist, was talking to Matron and others when at 12 noon a silence fell upon the gathering. Believing a social disaster had occurred, my dear mother launched into a shrill burst of social babble, till someone could explain the Angelus to her.

Confession happened every 3 weeks. A nicotine-stained priest used to hear our confessions. After morning chapel two of us notified for the sacrament of confession would remain behind with our prayer books in which were listed incomprehensible sins. "Winkley, what are lustful thoughts?" a boy would ask me. When we had achieved a decent number we were ready for the ordeal. "I have had lustful thoughts, I have committed the sin of envy." Father Van Der Meulen would stay for lunch. Unaware of the sanctity of the confessional we would watch him talking to Father Blofeld. "Watch out for Winkley," he would be saying, "He's had lustful thoughts."'

**Stephen Winkley 1954/57**

'I remember that teacher Mrs Wagg was unwell during one term, so it fell to me to take her place on the organ stool in Chapel. My short legs found it hard to reach the pedals to pump the American (Harmonium) Organ so others were seconded to help in that way while I looked after the manuals!'

**Charles Masheder 1957/62**

# ~ 10 ~

## Father Thomas Guest Blofeld

### Warden from 1939 to 1964

Thomas Guest Blofeld was born in Whetstone, Middlesex in 1884. His parents were Thomas and Ellen Blofeld and he had an older brother, Charles Harcourt (the previous Warden at St Michael's) as well as other siblings.

He wrote a brief account of his life on the occasion of his Golden Jubilee Mass in 1961:

> 'My first memories of All Saints take me back to the middle '90s when, as a small boy, my family moved up from the country, to live in the West End of London.
>
> My Parents visited several Churches, but at last decided to attach themselves to All Saints, Margaret Street. For that decision I never cease to thank God.
>
> For the next 10 years or so I was away at school, and saw little of All Saints, except during the holidays. It was at the end of Prebendary Whitworth's tenure of the Benefice that I became more closely connected with the Church, becoming an Altar Server, and a teacher in the Sunday School. At this time I came under the influence of Father Arundell, one to whom I owe a great debt of gratitude. He it was who so greatly helped me to be quite sure of my vocation to the priesthood.
>
> Then came the Vicariate of Father Holden, one of the most saintly men I have ever had the privilege of being brought into contact, and his influence over me was immeasurable.
>
> At the beginning of 1908 I entered Kings College, London, in preparation for Ordination.'

Due to a staff shortage at All Saints, TG Blofeld was asked if he could take the role of Choir Master for a year. He duly took a year out from his studies and then after the completion of his course at London, he went to St Stephen's House, Oxford where he was prepared for Ordination.

'Towards the end of my time at Oxford, Father Mackay said 'When you are ordained we want you to return to All Saints, and resume your control of the Choir School'.

I was ordained in October 1911, and then began six of the happiest years of my life. What a happy family we were...'

Six years later he was appointed chaplain of Bloxham School, where he was also Housemaster of Crake House. Here is an extract from their Newsletter [Bloxhamist Vol.LII No.4044. February 1926]:

'He threw himself into our life with a quiet zest, displaying a wide range of abilities. He played hard, and in the days of Association Football with great distinction. In Cricket, too, he was a valuable slow bowler, a capable, sometimes clever bat, and a dependable fielder.

The scouts owe him much for his interest and especially his help at three successive camps. Those Masses he celebrated so simply and quietly in a tent are much cherished memories.

Then the Library, the Photographic Club, the Chess and Draughts Club, all claimed his interest and care.

In 1920 he became Housemaster of 'Crake' House – a perfectly voluntary addition to his duties which together with the Chaplain's work made life very busy for him. As a Housemaster and in the care of the Dormitories he was equally devoted and undoubtedly did a very great deal for the good of the School.'

In 1926, Father Blofeld was called away from Bloxham to become Rector of St Mary's and Headmaster of the Boy's Grammar School in Nassau in the Bahamas.

'We had known for some months that at an urgent call from his friend the Bishop of Nassau, the Chaplain had decided to go to Nassau early in 1926. But it is doubtful if any of us had quite realised what this would mean to us and so his departure at

Christmas time was an event which moved everyone with the deepest feelings of regret. In secular activities, as well as supremely in our religious life, we had all learned to respect him and to appreciate his constant loyalty and devotion to duty'

Many years later his stories about the Out Islands and Bishop Sheddon's sailing boat – there was an Episcopal veto on powered craft – and of the hurricane which ripped the roof off his church enthralled successive generations of St Michael's boys.

Father TG Blofeld returned to England in 1929 as Chaplain and Headmaster of the Gordon Boys School at Woking but 10 years' later on the death of his elder brother Charles, he succeeded him as Warden of St Michael's.

# Warden at St Michael's

TG Blofeld's appointment was decided during a meeting of the Board of Governors on 31 October 1931:

'The Board then proceeded to consider the names of applicants for the post of Warden of the School. After several names had been considered it was proposed and carried unanimously that the Revd. T.G. Blofeld should be appointed to succeed his brother as Warden. It was further proposed and carried unanimously that the appointment should be for seven years with option to renew on either side.' [TG Blofeld, in fact, lasted in the job for 25 years – until his death]

*'Thomas Guest Blofeld was a lean ascetic looking individual, generous with finance like his brother, but a strict disciplinarian. He was regarded with awe and respect. His courage in keeping the school together during the war was admirable. He smoked a pipe and lived to over eighty years old.'*

**Paul Barraclough 1935/38**

*'My mother thought that (other than my father) Father Blofeld was the most sincere and serene man she had ever met. She assured me that should I be accepted as a boarder at St Michael's, that this man with his kindly blue eyes, and lofty presence would be a man that I could have faith in, and trust, and go to if ever I had a problem as a new boarder.*

*On reflection I guess he was all those things but he failed to spot in the first two weeks of joining the school that my constant visits to his study with sometimes two letters a day to be posted to my parents (only he had stamps!) how desperately unhappy I was! Maybe he did know, and did not send the letters on, guessing what the content may be, and that in a week or two my sadness of leaving home would change.*

*He seldom took lessons, but if another master was indisposed, geography would be his next best subject. His speciality and best subject was VARIA: always the first lesson to be taught on a Monday morning. As the word suggests it roughly translated from Latin to VARIOUS and he would cover topics of global interest, politics, religion and sport. It was a marvellous introduction to the week, before we inmates struggled with Latin, French and History. The kindly manner encouraged us all to take an interest outside of the school, and he was more than able to hold our attention without resort to the "Belt or the Cane?"*

*His own interests were vast, ranging from the 3 main sports of Football, Rugby, Cricket, to stamp collecting - he had a fabulous collection of Bahamian stamps - reading, singing and story telling. He was also an unbeatable Billiards player and would often score 50 points or more, while we lads just waited our turn to cue next.*

*He devised a game for "LETTER BOYS". A letter boy was hand-picked by TGB once a month and was charged to go to his study before lunch, and, having been given a list of conundrums or puzzles, usually typed, in which was hidden the name of the lucky boys who had had a letter from home. He had the advantage over us with his experience of life and it often took a letter boy the whole afternoon to work out who had some post.*

*A simple typed example would be:*

1. *It could be the will is in the drawers.*

2. *This lad is on the up and up and keeps his spirits high.*

3. *Don't deny this lad his supper*

4. *This boy would be owing you money.*

*Answers: 1. WILLIS   2. RUMM   3. DENNY   4. OWEN*

*All good fun until one day something went wrong, and this allegedly kindly man went berserk. Being thrifty, TGB would often print his clues on the back of an envelope, and on this occasion someone had changed his name. Originally a letter sent to the Revd Father Blofeld....now changed to the Revd Father BLOWFLY! This was done by some unwitting boy as a bit of fun, but resulted in the worst show of bad temper ever witnessed by boys, staff and kitchen staff. The man was furious and although the culprit (George Denny 1942/49) owned up, it took several days to get back to normal.*

*A likeable young assistant matron named Miss Crozier was to fall foul of TGB's temper. At lunch one day, being in charge of a table of eight happy lads, eating and enjoying almost next to nothing, for some reason we all shrieked with laughter and Miss Crozier's voice, being female, hit the highest note. Poor lady! She was told off in front of all the school, and being freshly demobbed from the W.R.A.C, was not used to such a reprimand, and not surprisingly she did not return the following term.*

*These are the only two examples of my mother's misjudgment, but she was so right about his kindliness. We were all convinced that the school was poor, and that even the masters and the warden had no money, but this loveable man would often treat the whole school to a visit from a magician, or conjurer, but best of all, on his birthday, would somehow get us all to the cinema in Sevenoaks to see a suitable film.*

*We all knew that God moved in a mysterious way, but it was uncanny how one such treat was to "The Bells of St Mary's". I remember the theme of the film was a singing priest (Bing Crosby) trying to dodge the attentions of the best looking nun in the business (Ingrid Bergman). The result was that for the rest of term we poor lads were fantasising about, and totally in love with Ingrid Bergman, and we all prayed that a comparable Nun would join the staff next term.*

*It is hard to imagine in 2004 that TGB's car was the only car in the quadrangle or drive. He kept it garaged in the stables and used only by him on school errands. His main task was to go once a week to Sevenoaks with a shopping list and return with notepaper, pencils and other commodities. He would never shop for food, but relented during the summer months to bring back packets of lemonade powder to us thirsty lads.*

*I have been told since I left the school that TGB was a shy man and uncomfortable with women. I am now aware that I have no recollection of seeing him talk to the female staff, with the exception of Miss Stockwell, the official Matron. He would often have a re-occurrence of a tropical disease and would only allow Matron Stockwell nurse him.*

*The Reverend Father also had a fixation about the health values of freezing cold water! Twice a week (thankfully) he would officiate in the senior changing and bathroom after he had had his supper. Fortified with warm food in his belly he would take great delight in getting each boy, having had a hot bath, to drain the water and get back in and kneel in the empty bath only to have a huge bucket of freezing cold water thrown over him. His theory was that it was good for the circulation and even better for our health in general, and to make MEN OF US. None of us ever agreed and none of us ever argued and to this day I never take a cold shower!*

**Tony Rumm 1946/49**

*'I remember the somewhat imposing and rather aloof figure of Father Blofeld. I was very respectful of him and always considered it a great honour to be invited to play billiards with him.'*

**John Hutchinson 1949/50**

'*Father Blofeld was a kind and admirable man, a wonderful model for fifty young lads, and a devout priest into the bargain. The winner of the billiards competition would get to play him. He would take orders for all sorts of toys and gadgets and go into Sevenoaks on a Monday and come back loaded with Dinky Toys and plastic soldiers. He would invite his four prefects to his study on a Sunday night, when everyone else was in bed, read us a story, and serve us lemon barley water.*

*He was such an admirable man that I found it hard to believe that he could ever cheat, but he did once, in the nicest possible way. Father was also our Scoutmaster, and we had an occasional visit from the regional Scoutmaster or some figure of authority in the movement. Father taught us semaphore the day before the visit, but he made sure we knew the message he was going to give us which was "Put out the flags". Was the visitor really taken in by forty-odd boys all putting up their hands to say which message Father had sent us with his little flags? I still wonder.*'

**John Crowther-Alwyn 1957/62**

'*Father Blofeld was very enthusiastic about cricket and a great fan of C.B. Fry. He posted on the bulletin board pictures of C.B., as he was referred to, in the classic batsmens's address and 'loaded' positions.*

*Father Blofeld was strict but very fair and always treated me kindly. Generally he was very formal but he did allow himself to relax a bit on Sunday evenings when he used to read ghost stories to the prefects. He was an excellent reader and often had us quite scared. In retrospect I'm not sure that it was good for us but we always looked forward to it!*'

**Kendall Carey 1949/56**

'*I remember Father Blofeld's shopping trips to Sevenoaks. Twice a week after lunch, boys would queue outside TGB's study to place "orders". The Revd. would write them in copperplate into a small notebook: pens, pencils, rulers, and rubbers were ordered; balsa wood and glue, paperclips and sweeties. Horlicks tablets, Sharps Extra Strong mints, Cremola Foam and Chocolate Spread or a quarter pound bag of salted peanuts were among the favourites. Father Blofeld would trundle off to Sevenoaks in his faithful Austin motorcar for this twice-weekly errand. Upon his return the cost of each item would be meticulously entered in the boy's personal ledger. Collections of the spoils would be after tea on the same day.*'

**Roger Harding 1954/60**

*'Father Blofeld in his kindness used to mark his own Birthday in early October with a special treat for us; I particularly remember the deep-sea diver, who brought all his gear.'*

**Charles Masheder 1957/62**

*'Father Thomas Blofeld, the Headmaster, an elderly Anglican priest whose head at its elderly angle looked screwed on through his dog-collared priestly shirt.'*

**Colin Emmett 1960/65**

# A selection of Father Blofeld's staff

## Callow - Servant

*'[Fr Baring] was once attacked by an extraordinary servant called Callow, who I seem to think, brandished knives. Fr Baring persuaded him to come outside from the commotion he was making in the hall. Outside Callow appeared to be attacking Fr Baring and we appealed to Fr Blofeld for help.'*

**Paul Rose 1940/44**

## Carlos Twins – Music Teachers

*'We were fortunate in having the Carlos Twins, Robert and Edward, bachelors in their late thirties. These two would pay us frequent visits and befriend us in many ways, our favourite being when they would take 4 or 5 of us away in their car to their large house in Bromley for the night and the following day to Sandwich Bay for the day, bringing with them all the necessary food and drink. Edward was the resident organist of Bromley Parish Church. When I think of it now, the sisters must have been very trusting to allow these excursions ad hoc.'*

**Gerry Winter 1924/30**

*'Music was fed to us by the Carlos twins – dark skinned and as like as two peas except that one was the musician and the other had migraines. They did a lot of work for Sports Day, were the mildest and most genial of men, came from Bromley and even dressed exactly the same – a tendency to brown tweed coats.'*

**Paul Rose 1940/44**

## Colson - Servant

*'Dear old Colson lived up the back stairs and used to play a banjo – or was it a guitar.'*

**Paul Rose 1940/44**

## Cunningham - Teacher

*'Mr Cunningham viciously slapped the heads of those of us who hadn't learnt off Longfellow's 'Evangeline' to perfection. Some said that out of school he was much more human.'*

**Paul Rose 1940/44**

## Ellis - Music Teacher

*'The Carlos twins were succeeded by another mild, gentle musician, Mr Ellis, who played at St Mark's Bromley and lasted I think a good many years. These three men were a tonic because they were both friendly and gentle.'*

**Paul Rose 1940/44**

*'I remember the Music Master from Bromley, Mr Ellis, telling me that I had a voice like Gwen Catley'* [one of the best loved British sopranos in the era between 1937 and 1950. She won a devoted following for her attractive, pure, high flying and flexible soprano.]

**Tony Rumm 1946/49**

## Fargher, Mary – Cook (retired in 1966)

*'Mary was a wonderful lady. She used to look after Fr. Charles even to religiously (if that's the right word in this case) cleaning his car in the yard and looking after Irish terrier Micky. She used to make supper for him and visitors and when in the upper reaches of the school we used to wait eagerly to consume the leftovers. After the sisters departed Mary cooked for the whole school, valiant soul, and her roast potatoes were legendary. They remain the unattainable standard in this household. She used to be so tired that she frequently fell asleep in the bath. If anyone was a saint she was.'*

**Roy Haines 1932/38**

*'Mary was a conundrum which exercised our young minds. She would have been in her middle or late thirties, a sharp-boned angular woman with a leathery complexion. Certainly no femme fatale. She was the only link between the school and the kitchens. There must have been a cook and*

*perhaps a scullion or two, but we never laid eyes on such creatures. Mary served all meals, both to boys at three long refectory but also to the high table where Father Blofeld presided with staff on either side (and occasionally a visitor)...We always hoped that some evidence would surface of her being Blofeld's mistress, but it was always unlikely and it never did.'*

**Eric Crabbe 1934/38**

*'Mary, the cook, slaved and sweated in the kitchen with a huge old black coal or coke fired range. She also did a lot of nurturing and I suspect cleaned the chapel and was very devout. She ended her life rather crippled in a convent in Rottingdean. I called her a saint because she was wholly devoted and very loving to those of us who knew her. She regularly snoozed in the bath at 1am only to be up again at 6am. She can never have had much sleep in bed.'*

**Paul Rose 1940/44**

## Freeman - Servant

*'Almost stone-deaf, Freeman never managed to ring the magnificent church bell correctly for the Angelus – three sets of three dongs followed by a nine at 6am, noon and 6pm daily. He had a lovely smile, and he and Mary were quite friendly towards us.'*

**Paul Rose 1940/44**

*Freeman, a rather large unshaven man, who worked mainly in the kitchen had very poor hearing and wore an aid. Despite his enormous size, many of us reckoned that he could lip read, and for my 3 years at the school felt that he had had a special relationship with TGB. Rumour had it that he had been a Mountie in Canada and other stories confirmed that in earlier days he may well have been TGB's manservant.*

*What he actually did in the school was a mystery - he seemed to be around the chapel and the kitchen as well as helping to clean the school. For me, he is best remembered for his ability to say very little, but convey moments of joy! The teaching staff would have supper in the library from about 7.30 to 8.30pm, and Freeman would clear the room and take the 'left-overs' back to the kitchen. Within minutes he would return to the refectory with the rarest of commodities: 'food' and call out in a loud voice "SUPPRA-UPP!" Eagerly anticipating Freeman each night we 8 or 10 lads would be ready behind the classroom door to seize and devour the remains of the staff's supper.*

*I cannot recall that he had a Christian name, or that he was smartly dressed, or even seeing him in Chapel for a service, but I do recall this kindly man helped us keep body and soul together.'*

**Tony Rumm 1946/49**

## Haines, Roy – Teacher from 1947 to 1954 [pupil from 1932 to 1938]

*'I have an enduring love of history sparked one afternoon when Mr. Haines the history teacher took the class outside behind the school and showed us how a motte and bailey castle was built, using a pile of sand and matchsticks.'*

**John Wood 1947/53**

*'Fortunately, after junior school, I was taught most of my subjects by Roy Haines, who was a superb teacher (at least for me) and I thrived and enjoyed my classes with him enormously and as a result learned rapidly. He managed to make history fascinating by teaching us about heraldry, castle and cathedral architecture and how battles were fought in the Middle Ages. He was also a great Maths and English teacher. He was a cornerstone of the School's administration and his leaving in 1954 was probably why 'The Michaelian' [termly newsletter] was not produced for at least two years afterwards. Roy Haines also taught us rugby, which I greatly enjoyed, despite being only nine when we started.'*

**Kendall Carey 1949/56**

## Johnson, Jessie – Assistant Matron

*After Miss Crozier, the assistant matron who left at the end of summer 1946, Miss Johnson joined St Michael's and stayed at the school for about 30 years. A small lady, always in white uniform, she had lived in Cornwall and spoke with a trace of a West Country accent.*

*Like most of the staff, although she was kindly, she could be very strict and every boy knew the boundaries which could never be crossed. Her duties were mainly to keep the top floor of dormitories and laundry in order, and to supervise 'tuck' after lunch each day. Even though on the ration, sweets were in plentiful supply for most boys and they were locked away in a cupboard to be dispensed to hungry young lads. Only on rare occasions did she break the rule and give some fortunate lads two sweets!*

*She seemed to be a loyal cricket supporter, and would always sit and watch a home game during the summer, sympathising with the team whenever they lost.*

*At meal times, she sat at the end of the table keeping conversation interesting and not so loud as to upset Father Blofeld who commanded a low hubbub at meal times.*

*For many years she was delighted to welcome Old Boys who visited the school and it was only then that many of us realised that she was much more kindly and understanding than we had realised. During these conversations we then learned that she had not missed very much. She had turned a blind eye to many of the pranks and things we had got up to.*

*I believe too that she was a deeply religious lady and had the courage to stand up for herself and the boys when she felt the strong arm of Donald Cormack was unfair.*

**Tony Rumm 1946/49**

### Keatch, Miss Margaret – Junior Teacher from 1944 to 1951

*'I remember as I was in the front row leading the choir out of Chapel after Mass, walking straight into the cutting edge of the open door and falling over, while trying to get a better view of Miss Keatch's magnificent breasts.'*

**Tony Rumm 1946/49**

*'The junior school was taught by Miss Margaret Keatch, except for Latin and French, which were taught by Father Blofeld and Donald Cormack respectively. Miss Keatch was generally quite a good teacher but she was a strict disciplinarian and must have had a bit of a sadistic streak in her. She used to punish us quite frequently by rapping the backs of our fingers with the sharp edge of a ruler, which may not sound like much but was extremely painful.'*

**Kendall Carey 1949/56**

### Parkes, Father – History Teacher

*'Father Parkes taught history and was quite radical for the time in teaching that English history started before 1066. He was an underage volunteer in WW1 and his first hand experiences of trench warfare were as unforgettable as I am sure he intended them to be. He had been an RAF chaplain and also the chaplain of a borstal where he had to witness birching, another tale relived for us in graphic detail. At one time an impressive network of trenches dug in the school grounds with garden trowels at weekends were ordered to be filled in before someone was accidentally buried!'*

**Alec Stevenson 1954/60**

### Paton, Mr - Teacher

*'Occasional help was given by a former Manchester Grammar School Classics Master, Mr Paton, who was pretty elderly. Saturday morning extra Latin at his house on the way to Kemsing was a feast – I seem to remember some chocolate! A dear old man, we were cruel to him. I remember some boys pelting the blackboard with snow, to which he paid not the slightest attention; he did not deserve that – but he was not going to punish us.'*

**Paul Rose 1940/44**

## Pinney, Mrs

*'Mrs Pinney, who lived in the stables, took Sunday School every Sunday afternoon before (or after?) the weekly crocodile walk in uniform. She played the old harmonium rather too gently in the chapel – omitting her little finger because she had arthritis. That was quite a feat.'*

**Paul Rose 1940/44**

## Sankey, Mr – Head Gardener from 1953 to 1956

*'Shortly before I left St Michaels Mr and Mrs Sankey, who were both artists, came to live in the stable buildings. Mr Sankey was employed as a groundsman and I believe Mrs Sankey did at one time teach art at the school....I was very upset to hear later of the suicide of Mr Sankey who shot himself while out with a shotgun in the school grounds. Very sad.'*

**Alec Stevenson 1954/60**

## Sister Hilda (Lay Sister)

*'Sister Hilda always dressed in a lilac coloured habit. She did all the cooking with assistance from two young girls. She was a very likeable and friendly person and we loved her and she us. If you found yourself near the kitchen (which you made a point of) she would always give you some tasty morsel to make you happy.'*

**Gerry Winter 1924/30**

## Shepherd, Stephen – Art Teacher

*'We were taught art by an external teacher, Stephen Sheppard, who looked like a typical artist with dark hair and a beard and was very patient with us all. His classes were particularly well liked in the summer, when he would allow us to find something we wanted to draw or paint outside in the grounds. He also did a great job painting the scenery for the school plays.'*

**Kendall Carey 1949/56**

## Stockwell - Matron from 1943 to 1957

*'Matron Stockwell came from a London teaching hospital, Guys I believe, and had all the characteristics of a strict hospital regime: upright, starch and hygiene. She was responsible for a change in school life: the introduction of cod liver oil, Vitamin C jelly and a balanced menu (on limited funds and rationing).*

*She was a very sensitive and lonely person, finding life at St Michael's, where women had little standing, very difficult. However, I recall it was always a race to see who would finish the crossword first – Father Blofeld, Father Wyman or Matron – so she was no one's fool.*

*At the end of term the whole school was squeezed into the senior classroom, together with the teaching staff. Father Blofeld would recall the more successful dates during the past term, ending with prayers and the singing of the hymn 'God Be With You 'Til We Meet Again'. This hymn was the climax of terms, when we all forgot bullies and who was the brainiest lad. All of us, the whole room managed to keep a stiff upper lip, until the most kindly of all staff in the room – Matron Stockwell – finally gave way to tears.*

*It was a very emotional hymn and to see this wonderful lady, who had been strict (but fair) breakdown, was the signal for practically all of us to cry our eyes out - even Father Blofeld and Donald Cormack.*

**Tony Rumm 1946/49**

*'Matron Stockwell was a splendidly old fashioned lady who always walked like a clipper ship under full sail, an image aided by the formal uniform she always she wore, with the white crisply starched triangular shaped head covering, her cloak and red belt! Her treatments were generally painful but effective. She was particularly keen on iodine and there were generally a few boys with brown blotches on their skin. Miss Johnson, the Assistant Matron, was a decent soul, who at least did not make our lives more difficult.'*

**Kendall Carey 1949/56**

*'Why did a school of fifty boys need two matrons? Matron Stockwell had been a real hospital matron and acted as if she still was one, supervising everything whether or not it required it. The planning and cooking of meals, the cleaning of the rooms, our nightly bathing, laundry shipments, dispensing vitamin pills or sweets "banked" in the sweet cupboard, our dress and etiquette. Arguments were frequent and those with Jessie Johnson particularly explosive, ending with "And who is the SENIOR matron?", followed by some muttered obscenity from Jessie Johnson, probably learnt from her time as an army nurse. An alternative parting shot was "Well, we'll see what Father Blofeld has to say". I felt rather sorry for Father Blofeld!*

*At the beginning of one term when I was eight or nine years old, I arrived back at the school with my mother and went upstairs to put away my hand luggage. Meanwhile my mother made the mistake of arriving at the front door with a handkerchief in her hand. Matron Stockwell, who was supervising our return, stopped her from coming in with "You cannot come in Mrs Stevenson, you have a virus. Mr and Mrs whatever-their-name-was are driving back through Sevenoaks, they will give you a lift". This fait accompli was relayed to me in the same blunt manner and I was so incensed by the injustice of it that I walked straight out of the school. By the time I was missed, I was halfway up the long hill leading to Sevenoaks town centre. Once I had had my say and a chance to say goodbye, I returned quite happily to school and nothing more was said. Father Blofeld's only comment to my mother was "That woman!"'*

**Alec Stevenson 1954/60**

*'Matron retired perhaps a year after I arrived, after teaching me to close my mouth, by saying "close your mouth" every time she saw me, and that's about all I remember about her.'*

**John Crowther-Alwyn 1957/62**


## Wagg, Kathleen – Teacher from 1951 to 1973

*'I remember the death of King George VI. We knew something was amiss because Mrs Wagg, our form teacher, was late; something that had never happened before. When she did arrive, she had clearly been weeping and, having told us of the King's death, she again wept, the first time that I had seen an adult cry. The Coronation was marked by an exeat but my parents being abroad, my brother Michael and I remained at school and, a huge privilege, we were permitted to watch the ceremonies on the (black and white) television. Later we went to the cinema in Sevenoaks and saw an extended newsreel of the Coronation in colour.'*

**Paul Hoddinott 1950-1955**


*'Mrs Wagg was a second mother to junior boys. Which didn't prevent me, when I was thurifer, making so much smoke that the poor woman had to use her smelling salts to help her keep at it on the organ, until she complained to Father who made the boatboy and me go out when not needed.'*

**John Crowther-Alwyn 1957/62**


## Whitling, Margaret – Lady Housekeeper from 1936 to 1943

*'Miss Whitling, being a very good Anglo-Catholic, always wore a veil. She was very small, and we really had I think no relationship with her. One morning she had died, and really we knew nothing more about her.'*

**Paul Rose 1940/44**


## Wyman, Fr Sydney – Teacher from 1943 to 1947

'It is with great regret that we said good-bye to Father Wyman at the end of the Summer Term [1947]. He had been with us for 4 years – and it is gratifying to know that he was very happy here. We owe him a great debt of gratitude, not only for his work in the schoolroom, but for producing the English Play so magnificently, at each of the four Prize Days he was with us, and for the many enjoyable evenings he gave us with his Talkie-Cinema. Father Wyman is now Chaplain of a Convent in Buckinghamshire, and we wish him every happiness in his new work.'

**The Michaelian – Christmass 1947**

*'Jolly and universally popular was Fr Sydney Wyman. He initiated stage musical productions – I can only recall a sort of Chinese effort in which the chorus was 'Lu San'.'*

**Paul Rose 1940/44**

Lu San produced in 1947

# Thomas Guest Blofeld 1939/64

**1939** – Father Thomas Blofeld becomes Warden on the death of his brother Father Charles Blofeld. There are just 27 boys on the register.

**1939** – Portraits of Arthur Tooth and Charles Blofeld (painted by renowned portrait painter Hugh Riviere) are unveiled.

**1941** – The Headmaster Michael Cork resigns and the Second Master Donald Cormack is called up to the war.

**1945** – The school is put on the list of 'Preparatory Schools recognised by the Ministry of Education as efficient' – and becomes a member of I.A.P.S.

**1946** – As recommended by the Ministry, Art is put on the curriculum with Mr Binns as teacher.

**1947** – First School Camp is held at St Ninnian's, Edinburgh coinciding with the first Edinburgh Festival.

**1947** – The War Memorial is unveiled.

**1947** – The termly newsletter 'The Michaelian' is launched.

**1960** – Beverly Cross [OM 1939/44], playwright and screenwriter, invited to open the New Hall.

**1961** – Father Blofeld celebrates his Golden Jubilee Mass at All Saints, Margaret Street.

**1964** – Father Blofeld dies aged eighty-one.

# ~ 11 ~

## The World War II Years

In 1939 Father Thomas Guest Blofeld succeeded to the Wardenship of St Michael's on the early death of his brother Father Charles Blofeld. With war breaking our in the same year, Father Thomas had to deal with some very difficult conditions.

> During the difficult war years he coped successfully with air raids, rationing, staff shortage and doodlebugs, and each crisis seemed to tap fresh reserves of strength, both spiritual and physical. It is in large measure due to his inspiration and indefatigable labours that St Michael's holds the position it does today as an outstanding preparatory school in the Catholic tradition.

**The Church Times 1964**

*'Father Thomas Guest was my guardian throughout the war as my father was based in New York (British Trade Commission). He allowed us to listen to all Churchill's speeches – very moving, particularly after Dunkirk and the Battle of Britain. Many of us stayed at the school throughout the school holidays – we were already 'evacuated'. We had the privilege to see the whole of the Battle of Britain from May to the end of September 1940. The V-1s and V-2s were all very spectacular and frightening – to say the least.*

*We did have the experience of seeing Dad's Army in practice: first the LDV [Local Defence Volunteers] then renamed the Home Guard. One guard would have a Lee Enfield Rifle (from the Boer War) and the rest had clumps of wood! Serious then, but amusing in 2004'*

**Tony Harrison 1937/43**

*'References [in the Old Michaelian 50th anniversary leaflet] to the demise of the ornamental fishpond are personal for me as I was 'firewatching' in Father Blofeld's study when it happened. Each of us did a couple of hours and we were provided with a hot drink in a thermos, cocoa I think, and chocolate wholewheat biscuits. On this particular night, I can't remember whether the 'siren' had gone or not, but it was thought that a limping German bomber who was in difficulties getting up over the downs decided to drop his bomb load over the school grounds.*

*There is no doubt that we were very fortunate: a quite small variation in his course and the whole stick of bombs could have fallen across the school. Strangely, next morning we saw a number of piles of earth scattered across the grounds. The bombs had dug themselves into the soft earth and had then exploded producing a large lump instead of a crater and the last one fell on the fishpond and demolished it.*

*In the morning we found one surviving goldfish which was flapping about in a tiny bit of water. I believe those were the days when all of us were sleeping in the cellars, an experience which was exciting but not too pleasant or comfortable.'*

**Jeffries Stratton 1937/41**

*'I remember the first doodlebugs coming over the school on a cold and wet Friday night at, I believe, the beginnings of a monthly exeat, many not getting as far as London but coming down in Kent as the Germans had not got the range to start. We were once again down in the cellars with that coke fired boiler and all those sulphurous fumes – no good for an asthmatic!*

*There were barrage balloons in the grounds and one called 'Lucy' was sighted at the end of the Kemsing drive. I'm not sure if it was 'out of bounds' but I know that we went down to see Lucy and those large cylinders that had the helium gas for inflation. Of course we also saw the chasing & interception of doodlebugs by RAF Typhoons (or was it Tempests?).*

*I recall cricket practice and seeing the Air Invasion Armada at the start of D Day. When VE Day came we had a bonfire on the warren in the evening which if I recall correctly was damp and the fire had to be encouraged by petrol from Fr. S Wyman's Hillman car.'*

**J. Martin Beech 1943/47**

The logbook entries for the early war years give a glimpse of some aspects of life at St Michael's during that time:

---

**20 September 1939**: Term started under war conditions, but we have a record number of boys - 43 - and a new dormitory has been established. The cellars have been turned into a "dug out" and the duties of Private Air Warden are being efficiently undertaken by Mr Cormack.

**29 September 1939:** St Michael's Day. Our Patron's day was kept as a whole holiday as usual. The weather was lovely and there were no bounds within the premises. Mass was said at 8 and sung at 10. No goose this year, but pork makes an excellent substitute.

**29 June 1940**: The weather was ideal for our first war-time Sports & the contests gave evidence of the keenness throughout the school.

Despite the war we had some 80 visitors & after tea we went down to the Badminton Court to the Presentation of Prizes. Commander Bull R.N. gave them away & he must be as proud of his son as his son was proud of him.

**16 September 1940:** Term started under conditions of "Total War". Air Raids at intervals of 2 hours in the day, and all night raids as well. The boys are sleeping in the cellars & the top of the house is unoccupied. Morale magnificent.

**30 September 1940:** As the Patronal Festival fell on a Sunday the holiday was kept on 30 September when a happy day was passed wandering over the ground & playing the "War Game". No goose......pereat Hitler! but a succulent pig & jellies of all the hues of the rainbow & blancmange which belied its name. S. Michael's Day has been kept in traditional style.

**21 January 1941:** A visit by the whole school to Sevenoaks to see Charlie Chaplin's latest film "The Great Dictator". No private buses now being available we were accommodated with a "duplicate". We just had time to inspect Messrs. Woolworths before going to the Majestic, and everybody thoroughly enjoyed themselves.

**28 April 1941:** We began with new faces. Fr F. G. Baring, my old colleague at Cambridge, took the place of Mr D. Cormack (called up) and Mr J. Paton kindly stepped into the breach with the senior Mathematics.

**14 June 1941:** Corpus Christi Festival. This was held despite the war - about 100 people were able to turn up. Those who had brought tea ate it in the grounds.

---

*'I was aged 9 years and 3 months at the outbreak of the Second World War on September 1939 and I suppose my earliest memory was that on returning for the autumn term my mother had to remember for me to take my gas mask and identity card; ration books were added to the list in January 1940.*

*Following the nine-month's quietness of the 'phoney war', in the late summer of 1940 the German bombing raids started and Otford was in the flight path of the German bombers going to 'blitz' London. Before their arrival overhead the air raid sirens would go and I remember the intensely bleary-eyed feeling I had after the rude awakening in the middle of the night as one staggered down the two flights of the big main staircase from the top floor dormitories to the ground floor and then further down to the capacious cellars below where straw palliasses and blankets had been laid out for us to rest until the 'all clear' went. I think there was a period when we slept there all the time to avoid the night-time disturbance.*

*Later in the war in June 1944 the 'Doodlebug' V-1 flying bombs were directed from their launching pads on the French and Belgian coasts, their target being London and again Otford was on one of their flight paths. One of the defensive strategies was to bring them down on less populous districts before they got to London; this of course included Kent. One was worried to see a forest of barrage balloons spring up in the countryside presumably to catch them although I don't think they ever did.*

*More effective however were the fighter planes and in fact we were practising cricket at the nets (which were down in the hollow beneath the school) when a 'Doodlebug' came over pursued by fighter planes which shot it down over us. We all flung ourselves down on the ground. Fortunately the 'Doddlebug' did not make a vertical descent (or I would not be writing this now) but glided down gradually and reached the ground and exploded somewhere near Shoreham.*

**David M George 1938/44**

*'The war dictated our lives to some extent. Before I arrived [1940] the grounds had been pitted with small bomb craters, and I never saw the fishpond which was smashed by enemy action. What affected all our lives was the Battle of Britain, during which we slept in the spooky cellars whilst up above we could hear the bombs and the guns on many a night.*

*More scary was the advent of the V1 flying bombs one misty Saturday morning. The sound was very eerie – particularly as soon as we knew there was no-one piloting these noisy planes with fire coming out of their tails. The warning was to beware as soon as the engines cut out – and we were at one time under the desks almost every five minutes. You got used to it; but one of the worst moments I remember was one evening when I was on the terrace by the house – out of action with a leg bite? – and one of these horrors was aiming straight for the cricket pitch where Fr Blofeld and several boys were playing a game. Just before a murderous disaster a spitfire or hurricane tipped the wing of the weapon, and it landed near Sevenoaks gasworks! The pilot deserved more than a medal.*

*This brought about a forest of barrage balloons all over the grounds, manned by the odd soldier who on occasion used the grounds as a loo. The balloons were fascinating – but seemed to prove pretty ineffective. I believe a number had their lines severed by the doodlebugs, as we called them – and presumably ended up a long way away.*

*In the woods a fair amount of timber was chopped down, presumably for the war effort. Some of us helped Fr Blofeld to clear a little, but a lot of work was supposedly done by Italian prisoners of war, whom I remember vaguely. They were friendly, and I think it was helpful to us to realise that they were human beings at the height of war propaganda.'*

**Paul Rose 1940/44**

# The War Memorial

Five Old boys from St Michael's were killed in the Second World War. They were:

Stanley Preece [1931/34] – Royal Air Force
George Blythe [1927/33] – Honourable Artillery Company
Edgar Barwood [1932/36] – Royal Air Force Volunteer Reserve
Gordon Alexander Searson [1935/39] – The Middlesex Regiment
Peter Derek Jones [1932/34] – Royal Navy (Submarines)

It was decided in 1947 that a Memorial to the dead should be erected at the school in the form of a Flagstaff on the terrace, with a Bronze Tablet at the base, recording the names. A ceremony to unveil and dedicate the Memorial was held on 17 May 1947. This is the write-up of the ceremony in the introductory issue of *The Michaelian* - Christmass [sic] 1947:

The five Old Michaelians who sacrificed their lives in the 1939-45 war were commemorated at the school on May 17th of this year. After the special Mass in the School Chapel an impressive ceremony took place on the terrace.

A long procession consisting of Thurifer, Cross Bearer, Acolytes Scouts, the School Governors, the Warden and Bishop Walter Carey, wended its way from the Quadrangle along the terrace to the memorial tablet which was veiled with a Union Jack.

After Tennyson's "Crossing the Bar" had been sung, Bishop Carey gave a short address in which he told us not to sorrow for those Old Boys who had died, and who are now in the nearer Presence of God, but to sorrow for the incredible folly of mankind. After his address the Bishop pulled a cord and the Union Jack slipped aside, revealing the bronze memorial tablet.

When this was dedicated by the Bishop, buglers from the Gordon Boy's School at Woking sounded the Last Post. Patrol Leader Raffle hoisted the flag from half-mast to the mast-head, and the buglers sounded "Reveille". The School Song was sung and then Bishop Carey gave us his blessing and the procession reformed and returned to the Quadrangle.

# ~ 12 ~

## 'Morky' - Donald Cormack

### Senior Master - 1937 to 1964, Headmaster - 1964 to 1981

Donald Hope (or Hamish, as he preferred) Cormack was a dominant figure in the life of St Michael's from the moment of his arrival in 1937 until his retirement, forty-four years later in 1981.

He was born on 25 September 1912, presumably in Edinburgh where his family home was at 15 Comely Bank Place. His father was James Clark Cormack who was in service as a butler and his mother was called Maud Isobel. He had a sister called Dolly who settled in South Africa and also a brother.

Although details of his early life are sketchy, it is known that in his early twenties he was a teacher at St George's Prep, near Lincoln and then in October 1935, at the age of twenty-three he started at St Chad's College, Durham University, with a view to progressing to ordination.

The following extracts are from personal letters that Donald Cormack left at the school following his retirement. The letters are from family friends, colleagues and from the Principal at Durham University. They were not unearthed until after his death and reveal an aspect of Donald's life that many Old Michaelians will be unaware of:

**9 June 1934** 'Thank you for your letter. I remember our meeting at Lincoln. I send you a prospectus of the College, together with a copy of the regulations for Matriculation. You will note from the latter you will have to acquire a matriculation certificate in Latin. With regard to financial matters, I should say that the college is hardly ever able to provide the full cost of a student's training. All we can do is make a grant of about £50 per year: so it would be necessary for you to find some other resources, either from Diocesan or Central funds. We never adopt the system of repayment after ordination.'

**The Principal, St Chad's College, Durham.**

**22 April 1935** 'It is most sad to think that this coming term will be your last at St George's. You seem to be so much one of us that we shall miss you more than we can say......You have always been so good to me and done so many things for me that I am sure nobody else will do. I really am grateful for all you have done & shall always remember your deeds of kindness.'

**Evelyn Heaton, wife of Edward J Heaton, Headmaster of St George's Prep School, Riseholme Grange, Lincoln**

**October 1935** 'See the result of prayer and faith. Glory be! I am so thankful you got through the Greek. I think great praise is due to you – you had so short a time. Now do swat at the organ, so that you can get some more taken off your fees. I think you told me the succentorship *[The position of succentor: A chanter who takes up the chant after the precentor (choir leader or director), or who presides over the left choir]* was worth £50 so it all helps. Don't get in with a fast lot of men, stick to those who mean to get on and make their way.'

**Susie Holt**

**17 April 1936**: 'I was interested but not a bit surprised to hear of your experience with regard to work. When you say, though, "It is not in me to work...get thro' in June", I just don't believe you, and in any case an attitude like that is quite indefensible. The statement anyhow is just indefensible rot! I often get bored stiff myself with work and any little interruption or distraction is enough to stop me doing any for a day or two. It's really a very good thing to have a spot of vision and take the long view; I mean it will be a case of to be or not to be ordained to the sacred ministry, in your case, I suppose, depending absolutely on what happens in June or September. This thought should have a galvanizing effect.'

**Eric**

**21 August 1937** 'How are you getting on? We were very sorry to hear that you had pipped.'

**Kath and Mary (Teacher friends from St George's Prep School, Riseholme Grange)**

Unfortunately, Donald failed his second year exams, and then again failed his re-sits in September 1937 and with poor finances, he had no choice but to apply for paid employment, with every intention of continuing with his degree at a later stage. How he obtained his position at St Michael's is not known, but on 1ˢᵗ November 1937 he commenced as Teacher at St Michael's under the Wardenship of Father Charles Blofeld.

**7 October 1937** 'I was very relieved to hear that you got the post, and more than relieved that it is such a nice school. I suppose it is St Michael's Oxford [sic] Court as you told me on the phone?'

**Graham (a friend from Durham)**

**21 November 1937** 'I was disappointed you failed in your Greek exam, but better luck next time let's hope. Still I feel if you had followed my advice & kept your nose to the grindstone, you would have got through. Coxing, cross country running, visiting etc - excellent in their ways, but no good to you until you had passed your exam. I am glad you are so happy at your new post – you were lucky to get a job so easily.'

**Susie Holt**

**19 December 1937** 'I was awfully sorry to hear you had failed last time – what rotten luck. I hope you like your new post. Don't suppose teaching goes down very well though when you have set your mind on the church. Is it only a temporary measure?'

**Mary Croft (friend from St George's Prep School, Riseholme Grange)**

**23 Jan 1938** '….you have been very ill with some poisoning. I am awfully sorry and do hope that you'll soon be really well again. You have truly been most unfortunate what with financial worries and then a nasty illness on top of it all…I hear…that you are teaching at a school near Seven Oaks…I was sorry you didn't get through the Greek. It does seem such a shame.'

**Kathleen Hammersley, a friend from St Georges Prep School, Riseholme Grange, who later married Rev Henry Thurlow Wagg, and later still became a teacher at St Michael's. She was widowed in 1944 and later married Father Whittaker, the then Chaplain at St Michael's.**

**3 June 1938** 'It must be for you to decide whether it is of any use attempting the examination or not. I am exceedingly reluctant to give you another chance in September – and but for your illness in the winter certainly should not consider doing so. If you are determined in your own mind that you won't fail now, I will give you a chance in September, but I cannot possibly guarantee a place or a grant in 1938-9. I might consider, with reluctance, giving you a place here in October '39 by which time you will be right out of your element...I meant what I said in the Autumn, and your only real excuse of some ill health is not a very strong one as it is Revision Work for an exam you should have passed last June...I am not at all sure that if you are to be ordained this is necessarily the best place for you to train in.'

**The Principal, St Chad's**

Donald decided not to sit his Greek Exam in June – perhaps still with the intention of sitting it in September.

**18 June 1938** 'Could you not go to a Theological College & do the last year there, get ordained and let your degree go hang?...It was a thousand pities you did not scrape through last June – I am sure you must have brains enough if other boys can get through. You must have been foolish – they are wanting priests so badly that I am sure some Bishop would ordain you…'

**Susie Holt**

**3 July 1938** 'You seem very happy at the school, and perhaps it is the best thing at present. Are you thinking of trying again for ordination in a few years or are you going to continue to teach? It is queer the way things work out – you seemed to have such a clear call to the Church, and now all these obstacles have arisen.'

**Joy (a friend from Durham).**

**29 April 1939** 'You have had a dreadful term, and have been nearly worked to death and I don't think it is at all fair on you, and then after such a strenuous time to cut your holidays to a bare fortnight. They seem to me to be exploiting you. They certainly ought to give you a handsome bonus for all you have done. I thought Blofeld was your Headmaster not Cork, I suppose B. is the Warden. I do hope in some wonderful and mysterious way a plan may be devised for you to obtain your goal. It is very difficult. How is your Greek getting on? Could you pass the exam more easily now, than when you were at Durham, or do the papers get more difficult every year. I am so glad your faith is strong.'

**Susie Holt (friend from St George's Pre, Riseholme Grange)**

**19 July 1939** 'The question about ordination is not a simple one, because there are two quite different questions involved: one is whether you are going seriously to attempt to obtain your degree of B.A., the other is whether your are going to obtain the theological training required for holy orders; the courses for these two things being, of course, entirely different…If you still are convinced that it is in your interests to train for a University degree, there is no way out of it but residing at Durham for another year. But you can not do that till you have passed your second year examination.'

**The Principal, St Chad's**

By March 1940, Donald Cormack was still paying off his tuition fees for the two years he attended St Chad's (*'It was so nice to hear from you and the cheque most welcome,'*) and also paying Susie Holt back for the £100 loan she had made him, but the war finally ended his dreams to gain a degree and to be ordained.

Paradoxically, these failures seem to have intensified his determination to enable others to achieve academic success.

His lack of a degree did not stop him from wearing gowns or putting "Durham" after his name on the school prospectus!

## Cormack's Early Days at St Michael's

Donald Hope Cormack arrived at St Michael's in Otford on 1ˢᵗ November 1937, at the age of twenty-five. He obviously made a strong early impression on the school despite his illness at the end of 1937 which presumably meant a period of absence shortly after his arrival.

By the end of 1938 he held a very significant role in the school, which became apparent on the death of the Warden who employed him. Father Charles Blofeld's brother Thomas Guest wrote to Donald Cormack in October 1938:

> 'Now that the first shock of my brother's passing is over I am able more fully to realize all that I owe you for your strong steady sympathy, and all your help during that trying time. I do thank you most warmly.....if I should be deemed worthy to carry on my brother's work at Otford I cannot imagine anyone I would sooner have with me than yourself – I really mean this. I know so well how greatly my brother valued your work & friendship.'

Cormack was called up to the forces in 1940 and stayed away until 1946. His years away were with the Royal Artillery (the Bofors anti-aircraft gun crew) which saw action across the Middle East, North Africa, and Europe including the landing at Sicily. His war years were traumatic for him. As well as the horrors of active combat, other soldiers bullied him, perhaps because of his diminutive height. His war stories recounted to pupils on his return (in place of the duller Latin lessons) were graphic and Old Michaelian Tim Brennand [1942/49] vividly remembers Cormack's tales of burying rotting bodies and other gruesome activities.

Cormack returned to St Michael's in 1946 and became Director of Studies (otherwise known as Headmaster and second in command to the Warden Father Thomas Guest Blofeld).

## The Old Michaelian Association

In 1947, Donald Cormack was instrumental in organising the unveiling ceremony for the Memorial to Old Boys who had been killed in World War II. It was whilst tracking down Old Boys to invite to the event that the idea of forming an Old Michaelian Association came to him.

At the same time, the concept of a termly newsletter, which could be sent out to Old

Michaelian's, was conceived (with the help of teacher Roy Haines). The Introductory Issue was prepared by the boys during the Michaelmas Term and was distributed in time for Christmas 1947. The editor was Wyndham Freyer and Timothy Brennand designed the cover. Contributions by the boys included articles on Stamp Collecting, Bird Life in Kent and reports on scouting and sporting activities. Mr Cormack himself wrote the news of Old Michaelians and included reports of any visits to the school by old boys:

> P. BARRACLOUGH is now living in Surrey and visits us frequently. Some of his indoor photographic efforts have been most successful, albeit somewhat disconcerting to certain members of the staff.

In 1948 Donald Cormack organised the first ever meeting of the Old Michaelian Association:

A meeting of Old Boys took place at St Ermins Hotel, Westminster, on Tuesday, 13th January, under the chairmanship of the Warden.

It was unanimously decided that an Old Boys' Club should be formed and that it should be called "The Old Michaelian Club"
The following officers were elected
Hon. President: The Rev. H J Fynes-Clinton
Hon. Vice-Presidents: The Rev. J. W. Mills; Commander C B Fry, R.N.R
Chairman: The Rev. T G Blofeld
Hon. Sec. And Treasurer: D H Cormack, Esq
Council: P Barraclough, Esq., B P Henharen, Esq., Beverley Cross, Esq

It was decided that the club should possess distinctive colours but after much animated and amusing discussion the final selection was left in the hands of the council.
The future activities of the club were discussed and it was agreed that these should consist at present of an annual re-union dinner to be held in the Christmas holidays and a summer function to be held in Otford.
The Secretary informed the meeting that the Rev. J Mills had offered to donate to the club a Georgian silver porringer which could be used with traditional ceremony as a "loving cup". This gift was accepted gratefully and the Secretary was instructed to convey to Father Mills the appreciation of the members.

For many years the Loving Cup, filled with wine, was passed from Old Michaelian to Old Michaelian in a moving ceremony which signified the solidarity of the association, and each Old

Boy's responsibility to one another. Nowadays the ceremony is unable to go ahead as the numbers attending the annual dinner (nearing the 100 mark) has meant that the procession of the cup would take up most of the evening! However, the cup still takes pride of place at the event.

The Inaugural Meeting of the Old Michaelians Association

The first Old Michaelian Day was held in the summer of 1948. This is Tony Rumm's account of the occasion:

### How to get a decent meal in 1948

*'The food ration in 1948 was little if any more than it was throughout the war. One wondered how Mary the school cook managed to provide a decent meal at all with 1 egg, 4oz butter, 4oz margarine and meat varying between 9d and 1/1d per person per week. We seemed to have plenty of bread and extra jam and the ever-popular marmite brought back to school at the beginning of term. The school garden provided ample vegetables and some fruit, and once a term some kindly fishmonger gave the school a huge box of herring.*

*That was until 24 July 1948 when at 6pm Mary provided a feast for 22 hungry cricketers, 2 umpires, a scorer and half a dozen Old Michaelians who needed sustenance. The feast was to celebrate the first Old Michaelians' Cricket Match against the school; a HOT sunny afternoon, the cricketers encouraged by warm applause from the remaining 37 boys made to watch from behind the wire.*

*Cricket was not compulsory but was unavoidable, and the build up to the match a week or two beforehand even got to DHC as he forgot about Latin and French and romanticised about a cricket match for us all to remember.*

*Terms of engagement were not agreed until just before commencement of play, when knowing how many OMs turned up, the teams were picked. Most matches for some years had 12 or 13 players each side to accommodate OMs who had made the special journey and those who had brought 'whites'.*

*I was too young to play, but remember clearly the enormous height of the OMs, and despite being a complete failure at both English and Maths, clearly made up my mind that the school could never win against such giants.*

*Terms of engagement also included:*
1. *The coin spun by DHC fell in favour of the school.*
2. *All OMs should bat left handed.*
3. *Positively no fast bowling by OMs.*
4. *Every OM should bowl one over whether he could bowl or not.*
5. *That any OM was to be given out lbw if the ball hit him anywhere on the body.*
6. *To keep a balanced game the umpires were empowered to call an occasional Wide or No Ball.*
7. *That during the tea interval, Matron would provide gallons of sickly sweet lemonade made from powder.*

*John Bull captained the First Eleven which consisted of several pre-war lads together with OMs released from King's Taunton and Kings Canterbury. They treated the spectators to an exciting afternoon, using all his bowlers to defeat the school. Paul Barraclough, a future OM captain, hit an enormous six, and had obviously practised beforehand.*

*The OMs team was made up from: J Bull, P Barraclough, J Allart, M Phillips, J Stratton, S Brennand, D Peebles, M Nowers, I Lockie, B Henharen, N Raffle, P Arden, R Willis, V Trehearne, A Campbell, G Perry, M. Pope.*

*Back in the refectory the two teams sat down to a scrumptious feast of: cold beef, sausage rolls, cheese, salad and ample supplies of jam followed by cakes and jelly, fruit salad and apple pie.*

*After the meal, the two captains and the Headmaster made speeches. The use of a few Gaelic words proved that the school captain had a superior speech writer.*

*Along with 36 other boys, not included in the proceedings, I rushed to the refectory to gather up some of the crumbs when the OMs departed – alas there were none! It is very hard to imagine in 2004 when many people today leave more on the side of their plate than we ate in a whole day, that we survived at all.*

*One lesson we younger lads did learn and that was to improve one's standard of cricket for the following summer, so as to get a decent meal!*

\* \* \*

Donald's 'favourites' remained very special to him throughout his life and many continued to correspond with him up until his death. They would also go out of their way to visit him, and he would reciprocate by attending weddings and other family events. He followed the careers of some OMs with keen interest and even attended the Cable and Wireless shareholders meetings in Scotland to support Gordon Owen [current Chairman of the Governors, pupil from 1946 to 1951].

However, this 'favouritism' did eventually cause the dwindling of numbers of those attending the Old Michaelian Dinners:

*'As the years rolled by he only seemed to invite his 'special lads' to the St Michael's Annual Dinner and in the end we dropped down to 28. It has taken Peter Bull (our Secretary who recently retired to try and claw back 25 years of missing boys. No one was allowed to interfere with his Old Boy lists. It was only in recent years that a new Old Boy Committee eventually took over from Donald after he retired.'*

**Tony Harrison 1937/42**

*'Towards the end of 1999 and into 2000 the 'Old Guard' Old Michaelian Association committee of Roy Haines (Chairman), Peter Bull (Secretary) and Tony Harrison (Treasurer) decided to retire. They had held the association together admirably since the 'dictatorial' days of Donald Cormack, who to my recollection was secretary, treasurer and chief organiser for some years.*

*Martin Picket (Secretary) and Anthony Wattenbach (Treasurer) were joined by Tony Rumm, the new Chairman in 2000 and within weeks had increased the size of the committee, being joined the Revd Paul Rose and two very welcome new and much younger faces of Verity Hall and Gemma Lewis. 'The Bull' in Otford proved an agreeable venue, for now all the committee lived within half an hour of St Michael's and had immediate access to the school and the Headmaster.*

*Its aims were to:*

1. *Create a positive bond with the school and present day parents*

2. *Increase the membership of the OMA by trying to recover previously lost records of the school leavers.*

3. *To encourage all school leavers to join the association and share its considerable benefits.*

4. *To award an annual 'Essay Prize' for English students*

5. *To maintain a website for the association: www.oldmichaelians.org.uk*

6. *To find better and larger premises at present held in London for the annual dinner and agree with the Headmaster that it should be held on the Friday before the school breaks up for the Easter holiday.*

7. *Ties for the boys and pins for the girls should be available, so that the school could present every leaver with the same on Prize Giving Day*

8. *That the last Sunday in June shall be known as MICHAELIAN DAY and that*

   a. *Two cricket matches should be played. 1. The school to play last years XI during the morning and 2. The Chairman's XI should challenge the Headmaster's XI for the Old Michaelian shield.*

   b. *Netball, rounders and other activities should be included*

   c. *The school shall be open for all Old Michaelians' to visit*

   d. *At the end of the proceedings a Service of Thanks Giving should be held in the Chapel*

**Tony Rumm 1946/49**


# The Blofeld Memorial Building

On the death of Father Thomas Guest Blofeld in 1964, Donald Cormack became sole 'Headmaster' of St Michael's – ending the use of the title of 'Warden' (associated with the era when St Michael's was an orphanage rather than a school). He set about his new role with gusto. His first project was an ambitious one. His plan was to build a second storey to the existing Hall which had been built in 1960. The Hall had been funded in the most part by donations from Old Michaelians and parents, and Cormack again had to resort to requesting contributions to meet the estimated building costs of £10,000. This time a glossy brochure was produced and specialist fund-raising consultants were used to approach potential sponsors directly.

The new building was designed to house several classrooms, one to be used as a science laboratory and the other to be used as a modern language laboratory. The leaflet stated, "provision of such specialized teaching units is essential in view of recent and forthcoming changes in education. For example, in order to implement the recommendations of the I.A.P.S (Incorporated Associations of Preparatory Schools) on the Nuffield Project and introduce general science as a subject, laboratory facilities will soon have to be provided."

The fund-raising leaflet emphasises that the new extension was to be built in the memory of the previous Warden of St Michael's and would be named after him:

> For some time now many of you who knew Father Blofeld have considered how best his devoted service to St Michael's and its boys could be commemorated. The provision of new teaching accommodation is surely a memorial which would have appealed to him.

The extension was completed in 1969 and on Saturday 27 September of that year, the Blofeld Memorial Block was officially opened with a dedication ceremony conducted by The Right Reverend Graham Leonard, Lord Bishop of Willesden (later to become Lord Bishop of London).

## Battles with the Planning Department

St Michael's School had long been financed by the legacy of Arthur Tooth and the investments of the three Sisters who helped to run the school until the 1930s. Upon the deaths of the Sisters, the Trustees of the school decided to sell up their shares in tea, rubber and diamonds to buy shares in the railway sector. This proved to be a costly decision upon the nationalisation of the rail network in the 1960s.

By 1970, the annual income from the Trust Funds was a meagre £3,500. In accordance with the principles set down by the founder of the school, Arthur Tooth, the fees for the pupils were kept to as low as possible (£120 per term), and 20 out of the 50 boys were assisted by the fund to the tune of £1500 per year.

The income from the fees and the fund was only just enough to pay the staff wages of a Headmaster, four full-time teachers, five part-time teachers, two matrons, a part-time secretary, a chef, a gardener and two full-time male domestic staff. Donald Cormack realised that the only way to make the school a long-term economically viable unit would be to take in a further 15 to 20 boys thereby necessitating new dormitories and a full-time resident master.

In 1970 Cormack decided to sell off a portion of the 88 acres of grounds to provide private housing, thereby making enough money to secure the future of the school for many years to come. The application was for 17 private houses to be built on 8.6 acres of scrubland, in the middle of which was the football pitch. The proposal was that two of the houses would be retained by the school to provide accommodation for members of staff and the rest of the money would be used to provide additional dormitories and classrooms; to move the football pitch; and to build a swimming pool.

However, the Sevenoaks Rural Council refused permission for the sell-off and Cormack was forced to go through a lengthy appeal process. In February 1971 a public inquiry was heard. The 160 strong Kemsing Society, which had recently formed to fight for the protection and conservation of the North Downs, listed several reasons for their opposition to the scheme. They stated that the Otford Court estate was in an area of outstanding natural beauty within the Green Belt area. They also claimed that the proposed development would add to traffic hazards and would even increase the crowding on commuter trains to London.

The forces against the development were too strong for Cormack to fight against and his lack of negotiating skills made matters worse. Eventually in May, the appeal was turned down by the Department of the Environment with the conclusion that:

> Although situated partly in a slight hollow, development on this site would nevertheless appear as a further encroachment on these downland slopes both from the adjacent section of Pilgrims Way and from a number of public viewpoints.

> I do not consider that the appellants' reasons for wishing to develop this land amount to a case sufficient to justify permitting such a substantial intrusion into this important green belt area.

Without the hoped for cash injection, St Michael's struggled financially for many years and any improvements to the school had to be financed through appeals to family and friends.

# Michael Bond

A handsome young graduate called Michael Bond joined the teaching staff in 1956. He was highly educated and a talented sportsman and he quickly became very popular with all the residents at St Michael's. As a fellow Scot from Edinburgh, it is highly likely that Cormack knew his family and invited him to Otford to help out between school and university. [This arrangement has long been part of the St Michael's tradition. Known as 'Gap' students for many years, they are now referred to as Teaching Assistants and three are employed every year – usually from Australia.] Michael Bond became part of the local community and enjoyed an active social life – often at The Bull in Otford or playing cricket at The Vine.

He was a dedicated and popular teacher. There seems to be no doubt that DHC had the greatest respect for Michael and was grooming him as his successor. However, this was not to be. Michael tragically died of a brain haemorrhage in the summer of 1976 whilst on holiday in Somerset, aged just thirty-nine.

The *Sevenoaks News* carried this obituary:

> Mr Michael Bond, a schoolmaster at St Michael's School, Otford, died recently while holidaying in Taunton, Somerset. The 39 year old teacher had taught at the school for 18 years.
>
> Mr Bond was educated at the Edinburgh Academy and Selwin College, Cambridge. He spent one year at St Michael's School as a student *[presumably between school and university]* and later returned as an assistant master.
>
> He played full-back for the Sevenoaks Rugby Football Club and had recently returned from the Buccaneers cricket tour shortly before his death. At St Michael's School he coached the boys at cricket, rugby and soccer.
>
> School Headmaster Mr Donald Cormack said: "Michael Bond belonged to the declining race of dedicated School Masters and St Michael's owes much of its success in the academic field as well as on the games field to his devoted efforts.
>
> "The loss to the school by his death is incalculable and his memorial service will be held locally at a later date," he added.

As a memorial to Michael Bond, DHC immediately set about collecting contributions to finance the building of an open air swimming pool which was opened in 1978 at a cost of £15,000.

*'I remember Mr Bond's room had a wall covered in match books from all over the world. He was considered something of a playboy by us at the time, and we Oohed and Aahed when he got his new Ford Cortina 1600E.'*

**Peter Hardy 1971/73**

*'I remember vividly the tragic early death of Michael Bond which was a shock and we were all, staff and boys, very upset...he was a genuinely nice guy who loved his sport, cricket in particular, and loved St Michael's. It is hard to think of any other teacher, either at St. M's or anywhere else that I looked up to quite as much. He used to do the Times crossword every morning after breakfast and I used to watch him, fascinated, complete it really quickly...I did offer some solutions to difficult clues but somehow I don't think he ever used them! His collection of match boxes on the wall was also something to behold. I remember meeting his brother at Michael's memorial service and he was equally as approachable and friendly. Michael did also enjoy a pint in Otford and used to drive back to St. Ms zig-zagging across the drive up to the White Ladies (as the entrance to the school was called).'*

**Simon Maurice 1974/79**

\* \* \*

In 1979, on a trip to South Africa to see his sister, Donald Cormack met up with an Old Michaelian called Michael Thurlow, the son of his friend Kathleen Wagg who had been a teacher at St Michael's. Michael was also a teacher and Donald Cormack invited him back to England to be his successor as Headmaster of St Michaels. The offer was accepted - although a request for proper accommodation for his family was an obvious necessity.

On his return to England, Cormack commissioned the building of a very modern 'Colt' modular house in the grounds of St Michael's School - which was to cost in the region of £45,000 - to be built. It was named Hatcham House after the district of New Cross which had been so important in the life and career of the founder of St Michael's, Father Arthur Tooth.

Unfortunately for Cormack, after a year as 'Headmaster Designate' Michael Thurlow and his family decided to return to South Africa, and the hunt for a new Headmaster began. An advertisement was placed in the Times Educational Supplement in March 1980 and the Reverend Paul Cox was appointed Headmaster designate in the same year.

After two terms of working alongside Paul Cox, Donald 'Hamish' Cormack resigned as Headmaster of St Michael's after nearly forty-five years' association with the school.

## On Donald Cormack's retirement in 1981, Old Michaelian Tim Brennand [1942/49] composed the following poem

Donald, you have for many years
Dinned verses into youthful ears,
Of Brooke, Shelley, Burns to name a few,
Have patience with some lines on you.

Time is a grasping robber king
Who has his way with everything,
Annually he commandeers
Each new sixth form that appears,
And without scruple even rips
Headmasters from Headmasterships!
Now Donald, whom we'd thought immune;
Can we believe you've gone so soon?

To us your progeny the thought is dire;
Mortals, Englishmen perhaps retire,
But Scots? They are a race apart!
So stiffened in old Gaelic art
And Pictish ways, they say, that some
Can keep on going till Kingdom come!

Few can name more rugged men
Than your native Edinburghian,
And more particularly he,
Who thrice a year, by Waverley,
Night-sleepered to and fro to Kent,
Every Summer, Winter term and Lent.
Could we but hold him fast we would;

## Morky - Donald Cormack

As in each remembered boyhood's
Place, lodge either in that booky room,
Savoury with Saint Bruno's fume,
Crying "Avaunt!" to each marauder
Who dares touch the holy disorder;
Wherein, geologically impressed
Lie "Michaelian" and last week's test.

Watching long-shadowed, at Sundown
Boys pitching lengths to win half a crown,
Or rubbing gleeful hands the exhorter
Of many a shivering three-quarter.

Faced with the giants of Bickley Hall –
"The bigger they are, the harder they fall";
Long-shadowed words we found as men
Life's game renewing those trials again.

Will there be boys like us to shrink
Before another's scowl, and red ink
Illuminating last night's prep?
To start at a different step
Hurrying down the corridor
To visit wrath or class uproar?
A thousand fledglings long since flown
Would not admit another's tone
Could half the awe inspire as his
"See me! That's pure carelessness!"

He took us through his Punic War
In a bofor's crew, where long before
Had Caesar fought; he urged us on
To cross our Latin's Rubicon,
Surmount the Frenchman's palisade,
Invest the poet's magic glade.
His lifetime of teaching's paid
Brilliance will earn it's accolade.

So must we now, with due applause,
With past champions of Saint Michael's cause,
From Father Tooth to T.G.B
Inscribe, with love, our D.H.C.

## Memories of DHC

*'To me Corky [Michael Cork] was a great contrast to dear, legendary Donald Cormack – a lifelong friend, whose slap was always followed up with a delicious piece of fudge.'*

**Paul Rose 1940/44**

*'I remember being mesmerised by Donald Cormack when he read Don Juan of Austria, Rupert Brooks' Granchester and readings from Goldsmith, Shakespeare, Wordsworth, GK Chesterton and many others. The man was a genius for getting the beauty of English Literature into my thick skull. The fact that he failed to fill my brain with Latin and French was due entirely to his extreme methods of teaching a terrified pupil.'*

**Tony Rumm 1946/49**

*'It was Mr Cormack who was the most 'feared' there as he took such hated subjects (for me anyway) as Latin and French, and was very strict, to the point of giving the 'strap' to those he felt should be doing better in these subjects. I was not one thank goodness!*

*There was a large entrance hall in which we would have all our meals, and the breakfast after 'Latin' and 'French' prep the night before was always the worst. We all dreaded the breakfast times when Cormack would arrive with last night's Latin prep in his arms, indicating he must have been up half the night correcting it, and look meaningfully (and with a heavy scowl) at certain boys. This ruined their day until Cormack's class just before lunch (it often ruined the rest of their day too!) This applied mostly to boys who were meant to be 'good' and who had made the fatal error of getting less than 100% for their prep work. The big trick in his classes would be to try and get Cormack to recount some of his wartime stories, and once started we would be desperately trying to think of questions to keep him going rather than let him get back to the far less interesting topic of Latin or French. Who was kidding who?*

*He was also what might be known as the Physical Education Master, and every day we would go for mid-morning marches with him (he was ex Army) half way down the drive and back, which doubled as exercise. I remember my Cousin George volunteering a 'chant' one day. I can't remember the words but it was a sort of skit on Cormack. I can remember him laughing, then ordering us down to the end of the (very long) drive "At the double!" and back.'*

**John Read (Read 1) 1946/49**

## Morky - Donald Cormack

'*The teacher who was quite unforgettable was Donald Cormack. I have vivid memories of this short and busy man who was always bustling around in a great hurry, full of energy and an enormous determination to teach. He must also have had a degree of prescience as he gave me a book entitled 'Mach One' by a Test Pilot called Mike Lithgow. In it he had written 'To John Hutchinson, in the hope that he too will fly at Mach One some day.' Not bad, considering that I became a Concorde Captain for the last 15 years of my flying career!*'

**John Hutchinson 1949/50**

'*Father Blofeld was fine but Cormack ('Morky' to us) was a very moody person with a vicious temper, who scared the daylights out of me and was not a good teacher, at least as far as I was concerned. I remember distinctly, when we were learning the meanings of voici and voilà having a full fifteen minutes of being berated by him because I was confused by their English meanings. My problem was that I was trying to make a direct literal translation, which is of course impossible, but instead of Cormack explaining that 'voi' means 'see', 'ci' means 'here' and 'la' means 'there', he tried to make me learn them by rote. Similarly, even when I was in my last year at St Michael's, having been taught French by Cormack for seven years, he had never explained that a circumflex was the result of adapting a Latin word to French and meant that the Latin 's' had been left out - or if he had, I had missed it.*

*I lived in fear of Cormack all the time I was at St Michael's, even when in my last year I became a 'favourite' of his, which was a dubious honour. Cormack's credo can best be summed up by his oft quoted Latin teacher, who used to say 'Give me a Kennedy (the author of our Latin grammar textbook) and a tawse (Scottish name for a leather strap for punishment) and I can teach Latin grammar to anybody'! He did indeed have a tawse, a nasty black thick leather thing with a split end and he did use it for punishment, generally on an upturned hand!*'

**Kendall Carey 1949/56**

'*Although we ate together as a school, I cannot recall meeting 'Morky' until about a week after my arrival. I soon learned he was a figure to be reckoned with. In my childish mind I worked out that he had three suits by which I could gauge his moods: bottle green meant good; brown, so-so; and black – watch out!*

*Donald's idea of geography was to do what he was superb at: telling stories about his war experiences and the places he visited and use his superb knowledge of Scotland and the Isles. National Curriculum would not have approved, much less H.M.I. No notes at all. This was interspersed with the odd map spotting exercise. "You boy, find the Bog of Allen, Magillycuddy's Meeks, and the Knockmealdown Mountains".*

*I left with two abiding memories. One was of the football team which Donald ran. Now one of the few things he could not teach was football, although he would never have agreed.*

*Gazza would never have made the St Michael's team. "Don't dilly dally boy – big boot!" I inclined more towards rugby which his young assistant, the late Michael Bond, dealt with.*

*The other was the school plays which were performed on the last day of the Christmas term. Rehearsals never started more than four weeks before the end of term. Chunks of dialogue were cut from the Bard or Moliere or whoever. I remember one character's part disappearing altogether because he went sick and there was no understudy. Incredibly though, they always came off!*

*Donald was an incredibly kind, generous man who under a gruff exterior was extremely sentimental. His wardrobe housed clothes given to him many years before, but kept as momentos. He had a mac Columbo would have been ashamed of!'*

**John Wright 1954/60**

*'Donald Cormack was completely unscrupulous. I got a special scholarship to St Edwards, Oxford, as did my brother later. Donald hired a deaf invigilator, and I sat in the library writing my papers while Donald went through the paper very loudly next door, belting out the answer "Yes, that's right, Hoddinott, the formula for the circumference of a circle is....."'*

**Stephen Winkley 1954/57**

*'What I dreaded most of all was Mr Cormack, in or out of class. He doubtless still has a reputation for getting countless boys through Common Entrance and Scholarships. It's true he could teach a good lesson, like the one on "me, te, se, nous, vous, " before "le, la, les," before "lui, leur," before "y" before "en" – see, I remember it to this day! But this was his only perfect lesson, the one he always did in front of the inspector, the one he practiced carefully with us the day before the inspector came.*

*Otherwise he was either in lazy mode, came in, ignored us, rattled his false teeth a bit, and read the Times, while we sat and not so much as twiddled our thumbs in total silence. Or in a foul mood, in which case it was "Belt test number one", usually on Latin vocabulary which we hadn't been warned to revise, and which involved a stroke of his thick leather belt on the hand for each wrong answer. Or in eccentric mode, which meant him standing in front of the whole senior school conducting us, sitting silently bemused, doing nothing, while the music teacher played 'The Queen of Sheba', or some other lively piece. Or even, once, pushing the very strict Nurse Johnson, the assistant matron, and a tiny but in our eyes formidable woman, round the top landing in a laundry basket.*

*Every so often he (DHC) would take us out for walks on Sunday afternoons - the whole school, all fifty of us, with our caps on, and we would all fifty of us raise our caps in greeting to whoever we met and say good afternoon. Except people whom Mr Cormack didn't recognise. He would send a small delegation of senior boys to these people to ask who they were, and what right they had to walk on our land. Fortunately for them, they always seemed to have this right.'*

**John Crowther-Alwyn 1957/62**

*'The academic education was pretty sound though 'Morky's' Geography lessons seemed to have a strong bias towards Kent and, not surprisingly, Scotland! The Tables tests always seemed to follow the same pattern for the first three questions: 7 x 8; 3 x 9; 12 x 11, so one learnt to write down 56, 27 and 132 immediately! I remember too his posturing that the three words you should never use were 'got', 'lot' and 'nice'!'*

**Charles Masheder 1957/62**

*'Mr Cormack, a small bodied, large headed Scotsman fond of his pipe and whiskey, prone to rattling his false teeth in his mouth, who walked with a limp, steel heeled brogues going thud click, thud click, in the long corridors.'*

**Colin Emmett 1960/65**

*'In many ways, St. Michael's was just a step ahead of being something straight out of Tom Brown's school days or from Billy Bunter and the boys of the Remove. Donald Cormack ruled with fear and trepidation but always with love and care for the boys. He would devote hours of his time to educate and develop the boys and never stopped believing that every young child had seams of potential waiting to be tapped. He never gave up on a single boy.*

*We kept in touch through senior school and university and he spoke at my wedding in 1991, a year or two before he died. I remember passing Comely Bank Place in Edinburgh, where he used to live, a few years ago and thinking of the great man and how very Scottish he was. Not only did he teach me "amo amas amat" but also he introduced me to haggis, tatties & bashneeps. All the boys to varying degrees of success tried out their impersonations of DHC from "broa' bricht nicht" to "wee Rabbie Burns".*

**Rashid Chinchanwala 1972/77**

*'Cormack (as we affectionately called him) was a legend. Fluent in Latin and French. A master of mathematics and just about every academic subject. He was fond of his cigars and scotch and*

167

*particularly keen of the most astonishing amount of sugar in his tea. We all respected him and rarely dared to daydream in his class for fear of that leather strap he carried in his pocket.'*

**David Humphreys 1974/79**

*'Initially one of the most terrifying men I have ever met! It took me a few years to discover a heart of gold. Amazing to think we sat in lessons where the sun lit up multiple cloud layers of pipe smoke in the senior classroom. That wouldn't be allowed now. The angry face he could make as he clacked his false-teeth around was impressive too.'*

**Steve Bolton**

*'I was 10 when Mr Cormack introduced myself and my parents to the School. The one vivid memory I have is that of Mr Cormack smoking his trademark pipe and having no ashtray. He proceeded to take a rare vase (so I thought) off his cluttered desk and empty his pipe into it. Then he carefully replaced the vase on the spot where it came. It must have made an impression on my parents because I stayed there boarding for four years!'*

**Greg McKeague 1980/84**

Donald Cormack with his staff (including his successor Paul Cox) in 1980

Donald Cormack & TG Blofeld with the 1954 cricket team.
(John Hurt is second from the left on the front row)

Donald Cormack with the 1978 rugby team

# Donald H Cormack 1937/81

**1937** – Donald Cormack is offered the position of Master at St Michael's.

**1940** – DHC is called up to war and serves until 1946.

**1947** – The War Memorial is unveiled and dedicated by Bishop Carey.

**1947** – *The Michaelian* newsletter is launched and continues to be produced until 1954.

**1948** – The Old Michaelian Association is launched.

**1968** – The Science Block is built in the form of a memorial to Thomas Guest Blofeld at a cost of £23,000.

**1971** – St Michael's attempts to sell off a large amount of land adjoining Pilgrims Way for the building of 17 houses.

**1976** – Michael Bond, the popular teacher who was most probably being groomed as DHC's successor, dies of a brain haemorrhage at the age of 39. DHC is devastated.

**1979** – DHC seeks a successor for the Headship, Michael Thurlow, and builds Hatcham House in the grounds to accommodate the designated Head's family.

**1980** – An alternative Head is appointed and Reverend Paul Cox works alongside DHC for two terms.

**1981** – Donald Cormack resigns as Head of St Michael's.

# ~ 13 ~

# Sport

### *'The match in our pockets'*

Cricket was first introduced into the life of the pupils of St Michael's in 1916, very soon after Charles Manning Jaggard took over as Headmaster from Frederick Wareham. Jaggard was a Cambridge Blue who had bowled out the great WG Grace (or so he claimed…). He must have been instrumental in persuading Father Tooth, himself a keen and able sportsman, that sport was a healthy recreation for the boys:

---

**12 May 1916:** Revd Father presented boys with a cricket set for which they were very grateful.

---

and the boys managed to play some school matches on their existing sports field:

---

**17 May 1916:** School commenced half an hour earlier & closed the same to enable the boys to play a cricket match.

---

**19 May 1917:** Tomorrow (Sat) I have arranged to supervise the boys recreation - a cricket match - Choristers v The Rest.

---

The boys were unable to spend much time playing sport during the war years as they were busy working in the gardens providing fruit and vegetables, in the fields gathering hay and in the woods chopping and sawing. In 1918 their recreation field was taken over by Croydon Council for allotments so all outdoor sports came to an end.

In 1919, after the war was over, Father Tooth acquired a cricket pitch for the boys:

---

**16 May 1919:** Have been able twice this week to take boys to cricket ground for recreation — much needed. The Revd Father has given us quite a good pitch which we very much appreciate.

---

The first match against an opposing school was held in 1920 and seems to have been a great success for the school:

---

**7 July 1920:** This afternoon at 3 we started a Cricket Match with Bedford House School. This was easily won - although the average age of our opponents was the greater. The game was very enjoyable & much enjoyed.

---

Football also got off to a rather hesitant start at Woodside, obviously the war caused great disruption to the recreational life of the boys. As well as a cricket pitch Father Tooth was also able to purchase a football field for the boys and, as in the cricket, their first match was a triumphant win over Bedford House School, a score line which was repeated almost exactly a year later:

---

**12 November 1919:** Began school earlier in the afternoon. Later we played Bedford House School at Football and won by 11 goals to 2.

**1 October 1920:** A very enjoyable football match took place in the afternoon versus Bedford House School. We won easily by 11 goals to 2.

---

Other sports to take place at this time were athletics meetings (annually against Bedford House), an annual cross-country event, and in 1924 a tennis court was established. After the initial flourish of success in all sports, standards started to slip and defeats came thick and fast:

---

**10 June 1921:** We have lost both matches we have played so far. The Revd Father says it will do them more good than always winning as we did last year.

**25 November 1921:** We played a Football match versus Clark's College on Wednesday & sustained our 4th defeat in succession. Last year we won 17 out of 18 games - a difference.

---

One of the major problems that faced St Michael's was the smallness of the school in relation to their opponents, and also the youth and small stature of the pupils:

---

**15 October 1924:** Played our first football match against Chester House School. They were a much heavier lot than our boys who were also short of practice. Consequently we were seriously beaten.

---

**9 October 1925**: We are having Football Practice but boys are too small to get a decent XI.

With the move to Otford in 1925, a new optimism began to be felt by the boys and their master in both football and cricket:

**15 May 1925:** During the present we have been able to appreciate the benefit of our large grounds. Cricket has been in full swing and the boys have thoro'ly enjoyed themselves.

**29 May 1925:** We won both our Cricket Matches last week beating Kemsing by 6 runs and Shoreham by an innings and 47.

**26 June 1925:** The boys have had plenty of cricket throughout the term and the XI have done well. We have won 7 of the 8 matches we have played so far.

Unfortunately, the footballers did not do so well during their second season at Otford:

**3 December 1926**: We played our second Football match this week & lost again. A contrast from last season when we won 14 out of 15. There is neither quantity nor quality in present boys.

**10 December 1926:** Played a football match yesterday afternoon versus Kemsing & lost. They had never beaten us before. Our team this Term is useless.

In 1931 Father Charles Blofeld became Warden at St Michael's, and reinforced the school's dedication to sport. After all, in his job as Chaplain on the Training Ship Mercury from 1907 to 1917, Blofeld had worked closely with the sporting legend CB Fry who was a genius at many sports, but especially cricket.

Michael Cork who succeeded Charles Jaggard as Headmaster in 1932 was equally interested in sport and the log books from this year until they end in 1941 are dominated by accounts of matches, comments about the players and lists of school records.

The main feature of Michael Cork's accounts are his forthright attacks on the skills of the boys when the standard of play had been less than he had hoped for, obviously assigning himself the role of expert coach in cricket, football and rugby:

**15 May 1935:** 1st match v All S.S. Margaret Street. We gave a very poor and unconvincing display. Wall ran himself out. Burkitt and Heron were both out to half-hearted attempts. The rest of the side can only be described as feeble. The great fault in the batting is that boys do not lift their bats soon enough. Every shot practically is made too late. Result - either the ball is missed altogether, or an easy catch is put up. Our dismal innings closed for 31.

**5 June 1935:** Match v Merton Court at home. A very weak display. Our team have not the determination to win - they are pessimists - they think they will make nothing therefore they do make nothing. We should have had Merton Court out for under 50, but we let the last pair make 20. Their bowling was mediocre in the extreme but we hit up little silly catches & scratched away like a set of hens......

**27 June 1936:** Match v Bassetts at Farnborough. A singular game! They won the toss and batted first. They lost 8 wickets for 24 and we let them make 54. A small enough total for so strong a school. At tea time we had lost 2 wkts for 34 of which Burkitt had made 33 not out. The prevalent idea was that we had the match in our pockets. Alas, our pockets had holes in them - for - after the resumption Burkitt was caught at silly point from his second ball, and in another 15 minutes the whole side were out for 36!!! The ten alleged batsmen made 2 between them!!! There was one leg bye and Burkitt's 33. Infantile paralysis best describes the performance.Three new Caps were all speedily christened with the sign of the Duck's Egg — one miserable single. Haley and Burkitt bowled with great accuracy and pluck.

**1 March 1939:** Rugger match v Bassets. We were well & truly beaten by 37pts - 11. Bassets were in every way the better side & it will take all we know to turn the tables on them when they come here. Our mistakes were these:-

1st .The forwards did not play nearly hard enough. They did not follow up – they did not get round – they did not use their weight.

Remember: The forwards are the most important players on the field. They are the best and safest defence and all attacks must begin with them. A forward must be hardworking & brave. He must never pack up.

2nd We lost through childish tackling – each player must go low.

3rd The extreme poor marking – especially by the scrum half. He danced about like a girl at her first dancing class and he never got the ball out of the scrum for us – or smothered the Bassets scrum-half.

Although Michael Cork was happy to praise when praise was due, his preferred method of motivation seems to have been public ridicule and blame. The boys were encouraged to read his logbooks where their failures were detailed. 'Erratic', 'feeble', 'incompetent half-witted', 'awfully bad', 'an Aunt Sally', 'lacks brains', 'lacks thrust and dash', 'danced about like a girl at her 1st dancing class', 'his fatness [is] a hindrance in the field', 'lackadaisical', 'little power of concentrating', 'a clockwork dummy', 'quite incapable of any energy', 'too lazy to stoop', 'too dreamy'.

However, there were several major triumphs during this era:

---

**17 July 1935:** Final match of the season V. Ravenswood at Tonbridge. This proved one of our overwhelming successes - they won the toss & put us in! After losing Haley at 13, Wall & Heron proceeded by nearly faultless batting to take the score to 112 for 2! Heron made 67 largely on the off - his cutting being very good. Wall made 50 which included several long drives. With William 1 and Burkitt 4 we declared at 147 for 3. They made 31 & 12! Burkitt & Heron bowled magnificently & Haley was a help in the 1st ins. Haley then brought a very successful season to a close by a very fine win indeed, in which he played a Captain's part with bat, ball & in the field.

**8 July 1936:** Match v Hazelwood. We amply took our revenge for our previous defeat. Burkitt broke another school record by scoring 104 not out. This is the first time a St Michael's boy has made a 100 in a match. We declared at 132 for 6 wkts. Burkitt laid the foundations of victory after tea by bowling Martin Irving their best bat with his first ball. Johns caught three catches, and in less than an hour we had the whole side out for 41. A good day!

---

**15 July 1936:** Match v. Merton Court at Otford. This was a real triumph for us. We batted first on a "deadly" wicket & took 1¼ hours to make 28. The match seemed to be all over, but one of those cricket miracles took place - Burkitt & Haley assisted by some excellent fielding set all the Merton Court side back for 11! This was the smallest score they have ever made. It was also the first time that we have beaten them - a magnificent victory after a disastrous start.

*'Excitement came when Corky posted the team. Who would be on the list? Away matches were extra popular, such good teas and the fun of a drive to and fro, in the brothers Carlos' vehicle, John White's (guaranteed to speed) and, for the lucky few, the Jaguar, with hopefully a "ton" on the Bromley bypass.'*

**Roy Haines 1932/38**

In 1938, Rugby was introduced to the school and St Michael's had immediate success in their debut match against Pennthorpe School:

**12 February 1938:** Our first Rugby football match was played on our ground today. Our opponents were Pennthorpe, who like ourselves were playing their first match. The team which had been ably coached by Mr John White gave a very good display and we were superior to our opponents in all departments of the game. The forwards were quick on the ball and heeled well in the tight scrimmages. The backs were a little apt to run sideways, but in nearly every case they recovered in time. The final score was 50 - 0 (4 goals & 10 tries). Green was outstanding among the forwards & Crabbe did some very spectacular work at centre ¾, but everyone was good and the team are highly to be congratulated on gaining their first victory in such a convincing manner. Our side has much promise.

*'It was axiomatic in these surroundings that sport was manly. Down on the bottom field beyond the bank of stinging nettles was a dusty pitch with goalposts at either end. Whenever we could we would pump up one of the old footballs to be found lying in the games room chest, lace it up (there is a special tool for this, rather like a crochet hook), appoint a goalkeeper (an honoured appointment, and one I was always pleased to accept) and play with two teams into one goal. It would be five or six a side, and the goalkeeper would be the busiest player. Also he got to handle the ball and this I liked.*

*It was perceived (though I never heard anyone say so) that rugby was a gentleman's game, while soccer was the sport of the masses, otherwise thought of in those days as "the great unwashed". Someone moved the school management to espouse rugby. The soccer goalposts were replaced by rugby posts, mysterious oval balls began to appear in the sport lockers, and we were encouraged to nurture them with Dubbin and loving care. Although we were orphans it was being suggested that we regard ourselves as gentlemen. The rules of the Rugby Union code were explained as follows:*

- *Take the ball in your hands and run with it.*

- *Don't pass forward.*

- *Don't kick an opponent.*

- *Don't punch an opponent after tackling him. This rule and the preceding one, it was explained, were included for the sake of good public relations. After the match we would of course sit down and enjoy tea and slices of rather stale cake (it was the only time we might expect cake) with the opposing team. It was gentlemanly to be in a position to relate companionably with them.*

- *If you want to trip an opponent, do it with your hand, not your foot.*

- *If someone tries to tackle you place your palm on top of his head and press downwards so that his mouth connects with your boot. Next time he may choose to be not quite able to catch you.*

- *Interpret these rules in a gentlemanly fashion.*

*Which we always did, of course. So successful were we at it that we became the scourge of all the preparatory schools in that corner of Kent, often running up scores of 50 or 60 to 3. In those days, three points were awarded for a try and an extra two for a conversion. A penalty goal or drop goal also scored three points.'*

**Eric Crabbe 1934/38**

*'Games were taken very seriously and all matches were written up by 'Corky' in the logbook. When we played cricket against Merton Court, who always fielded a 'Silly mid on' and 'Silly mid off', we put up a miserable performance. 'Corky' was disgusted and his heading in the logbook of this match was: "Featuring the St Michael's Players in their now well known tragedy. JITTERS!"*

---

**17 July 1940:** S. Michael's v Bickley Hall featuring the S. Michael's Players in their, now, well known tragedy "Jitters". Let us hope that they may learn a lesson from Humiliation which apparently they cannot learn from Encouragement.

Score S. Michael's 9, Bickley 126 for 6.

---

*But on a happier note when we beat Bassetts, our toughest fixture, at Rugger, 9-6, 'Corky' was absolutely ecstatic. He sent me and Brian Henharen down to Lowry's (out of bounds in fact) to buy some chestnuts, but they were closed!*

*Home matches were very exciting. All boys not selected to play in the team, watched from the touch line along with Father, 'Corky' and the two matrons. In the cricket season, Father and 'Corky' umpired. I remember Peter Burkett [1934/36] playing cricket against Hazlewood and scoring 104 not out. And what a joyous moment about to leave school for an away match, four boys all with their white caps (cricket colours) sitting on the back seat of Father Charles 3 ½ S.S. Jaguar – as it was then. Later peering over Father's shoulder watching the speeds increasing to 80 m.p.h.!'*

**Peter Bull 1935/40**

*'Soccer was probably the sport we did best at as a school in that era. However, my impression is that we were the easy match for miles around! I recall the wait at dinner for the return of the team that had been "away". The sighing disappointment as the news of another defeat made its way through the refectory. I do remember one extremely foggy day when we won handsomely at home. Even our goalie scored, so thick was the murk!*

*Another soccer memory is the sound of boots on concrete-hard frozen fields. Getting hacked in the shins and ankles was an hibernal hazard. In my case the wounds to my ankles took forever to heal, the scabs pulling off each time I took my socks off at night. Can anyone say "surgical dressing"? It seems that those niceties were not forthcoming, or I had used up my allotment, or something. I have the scars to this day. Winter memories would not be complete without mention of chilblains. I have those scars on my toes too.*

*Dubbin - probably unknown to children whose football boots I suspect are of the Nike type, and dry off quite quickly. Our football boots were leather, and had to be made waterproof, and supple. This was done by rubbing in a waxy paste (the nearest thing I've come across since is the paste flux used by plumbers for preparing copper pipe for tinning). This was Dubbin. It has a smell all its own, I can almost smell it now. It brings back memories of picking caked-on clumps of grass and mud out of the spaces between the studs on the bottom of the boots with a penknife. The studs were leather too, built up in layers, I think, and were nailed into the sole with three or four nails per stud.'*

**John Wood 1947/52**

Other than Football, Rugby and Cricket, the boys enjoyed competitive Ping Pong tournaments against Pennthorpe, West Sussex and were exercised with regular physical drills which Donald Cormack orchestrated with relish:

*'It was a tiny school and very isolated. In 3 years we didn't win a single school match (it was like the Molesworth books – "We played Bickley Park and lost 15-0").'*

**Stephen Winkley 1954/57**

*'St Michael's in those days was a far cry from what it is today. There were barely 60 boys at the school, only a handful of whom were day pupils. We were much smaller than the schools we used to play (Hazlewood, Bickley Park, Yardley Court, Hill School) but would give a good contest on the playing field. I remember playing for the school in a home soccer match against Winchester House. At half time (score 1-1), one of our most infamous OMs, John Hurt, came over to deliver a pep talk to the boys. We ended up thrashing the opposition that day.'*

**Rashid Chinchanwala 1972/77**

*'Mr Good was the stern sports master who, although he ran most of school life as if it were an Army camp, shaped my love of sport and hunger for success in competition. I remember many a day playing 'hare and hounds' in PE lessons. The slower boys (the hares) were set off on an established run around the Warren (the huge hill beside the school) up to the reservoir; after a period of time the faster boys (the hounds) were released to catch up with and hopefully overtake the hares. Any hares that were significantly late faced a cold shower!'*

**Justin Ablett 1985/90**

It was not until the number of pupils began to increase during the 1990s, and a strongly sports-orientated staff team took over, that St Michael's began to shine on the prep school sporting circuit. Football, and rugby tournaments were arranged and an annual 'Jersey Tour' was established. With the introduction of girls to the school, pop lacrosse, netball and rounders were added to the sporting repertoire along with hockey for the older children.

Nowadays, children are encouraged to participate in sports that traditionally had been restricted to a particular sex, so girls now enjoy cricket and boys enjoy lacrosse, rounders and netball.

The new sports hall and swimming pool, opened in 1997, give all-year-round facilities which are the envy of many other schools.

## Sports Day

Sports Day has played an important role in the sporting calendar at St Michael's since the very earliest days. Most pupils look forward to the event, while others see the event as a trial.

*'A 'Red Letter Day' was the annual school sports day. I well remember going into Sevenoaks with Matron to purchase prizes, chiefly from Wooolworth's, and later winning one of their five shilling 'gold' watches as a prize in an event (probably the egg and spoon race, as I was no athlete.)'*

**Douglas Keddie 1923/31**

'Then came Sports Day: an annual affair with an extra competitive edge provided by the House Competition. For coaching the High Jump I even learned the "scissors", but couldn't manage the "western roll". I remember on one misguided occasion I organised a practice relay, only to be told scathingly by the Warden that to practice the relay was an unforgivable sin! (John Underwood remembers that incident as he bore the brunt of it.) In fact the final result did not mirror the practice performance.'

**Roy Haines 1932/38, teacher 1947/54**

'Sports Day was a miniature Olympiad. We were ill-prepared, often suffered awful cramp from suddenly dashing 80 yards (the cricket pitch could not stretch to 100 yards) and long and high jumping after sedate flip flaps on the badminton court! The grand finale was the Chariot Race – run between the three Houses (Greeks, Romans and Barbarians) – with three in front, two behind and a charioteer atop holding reins in the House colours with jester-balls attached to garters.

On one famous occasion I saw these sacred appurtenances waiting in a box outside Father Blofeld's bedroom on the Friday before the great day. Roy Haines thought a practice for the Chariot Race would be sensible. I told him I knew where the reins and bells were. Father Blofeld was in Sevenoaks buying the prizes for the next great day. We took the garters, reins and bells – and we practised. Father, returning in his venerable Austin paused only to hear, afar, the ringing of the bells. He was thunderstruck. I was summonsed. "How dare you trespass upon my private apartments? How dare you ruin the challenge of the race by preparation?". He was livid. I was mortified. Next day he realized that he had been very unfair. He registered his contrition by allowing me to help him mark out the white lines of the running track!'

**John Underwood 1948/52**

Sports Day is still an annual athletics event and each child must compete in at least two events. The competition is fought between the four Houses (Dover, Leeds, Rochester and Windsor) as well as on an individual basis.

## Sports Day Records

Records of Sports Day successes were not kept continuously from the 1930s to the 2000s, and of course most events are not comparable because of the differing lengths of races (the change from yards to metres). However it is interesting to compare four events by converting metric into imperial measurements. All boys in the following table are of comparable age.

| | 1941 | 2001 |
|---|---|---|
| **Long Jump** | 15ft 9in by Peter Burkitt (1936) | 15ft 0in by William Goulstone (2000) |
| **High Jump** | 4ft 3in by Ivan Green (1938) | 4ft 11in by Tarquin Glennister (2000) |
| **Cricket Ball Throw** | 80yds 6in by Michael Haley (1938) | 76yrds 8in by Martin Taplin (2001) |
| **½ Mile (804 metres)** | 2 mins 41 secs by Peter Bull (1941) | 2 mins 31.2 secs by M Rawlings (1997) |

# Sports Review - Trinity 2003
## (from the Director of Sports)

Another Summer Term has drawn to a close and another sporting year at St. Michael's has come to an end. A year filled with effort, excitement, enthusiasm, determination and real enjoyment of sport. A year full of excellence and tremendous sporting success and achievement, both individually and collectively. I would not have thought we could eclipse the success we bathed in last year, but I do believe we have, and in many different areas. This term alone, we have continued to win tournaments and trophies both in team competitions and individual events. A number of our pupils have achieved Sports Scholarships to their next school, including the first ever Cowdrey Scholarship to Tonbridge, an achievement of which we are extremely proud. This can only be put down to the outstanding efforts of not only the children, but also the staff, fully supported by you the parents. It really is a team effort and I, personally, am so proud to be a part of that team.

## Cricket

It has been a very short term for cricket and we have not been able to fit in the same amount of fixtures as we do in the winter term. We lose a number of match days to exams and trips, but we have achieved a lot of success when we have played. The U11 A team was particularly impressive this term, as they have been all year. They performed very well in the Summers Cup, got to the Final of the Sutton Valence Six a-side Tournament and won the Julian Parker Trophy at Sevenoaks Prep. Both the senior and junior teams continue to perform well, but it is the current Year 5 and 6 who seem to be leading the way. The U10 A team still maintain an unbeaten record now spanning three years. An amazing achievement!

## Rounders

Rounders continues to thrive in the Summer Term and, along with cricket, has become a real example of our Equal Opportunities Policy. All those involved have really enjoyed taking part and performed very well in school matches and tournaments. For the first time ever, the U13 A team reached the Plate Final in the IAPS Tournament held at Holmewood House. Another fine achievement.

## Pop Lacrosse

It has been a momentous year for our U11 Lacrosse players and the school. The team won the South East Regional Finals and qualified for the National Finals in Birmingham. For the first time ever the team got through the championship rounds and went on to contest the Final. This has never been achieved before. Congratulations to all the squad and, in particular Mrs Skelly. Believe it or not, this means we are currently the second best U11 Pop Lacrosse team in the country. A truly outstanding effort.

## Athletics

We have completed another excellent term of Athletics. At the Kent IAPS (Independent Association of Preparatory Schools) Championships we had five new champions who all went on to compete in the National IAPS Championships in Birmingham and performed extremely well. The efforts of all our children on Sports Day were quite magnificent and highlighted by 12 new school records.

## Sports Day

We have had some wonderful and generous feed back about this year's Sports Day and we are delighted that many of you enjoyed it and felt it was a really special day. We too felt it was a real success, full of outstanding performances held in terrific atmosphere and conducted in an excellent spirit. The sight of so many parents and picnics on the banks was so comforting and really added to the whole occasion. Thank you so much for your fantastic support and I hope we can continue in this vein next year!

## Michaelian Day

This term's Old Boys' and Girls' Day was one of the most successful and enjoyable I can remember. In the morning we had the girls playing Rounders and Netball as well as the 1st XI playing last years 1st XI on the cricket field. This was followed by an afternoon cricket match in which the Headmaster's XI defeated the Chairman's XI. It was a fun day with lots of family picnics and barbecues and I would like to thank all those who played and turned up to support the occasion. Please come and join us in the future.

## Outdoor Pursuits Year 6&8

The Outdoor Pursuits events that are conducted every Summer Term have become a real feature and highlight of our Physical Education programme. Year 8 returned to Bude in Cornwall for an absolutely outstanding week and Year 6 continued their annual trip to Blackwell Farm near East Grinstead. It is a vital part of the children's education, not only as a result of participating in some different physical activities, but arguably more importantly gaining the experience of being away from home for a period of time.

**Guy Drayton, Director of Sport**

U10s & U11s practice match

# Sporting Timeline

**1916** – Cricket is introduced to the school at Woodside.

**1919** – First football match against an opposing school. St Michael's wins 11 goals to 2.

**1920** – First cricket match against an opposing school. St Michael's wins 'easily'.

**1936** – First century in cricket for a St Michael's boy

**1938** – Rugby is introduced to the school. St Michael's wins its first match 50–2.

**1978** – Swimming is added to the curriculum with the opening of the Michael Bond Memorial Swimming Pool

**1982** – First Cross Country meet is held using the course cut through the woods (2.75 mile or 4 mile laps)

**1991** – With the introduction of girls into the main school, lacrosse, rounders and netball are now played

**1994** – The Donald Cormack Memorial Pavilion is opened by Richard Ellison (Kent & England cricket player)

**1997** – The Sports Complex (with swimming pool) is opened by Mike Denness (Kent & England cricket Captain)

**2003** – The U11 Pop Lacrosse team reach the national final.

# ~ 14 ~

# Drama and Music

## "The Thespian Tradition"

Perhaps it was the theatricality of the religious services that started the strong tradition of drama at St Michael's. The vibrant colours of the vestments, the varied sounds of bells; singing and rhythmic chanting; the smells of incense, rich mahogany and wax all lead to an intense experience for all the senses. To this day, the Eucharist is held weekly and is carried out as a ritualistic performance involving children in key elements of the ceremony.

This theatricality certainly made an impact on the life of one Old Michaelian. John Hurt [1948/54], multi-award winning actor whose numerous definitive roles have included Quentin Crisp in *The Naked Civil Servant* and John Merrick in *The Elephant Man*, has often credited the school for launching his acting career.

As he told critic Geoff Andrew in an on-stage Guardian interview at the National Film Theatre in 2000:

*'I first decided that I wanted to act when I was nine. I was at a very bizarre prep school at the time, to say high Anglo-Catholic would be a real English understatement. It was so high it was flying. So I already had an enormous sense of theatre, if you see what I mean, from an early age and the first part that I ever played was the girl in Maeterlinck's 'The Bluebird' and I felt an extraordinary feeling that I was in the place that I was meant to be.'*

From the early days, drama was used to supplement the academic teaching at the school and had the benefit of taming some of the more unruly pupils, as well as those who were not academically bright. The Croydon Reporter states in 1912:

When the boys leave the school, every effort is made to give them a good start in life, and many are doing well. One of [Father Tooth's] old boys is now an actor of much promise. He is "going straight, an abstainer, and looked up to by all his company."

187

The first drama production held at St Michael's was in 1932 during Mr Michael Cork's first year as Headmaster:

---

**14 October 1932:** First reading of the Christmass plays. The ones chosen are the Rehearsal and Interlude of the Clowns from Midsummer Nights Dream, and the Nativity Play of the III Rich & the III Poor men.

---

The two productions were held alongside the first ever prize-giving ceremony, and this combination became the custom for many years.

In Hurt's biography (by David Nathan), he credits Donald Cormack as the inspirational teacher who helped him to get into acting. Nathan states that Hurt played the main part of Scrooge in A Christmas Carol but in reality, he played a laundress! However, he did receive a mention in *The Michaelian* newsletter: 'A word of special praise must be given to Hurt for his portrayal of the laundress'.

Other plays performed by the 'St Michael's Players' have included:

| | |
|---|---|
| **1940** The Alchemist | **1972** Scenes from Toad of Toad Hall |
| **1947** Lu San | **1977** Charley's Aunt |
| **1951** The Comedy of Errors | **1984** The Insect Play |
| **1953** The Critic | **1991** Bugsy Malone |
| **1955** The Merchant of Venice | **1997** The Hobbit |
| **1959** St Joan | **1998** The Factory Children |
| **1967** Merlin's Problem Cap | **2000** Say Goodbye to Satchwell Road |

Nowadays, as well as the annual school play (directed by Peter Nixon), there are also form plays and every child is encouraged to take a speaking role. The Pre-Prep hold a Nativity Play each year.

Now that the school hall has been extended to provide room for a good size stage and a large audience, and high quality theatre lighting has been installed (donated by the Parents' and Friends' Association), there are plans for even more ambitious projects.

In 2003 the school achieved its first Drama Scholarship to Tonbridge School awarded to Miles Tanner.

Joseph from a Pre-Prep Nativity Play

*'I remember the wonderful sound of hammering as the stage was erected at night in the dining hall. This meant that it was getting on for the end of winter term, and then it would be home for Christmass. (Two 's's, we were Anglo-Catholic after all!).'*

**John Wood 1947/53**

*'I remember as a junior being warned not to bring penknives to school and shown a cupboard which was still there when I last visited in 1998 which had the name J. Hurt carved in it. This proved to be John Hurt the actor of 'Elephant Man' fame who used to return quite regularly in my time.*

*Indeed the thespian tradition in the school is significant. During the time I was associated with the school we had a boy who became an actor with RSC and another who went into stage management, but the best known was Patrick Ryecart who was to appear regularly on television in anything from thrillers to soap operas. Beverley Cross who married Dame Maggie Smith and was author of 'Boeing Boeing' and 'Half a Sixpence' had begun the tradition. Donald Cormack was fond of recalling him playing the ukulele during air raids.'*

**John Wright 1954-60**

---

**Young drama group tackle Sheridan with gusto**

ACTORS John Hurt and Patrick Ryecart have been among those to take the stage at St. Michael's School, Otford, and youngsters there recently tackled Sheridan's "The Critic."

To present an 18th century comedy about actors rehearsing a 16th century play was ambitious, but the enthusiasm with which the producer Headmaster Fr Paul Cox inspired his cast carried the audience with it.

Anchor man was Darren Pearce as the playwright Mr Puff. His play clearly bemused his friends Dangle and Sneer (Martin Pickett and Andrew Fleetwood). However his cast relished his farrago of passion and intrigue, even if they took liberties with his text!

Highlights included Ziad Nasr's confidante, mimicking the madness of her mistress (Tamsin Cox), and Darren Tigwell's revelation that he was Superman under his Beefeater disguise.

Jean Kelsey's striking costumes contrasted the two periods, and the atmosphere was enhanced by incidental music from a promising young oboeist and guitarists.

**Sevenoaks Chronicle April 9 1983**

---

*'Once described as 'the primeval hag' by one of the Chesshyre boys, Matron Stockwell achieved fame during a vigorous performance of a bit of 'Murder in the Cathedral'. I remember "Bar the door, bar the door!" "The door is barred – we are safe, we are safe". A moment later the allegedly barred door between the front door and the main hall was opened by Matron to admit some parents, who were greeted with laughter.'*

**Stephen Winkley 1954/57**

*'The School plays were always great fun and recently I saw a picture of the cast of my first Junior play; taking the part of a robin meant I am completely unrecognisable. Later I was an ugly princess but the highlight on the building front was the New Hall, when Beverly Cross wrote a special play. I was no great actor and it is only very recently that I have returned to the boards in the local Village Pantomime!'*

**Charles Masheder 1957-62**

# Music

St Michael's has had a long tradition of incorporating music into the school day. Indeed, the school was originally founded as a choir school and the earliest boys provided the choir for Arthur Tooth's church, St James' in Hatcham.

In 1878 the boys at Woodside entertained the public during a summer fete with 'A selection of part songs' and concerts such as this became a regular feature in the 45 years the school was at Woodside.

The logbooks, which were started by the Headmaster in 1916, indicate that the first individual music lesson was given to Douglas Keddie in 1929:

*'My abiding memories of the classroom were brought home by an extract from the school Log Book for 22 November 1929 which read "Douglas Keddie started music lessons on Wednesday, 20th inst.". How well I remember those lessons, held during the lunch hour! These consisted in elementary grounding in the learning of notes and the practice of scales, etc. etc., and although I never really became adept I eventually graduated to learning and playing hymn tunes from the English Hymnal, but woe betide me if I played a wrong note! Jaggy would break off from his lunch and perusal of the aforementioned sporting paper (we all believe he was addicted to "the horses"!) and shout "wrong note, boy; it should be E flat" (or whatever). I never progressed very far in my musical career, but I did learn - and came to love - many of the hymn tunes, and also how to read music.'*

**Douglas Keddie 1923/31**

Nowadays, all children learn the recorder and every child in Year 2 learns the violin! They are also encouraged to learn an additional instrument (or more than one) with tuition provided by a variety of peripatetic teachers. House points can be won at an annual House Music Competition which is open to all pupils and gives the entrants experience of performing solo.

A very special music teacher retired recently. Mrs Isabelle Peacock had been teaching piano at the school for 27 years and had seen many pupils through countless practical and theory exams, as well as coaching entrants to various musical festivals. One of the many highlights of her career was to see 12 year-old Benedict Vaux win the Duke of Norfolk Music Scholarship to The Oratory School in Oxfordshire in 1998.

In 1940 St Michael's produced its first School Concert:

---

**27 March 1940:** School Concert. This was the first we have ever given and the heartiest congratulations are due to Mr Carlos for the fine way in which he has trained the boys. Real purity of tone has been achieved. The programme began with songs and recitations by the smallest boys who were trained by Mrs Pedley - one other recitation "Sea Farers" spoken by R Thomson was a great success. The rest of the programme was vocal & included soli by Day, Campbell, Raikes, Bidwell, Gedge, Fairburn 2 and Johns. The programme was excellently varied and the items well contrasted. Mr Carlos himself accompanied in his own inimitable style.

---

Nowadays, both the Main School and Pre-Prep give regular concerts throughout the year and musical entertainment is always provided during the prize-giving ceremonies. There is a school orchestra and three choirs including the newly formed Chamber Choir. This choir is made up of twelve especially invited children and the small size allows them to tackle ambitious repertoires.

The school participates in several annual music festivals including the Three Arts Festival and the Tunbridge Wells Music Festival. Both groups and individuals take part and St Michael's usually wins an embarrassing number of accolades, though this was not always the case:

*'In addition to teaching history, I taught English and games, and I often conducted the choir. I remember our entering the Sevenoaks Music Festival for the first time with our 'Skye Boat Song'. We got off to a fine start, lost each other in the middle section, but managed to end strongly, together! I don't think we came in the top 3 that year!'*

**John Jennings – Housemaster and Head of History 1990/93**

The school choir regularly performs outside the school, and has performed in a variety of locations ranging from outside Sainsbury's to Disneyland, Paris.

## Clarinet Concerts Are Extremely Dangerous

There is, it seems, a symphony orchestra
Hiding in the bass drum of my heart,
CRASH! BANG! CRASH! As I fasten the reed in place,
Crouching behind the main wing door;
Clutching the clarinet close to my chest,
I totter dazedly onto the stage,
Squinting into the glare of the harsh blinding lights
I pray,
*'Come on B key, come on B key,'*
And close my eyes and blow.
My clarinet responds with a noise like sheep in a blender.
Five hundred eyes boring into the back of my head,
I try again,
I say to my mouth, *'Nice smile now,'*
I say to my heart, *'Get out of my mouth,'*
But no sound appears so I must join the audience's joke,
I giggle, bow scamper off, and slam the stage door,
"OH GOD, NOOO!"
Two minutes later and everything is fixed,
The blasted B key successfully unjammed,
(Thanks be to you, Mr Summers, hallelujah amen etc.)
The piano plays once more, here comes my entry and –
"SQQQUUUEEEAAAK!"
I say to my mouth, *'Nice smile now...'*

**Catherine Gluckman 2000**

1988 Recorder Ensemble

(Below) 1988 School Choir

# ~ 15 ~

# Reverend Paul Cox

## Headmaster and Chaplain – 1981 to 1990

***Could you tell us a little about yourself and how you came to be Headmaster of St. Michael's?***
West Kent was the area in which I was brought up. I went to The Judd School Tonbridge with
my twin when we were living in Tunbridge Wells, following in our father's footsteps. After

University and a year in Nigeria I lived in
Kemsing whilst teaching at Bromley Grammar
School. Then I moved to be Head of Economics
and Business Studies at Tonbridge School where
I stayed for ten years, during which time I was
ordained.

I had been thinking about moving into
teaching younger people when I saw the
advertisement for the Headship of St Michael's
in the Church Times. I applied; eventually was
invited to preach at an evening service and then
interviewed with ten others and was offered the
post. Donald Cormack wanted me to come to
the school for a year under him but this turned
out to be for two terms, which I valued, as it
helped me to gain a good "feel" for the school.

***What in particular did you bring to the school?***
The school in 1980 was run in a style that was suited to the 1950s - a small, boys' boarding prep
school with a "bachelor" feel about it. I was married and so with Jenny my wife, and Tamsin our
daughter, (now married to an OM), we were able to bring a new "family" feel to the way we
thought about the life of young boys. I introduced exeats with a night stay over Saturday - the
increasing number of day boys invited the boarders to their homes. Weekly boarding was
introduced and became appropriate for some families.

With just three boys to begin with we opened the Pre-Prep in 1982. Academically there were gradual changes with the use of computers and staff taking on particular responsibilities. As the school grew, so the administration needed to improve and this I did with the very able help of our School Secretary Mrs Judy Borrowman (using the backs of envelopes as Donald did for keeping accounts and the budget could not be continued).

Perhaps one of the marked changes that the boys appreciated was that I tried to improve the meals ensuring that there was a good variety of menu and the ending of "Nine o'clockers" having the leftovers from the staff evening meal and given a proper provision. Also I felt it was important that boys had somewhere to keep their belongings and so we gave them all cupboards by their beds replacing the wooden trays. We encouraged boys to bring bright duvet covers and the younger ones could have a soft toy in bed.

A nature lesson in the grounds

### Were there other changes that you introduced?

I felt that the boys needed to be aware of a wider environment than that of school. Other than those who sneaked out and went to the shops in Dynes Road, the only boarders who went out from school were team players in away matches. So we introduced trips to London taken by my wife to the Children's Concerts at the Festival Hall. We had School or Form day outings arranged once or twice a year for educational visits. Four-day field trips to Yorkshire (Ingleton/Malham area) including camping for some were certainly a new experience. Despite the rain, the boys remained cheerful and particularly enjoyed standing behind the waterfall at Thornton Force, and going down into the caves. On the first trip Jonathan Vokes shared the joys and burdens! Jonathan (an OM) was a house tutor who encouraged boys in their sports, but also helped some to come to know and appreciate the finer aspects of the countryside.

The Warren was a wonderfully full meadow of many varieties of plants and flowers. Tom Hart Dyke displayed his early love and knowledge of orchids pointing out different species just by looking at their small immature leaves. *[Tom Hart Dyke is a botanist and plant hunter, who has been described as the 'Indiana Jones of the Orchid world'. In March 2000 Tom went travelling in a notoriously dangerous part of the Colombia-Panama border, the Darien Gap. There they were kidnapped by a group of Marxist guerrillas - and held hostage for nine months.]*

Television had become the way most boys used their spare time so we opened up the cellar rooms for hobbies, had a computer club with Mr. Singleton, played indoor hockey and soft football, as well as table tennis, in the hall. Snooker continued on the Study Landing table given by Dr Campbell. Quite soon the amount of television watching reduced by the boys' own wishes. We introduced the weekly Newsletter which kept parents informed of what was happening in the school and of boys' achievements. A Stars and Stripes system was brought in as a way of rewarding boys for effort and consideration for others; there were very few stripes awarded. Although some boys gained a lot of prizes for academic achievement I was always keen to show everyone that other boys could be rewarded and acknowledged for their contribution to the life of their Form or the School. We altered the way the tuck was organised with a payment system that encouraged boys to learn the value of money, and reduced some bullying that occurred in the old tuck queues.

A Parents and Friends dinner, held in the entrance hall

The Parents and Friends of St Michael's began with Alan Simmons as its first chairman. Of the many happy occasions arranged by the committee the Summer Ball was a very happy annual event.

I am sure that I made changes to the Boarding at the school but my recollection is that I could depend upon Matron (Margaret Blackwell) to look after that side of school life. She was utterly dependable and caring, including ensuring boys got up for early chapel when they wanted to, and insisting that Dr Lothian saw me when she thought I might have had a heart attack (which I am glad proved to be a false alarm.)

### What changes did you make to the buildings?

I first had to tackle the Headmaster's study - which required a lot of tidying and clearing out! Much of the school needed painting, especially the Chapel, and everywhere needed a good clean. The changing rooms and bathroom for the boys were very old fashioned so we had showers fitted and new fitments. Unfortunately this meant the end of the Praes' (prefects') locker, which was turned into a kit store.

Then we built the Pre-Prep in the stable block. Later, having laid concrete (with the help of Mr. Good) in the old boot room we built new changing rooms by the Hall with foundations strong enough so that a second floor could be built on top. Building and maintenance was always within a tight budget but I never had to borrow money to do what we did despite a very expensive problem with dry rot over the entrance porch (£35,000).

All this may seem small beer now but when I became Headmaster the total school budget was £55,000 with £3000 allowed for building and maintenance. Donald as a governor was always reluctant when I tried to raise the fees. I became adept at clearing blocked drains - even at midnight! Having a tight budget meant that I did much of the maintenance work with some help from Tony Good and parents. I used to mow about 8 acres a week in the summer; I sanded and then varnished the hall floor - which was just as well as the following winter a burst pipe meant the whole floor was flooded! Many summer holidays were spent by having various people use the school (a good little earner!) which meant that Jenny and I were involved with some of the cooking and washing up!

In the grounds the changes were relatively small compared with what happened under Mr. Cummins *[the subsequent Headmaster]* but we opened up quite large areas of land by cutting down the cornus (dogwood) and by frequent mowing.

I cut out the route through the woods which provided an interesting and quite demanding cross country running course. In the walled garden we planted 180 Christmas trees which we gradually sold as they grew. (There had been no hint of these requirements of the Headmaster when I was interviewed!)

### Did you do all that you planned to do?

To some extent I achieved my first main objective which was to give the pupils an education meeting the demands of the last decades of the 20th century, within a friendly family atmosphere. I enjoyed helping children with particular needs and seeing them make real progress not only in academic results but as personalities with growing confidence.

But if I had felt that I had achieved all I hoped for it would have meant that I had too small a vision for the school. There was always more to be done. I hope that I maintained appropriately the Christian ethos of the school, for Chapel was very important to me. Sunday evening service was a wonderful mix of high Anglo-Catholic ritual, joyful hymns and lively visiting preachers - including my twin brother - which must have been a bit confusing! What a privilege it was for me to wear the fine vestments of Father Tooth and to use the chalice that was made using his mother's precious stones. The tradition of boys wearing white carnations for their confirmation was still remembered by Bishop David Say even when he was 87 years old.

I look back at our time at St Michael's with affection although realising that it was very demanding upon me and upon my family, as well as upon the staff. There was much fun, as well as moments of anxiety - our very sad time at the death of Mark Simmons, being one such occasion.

Memories of course are primarily of people: the boys (and later girls), the staff and the parents; and of events such as the 'Expotitions' [night camps in the grounds], the plays, Sports Days and saying compline with the senior boys in Chapel on Wednesday evenings. Of the many staff at St. Michael's, who really all deserve a mention, inevitably it is Michael Hatton who stands out in my memory. First impressions, I learnt quickly, can be deceptive, for Michael was a most caring, faithful member of the school with a vast knowledge of churches and a wealth of stories about people in all sorts of walks of life. Most days the post addressed to Michael was more numerous than the letters coming to the Headmaster!

It may sound trite but I am sure that in my ten years at St Michael's I gained much more through the boys, and all the people there, than I ever gave. By my last year the school had grown to about 90 children (45 when I started) and the staff had increased by 300%!

### Have you any anecdotes or memories you would like to share?

It is not difficult to make a mistake in pronouncing words, which can be especially embarrassing when doing so in public and in chapel! On one occasion during Benediction I heard myself thanking God for "these His Holy Mistresses". The following week I made every effort not to let it happen again - but it did!! Still I am very wary of any prayer or reading that includes the word "mysteries"!

Ferdi Keon was introduced to the school when we were blocked in by snow. The boarders had arrived but the dayboys could not get to school. We went down to the village with a toboggan to bring back bread and milk. It took about three days of clearing, much of it directed by Ferdi, before the dayboys could start term.

Jonathan Perry ran out of school on two occasions. Each time he ran home to Trottiscliffe and did it in such a fast time that I made him the captain of cross-country running!

Having lost a music teacher on the day I took over the school, Jenny and I had fun taking those lessons until we could appoint a new teacher, Mrs Kelsey. Individual music making in the school seemed to be centred on the wonderful teaching of Mrs Peacock who always blamed me if the boys did not practise the piano enough. Mrs. Kelsey was less ready to pass on the blame!

In fact Jean Kelsey allowed me to play the piano to accompany our school choir at festivals! I very much enjoyed playing the Steinway which OM Paul Barraclough gave the School and even composed two songs for one of the school productions - a play about Merlin and King Arthur.

Occasionally we had visiting speakers or films on a Saturday evening. Once we had a talk given by a man who kept reptiles that are heavier than humans. He brought a boa constrictor to school in a laundry basket moved on a trolley. Some boys did not feel comfortable with it but many held it along its whole length of 15 feet.

*'Father Paul Cox was Headmaster when I was at the school - a true 'father figure' who looked after all the pupils as if they were his own, yet preserved discipline at all times. He worked tirelessly to maintain the school buildings and grounds.'*

**Justin Ablett 1985/1990**

*'Nick was at St Michael's from 1985 to 1990. He had been at a prep school in Sevenoaks, Winchester House. When the school broke up for the Easter holidays all the parents received a letter informing us that the school would be closing down at the end of the summer term. All the prep schools in the area made themselves available over the Easter bank holiday, including St Michael's, to cope with frantic parents, us included.*

*When Nick started at St Michael's in the September it was a unique place. Only just over 50 pupils (Winchester House closing bumped the numbers up a bit, plus a couple of teachers went there as well), all in a lovely old house with 90 acres of ground.*

*Father Cox was Headmaster; he not only ran the school but taught, tended the grounds, preached at the school services (he also often preached in local churches as well) and was always available if you wanted to see him. It was a seven-days-a-week job as many of the boys were boarders.*

*We were a very close-knit group: boys, parents and staff which could never be repeated. My family all have very happy memories of the school.*

*Nick was involved in all the music activities, being taught by Jean Kelsey, recorder, clarinet and choir (he was in the school choir but not the chapel choir because he sang too loudly!), and Mrs Peacock taught him piano. He represented St Michael's in numerous*

*Sevenoaks Art Festivals though he nearly didn't manage it one year having fallen out of a tree at school and having broken his wrist! The plaster came off just in time.'*

**Susan Shillinglaw, mother of Nick Shillinglaw 1985/90**

# Parents and Friends Association

The inaugural meeting of the Friends of St Michael's was held on Monday 10 December 1984 during Paul Cox's Headship. The Chairman was Alan Simmons, Secretary Lyn Metcalf; and the committee was made up of Sheila Colthurst, Pamela Townsend, Ian McLaughlin and Roger Stubbs.

> 'The Association has been formed to support St Michael's School as a community of boys, parents and staff, to help maintain the Christian education, the Otford Court Estate and to act as a vehicle for communication and public relations within the local environment.
>
> Membership is automatic for any parent with a son at St Michael's and for Old Boys who wish to participate. Additionally, "friends" from the local community will be invited to participate, providing they are keen to be involved'

**The First Newsletter 14 December 1984**

The first social event was held on 2 March 1985 and included an entertainment provided by the boys. The Headmaster's logbook states "the evening was a success – a friendly atmosphere. The committee were pleased with the event".

The Friends continued to support the school by helping in the grounds, providing teas after matches and in the summer of 1985 they provided a barbecue after the annual Old Michaelians' cricket match. Again the Headmaster records his satisfaction in his logbook: "This was an excellent social event and is showing us that the Friends is an active and well worthwhile organisation."

The first fund-raising event was a raffle held in the Michaelmas term of 1985 and £300 was raised for judo mats.

Today, the Parents' and Friends' Committee is thriving and is extremely successful in hosting enjoyable events. The annual ball is sold out months before the event and other social events have included quiz nights, barn dances, and 'Murder Mystery' evenings. An annual Christmas Bazaar and Summer Fayre help raise significant amounts of money for the school and recent funding has been for an upgrade of the netball courts and new playground facilities for the Pre-Prep.

# Reverend Paul Cox 1981/90

**1980** – Paul Cox arrives at St Michael's as Headmaster designate. Donald Cormack remains for two terms before retiring from the Headship.

**1982** – The Pre-Prep department is opened with just three boys. Headmaster's wife Jenny Cox and Jan Anker share the teaching.

**1982** - Weekly boarding is introduced.

**1982** – The film *Treasures in the Snow* is shown at school. Pupil Timothy Fleetwood featured in the film which was partly shot at St Michael's using the rocks by the White Ladies (the entrance gates).

**1982** – The first Cross-Country meet is held along the newly-cut course through the woods.

**1984** – The inaugural meeting of the Friends of St Michael's (later to be known as the Parents and Friends Association) is held.

**1986** – Girls are admitted to St Michael's for the first time.

**1986** – A Fun Day in aid of the Mark Simmons Memorial Bursary Fund is opened by Olympic Gold Medallist Duncan Goodhew. The Red Devils Free Fall Team parachute into the grounds.

**1990** – Father Paul Cox retires as Headmaster and Jenny Cox retires as Pre-Prep teacher.

# ~ 16 ~

## Pre-Prep

### The Birth of Pre-Prep

#### by Jenny Cox

When Father Cox, as Headmaster designate, and I came to St. Michael's in January 1980, there were 50 boarders and 5 day boys on roll. We were to discover that no advertising or recruitment had been made for new members of the School and that the total number of boys for September, after "leavers" and a few others had left in July, would be 39! We started advertising and also decided to start a Pre-Prep department as soon as possible to encourage boys from 4 ½ - 7 years to join us and hopefully continue their education to the Main School. It did not seem appropriate for these young children to be housed in the main building, so our thoughts turned to the Stable Block.

By the summer holidays in 1982 we were able to start converting the accommodation into the Pre-Prep Department, having by then improved the bathroom/changing room in the main building. As we were working to a tight budget we knew that much of the work would be our responsibility. With the help of Jonathan Vokes, our House Tutor, we decorated classrooms and laid carpets, but before these jobs were done we had to have heating put into the building. The gas pipe was laid through the woodland and Hatcham House garden to the main in the Drive, and eventually after term had started it was all connected. A new wooden staircase had to be made and fitted from the Coach House to the first floor, as the narrow stone spiral stairs were not a safe, everyday route – although they provided a fire escape. The downstairs back room was then used as a dining room and art and craft room. On the first floor was our main classroom and two spare rooms. "Stable Court" was ready!

All this space for just three boys who started in the September 1982 – Anthony Handley, Mark Simmons, and Geoffrey Smith.

Two terms later Geoffrey's 4 ½ years old brother, David, joined us. Mrs. Jan Anker and I shared the teaching, two days and three days respectively. Those 4 children worked hard – almost individual teaching and no chance of skiving – but what lovely times we had.

Our lunches were brought down to us from the Main School, first of all by Georgie on her motorbike and later by Esther. As there were so few of us we did our own washing-up of plates and cutlery – a new experience I remember for one boy. I can still picture him spreading the tea towel out and carefully folding it over and over the fork to dry it. Daily hoovering and sweeping of the floors, and cleaning the toilets was also the responsibility of the staff in those early days.

There was no outdoor play area – the cobbled yard was part of the road from Row Dow to the Main School, so at lunch times the boys put on Wellington boots and tracksuits and we would go to the football field opposite Hatcham House, or walk through the woods and sometimes up the Warren – fun and Nature Lessons became combined! Mark Simmons recovering from his first brain tumour walked or ran slowly in those early days and most time I gave him a piggyback ride for much of our walks.

Our numbers began to increase with local boys and three or four young boarders who we thought would benefit from lessons with the Pre-Prep. So every morning and afternoon I could be seen leading a little crocodile of boarding boys, plus Geoffrey and David, who now came to breakfast, carrying their school bags plus Wellington boots and tracksuits between Main School and Stable Court. With more children there were greater opportunities for activities both in and out of the classroom, and Mrs Anker's artistic lessons with the children were a delight.

Sadly Mrs Anker decided she wished to do fulltime teaching and she left us in July 1985. During the summer holidays Winchester House School closed and we were soon

The first three boys started in
September 1982

receiving applications from parents for boys to attend St. Michael's. Our numbers grew and we were pleased to appoint Mrs Shipton, from Winchester House, and Mrs Rankin, to our staff.

We were now using most of the rooms for teaching, including a library/television staff room in the smallest room. Somewhere had to be found for playtimes, so we started clearing and mowing part of the overgrown walled garden. There was so much space for the children to play in: they loved it. Later we bought a climbing frame. It did mean, of course, that there was now an extra area for Father Cox to mow regularly, as well as the cricket field and two football pitches!

In 1986 we decided to admit sisters of boys at the school. That caused quite a stir the first time that they came to the Main School for their weekly Chapel Service. Girls at St. Michael's!

We used the Main School hall for P.E. classes and play productions, the outdoor swimming pool in the summer, and the Chapel for the annual Nativity Service in which all the children took part. We also had our own Sports Day. We had two outings a year. Our first, with the four little boys, (and a push chair for Mark or David), was to London – the train ride a new experience for

three of them – and then in later years we visited castles, the zoo, the seaside, and a lighthouse. We decided, in 1987, to start a Kindergarten class for 3 ½ – 5 year olds, mornings only, with Mrs Good as their teacher. We had to have more toilet facilities, wash basins, cloakroom and a classroom, so the Coach House on the ground floor was cleared, new windows, heating and a wall installed, noticeboards erected and furniture acquired and this became the new classroom for the oldest children. Mrs Richards came from the Main School to be their teacher. So from two part-time teachers and three boys we had now grown in 1989 to two full-time teachers, three part-time teachers and 30 children. In 1982 someone queried my intention to start a school with three boys – my reply was that if I didn't start with the three it wouldn't ever grow!

We were a very happy, hardworking unit, with delightful children and friendly, supportive staff and parents. Without these loving people the two sad occasions in my time at St. Michael's would have been even more difficult. The death of little Mark Simmons, aged eight, having watched him make so much progress in the three years he was with us, was like losing a member of my family –certainly a member the family of St. Michael's. Secondly, saying our goodbyes in 1990 to St. Michael's which had become our family for 10 years, and all that it meant to us.

A happier note to finish on. We were very pleased to welcome Mrs Anker back to the teaching staff just before we left – although I was sorry not to be working with her again. We are pleased to know that from our small beginnings a large Pre-Prep department now flourishes.

* * *

# Pre-Prep Today

### by Vanda Marchetti, Head of Pre-Prep

In 1990 when I took over from Jenny Cox as Head of the Pre-Preparatory Department, and under the new Headmastership of Simon Cummins, we were very keen to promote the admission of girls to St. Michael's which Jenny Cox had first started. The only remaining members of staff at that time were Flick Shipton and Jan Anker. Paula Pallett took over from Vickie Good in the Kindergarten. In January 1991 we opened our doors to children of two years old with Jocelyn Barton as head of the Nursery Department. The main part of the stables was opened up and became our Nursery Classroom.

We embarked on a very active campaign to raise the awareness of St. Michael's among the local community. Children were taught French from as young as Kindergarten. We introduced 'after school' activities which was quite innovative at the time and proved to be immensely popular. Children were able to learn to play the violin.

The numbers soon began to grow and swimming lessons which were run by Paula Pallett and myself began to prove quite difficult. The swimming pool was actually an outdoor diving pool which had a very small shallow end, and was obviously unsuitable for the growing numbers of very young children. We simply could not fit the children in. One of our governors, Paul Barraclough [OM 1935/38] was so keen to promote the swimming that he had the whole pool filled in during the half term holiday and it became a teaching pool almost overnight.

Vanda Marchetti

Swimming was a great success whilst the weather was good and then lo and behold during the next half term holiday a bubble was installed and we suddenly had an all weather pool. We swam at every available opportunity and on Saturday mornings too. We had swimming galas and of course no one would have expected that we were soon to out-grow that pool too.

In May of 1991 we entered our first ever float in the Otford Fete. With the help of Diana Binstead and her husband we constructed a small Greek temple on a trailer which had been supplied by one of the parents. It soon became an annual tradition for St. Michael's School to take part in the Otford Fete. As we reached the end of our first academic year, we had practically filled each class in each year group, and were about to add another Reception class. The classrooms in the original stable block were too small and parking was becoming very difficult in the courtyard. We had to find some extra classrooms very quickly and that was when we had the idea to reconstruct the old greenhouses at the top of the walled garden.

During that summer three new classrooms were erected and Rosie Anderson joined the staff as our parallel Reception teacher. The following year we added two more classrooms to the walled garden and Deborah Smith Joined, followed by Andrea Kirkpatrick who took over from Deborah. Karen David whose children Tom and Sarah joined Main School also became part of our team.

Our staff numbers had grown considerably and once again Paul Barraclough stepped in and converted one of the original classrooms into a staff room. The Pre-Prep grew much more quickly than we had expected and we soon became experts at utilising every available space. We continued to eat our lunches in the classroom and to reorganise all the chairs in Nursery each afternoon for our assemblies and music lessons. For computing and P.E we would walk to Main School to use their facilities.

St Michael's float at the Otford Fete

Now we have computers in each classroom. We have a Conservatory which is for our Additional Educational Needs Department. We have assembly every morning in our Pre-Prep Hall; we lunch every day in our dining room; we have a Library and a Music Room which is home for the thirty-six little violins. The Pre-Prep has its own Reception area.

Each year on the anniversary of the opening of the library, Pre-Prep children come to school dressed as their favourite character from a book. Alice in Wonderland is always very popular (probably through ease of costume-making!).

There are 180 children on roll and 23

members of staff including Liz Taplin, our Physical Education teacher whose son Martin was one of the first to join St Michael's in 1991, Sally Beesley who teaches Music from Nursery to Year 2 and Pat Whiting our Secretary, whose son Tom joined Kindergarten in 1995.

## A Day in the Life of Kindergarten Staff

Here we are the awesome four
Who every morning lock the door
To parents who attempt to bring
Far too early, their offspring.

And then at 9 o'clock we go
Off to assembly to see the show
With cherubs like dear Ben and Ted
Who come equipped with half their beds.

Then back we go to paint and glue
And write and sing and do a poo
And when the rooms are in a mess
Our Head comes in with a nice guest.

Playtime arrives without a care
Then milk and juice spills everywhere
And then it's time to have a wee
Be careful Jack! Now, look at me!

It's tracksuit time, "Whoopee we shout",
They're back to front and inside out
And when we think, "Right that is that",
Paula says, "They'll need a hat!"

We're out at last, we breathe and sigh
And then I feel that I might cry
For it has begun to rain
It's time to take them off again!!
The lunch comes in, the moans all start,
"I don't like beans"; "I don't like tart!"

Spaghetti covers half the floor,
And manners fly out of the door.

Our day of bliss comes to an end
With hats and coats and prayers to send
We can't believe it's come so soon
As we all say "Good afternoon".

And so you see why we all four
Turn up each day and beg for more
I'm sure that you will all agree
Our life in here is just pure glee.

So raise your glass as this term closes
As we can now release our noses
It's cheers to us in Kindergarten
The awesome 4 and Mrs Barton!!!


**Teacher Elaine Martin 1996**

# ~ 17 ~

## Simon Cummins

### Headmaster – 1990 to 1996

On the retirement of Revd Paul Cox, a twenty-seven year old layman called Simon Cummins was offered the Headship of St Michael's.

The school was at a critical stage of its development as it was not financially viable to continue as a boarding school for some fifty-plus boys. Change was required to meet the needs of local families who increasingly wanted day schooling for their children and were prepared to pay for the privilege of high-quality education and top-class facilities.

Mr Cummins set about transforming the school by recruiting a new staff team, landscaping the grounds and boosting school pupil numbers to well over the three hundred mark in just a few years. This transformation required an enormous amount of energy and passion from a dedicated team whose vision of a new-look St Michael's still encompassed many of the values and traditions of Father Tooth's school.

This is Simon Cummins' own account of his time at St Michael's:

'My wife Liz and I found out the news we would be moving to Otford at the wedding reception of a very good friend of ours. It proved to be quite a memorable night! We are still extremely grateful to John Bull, the then Chairman of Governors, for offering us the wonderful opportunity to follow the excellent work of Donald Cormack and Paul Cox.

I had visited the school previously on a sports fixture and had admired the outstanding location and obvious potential. Fortunately, the governors trusted my judgement on opening up the grounds to further admire the stunning site and to extend the facilities available for the pupils.

I must admit there were some scary moments as the digger dragged away the undergrowth and left what looked, at times, like a desert. However, when the site turned green, the vision for the campus began to take shape. Once the tennis courts had been added, the swimming pool renovated (thanks to Paul Barraclough), the cricket pavilion finished (a Herculean effort from the ever-industrious Ian Saunders), matters were well under way to creating a campus worthy of such a prestigious school.

But how I hated spending money on tarmac! However, with every car entering via the Pre-Prep courtyard, it was somewhat of a necessity. The new entrance onto Rowdow and the new car park had a marked effect on the daily morale of the parents and a noticeable contribution to the relations with the planning department at Sevenoaks; a relationship that was to be a very close one for some years to come! I can't remember exactly the total number of vehicles I anticipated would use this new entrance in the foreseeable future; let's just say I under-estimated it slightly!

The need to satisfy the increased demand for places at the school very quickly resulted in old storerooms becoming classrooms and garages becoming Kindergartens. Responding to market demand meant more day places and fewer boarders, more sandpits and playdough and a need for summer dresses and ballet shoes. I remember the school production of 'Bugsy Malone' doing more for attracting siblings to the school than anything else.

Greenhouses were converted into Pre-Prep classrooms (I think the official term was replacing old for new according to the building regulations form. Quite how old and substantial were the lean-to glasshouses was open to some debate!), cellars to music rooms and dormitories to subject rooms.

The moving of the dining tables out of the entrance hall at least took away the smell of baked-beans when prospective parents first arrived. Showing parents round a school with some classes having as few as 5 children challenged my powers as a creative salesman.

It was those early months that persuaded me to stand forever firm against future demands from staff for detailed job specifications. The school would never have developed as it did had it not been for the incredible flexibility and versatility of the staff, always willing to turn their hand to any profession that was needed at the time. I could not have dreamt of a more capable Senior Management Team: Paul Alford, Graham Malcolm, Vanda Marchetti and Jane Priestly were simply faultless. Anyone teaching at St. Michael's in the '90s is now a DIY expert and accepting of the most challenging of situations. Anyone who was a parent in the '90s is now a respected socialite or event organiser extraordinaire! The camaraderie developed into a team spirit that I've never since experienced and am never likely to ever again.

Open Air Concert 1991. Unfortunately it rained

I was extremely fortunate to have the most exceptional support from the whole community and especially the Parents and Friends committee who were simply incredible. Events that spring to mind are too numerous to mention but how diverse and exciting it was to attend an open-air concert from the Royal Philharmonic Orchestra and the unparalleled Summer Balls.

I'll never forget the staff/dads cricket team defeating Holmesdale in the Clarke Trophy or Jeff Thorne's version of 'The Billabong' following the Chairman of the P and F's 'Curiosity Killed the Cat' after the New Year Dance (he was our resident from Perth, Western Australia)!

The 'hands on' approach obviously served the staff well as four of them went on to secure their own Headships!

Facilities are clearly only a small part of any educational experience. Although the realisation of the full vision with the completion of the new sports hall and pool and the present theatre and science labs still excite me from afar, memories go much deeper than bricks and mortar.

We were excited when the numbers reached 159, from 59 on my first day; we partied when the Pre-Prep reached capacity at 180 and the full-scale madness that followed the 350th signature somehow led one to believe something was going right. To put one's finger on exactly what was causing 'The-Hoover-on-the-Hill' (as I was once called by an adjacent competitor) to continue to inhale the families as quickly as we did, is difficult to achieve but it lies somewhere in the beauty of St Michael's, a beauty that runs deeper than that which is tangible. The spirit that permeated from the chapel, the serenity of mind that drifted from the warren, the sense of belief from the staff and parents and the loyal sense of belonging from the pupils all contributed to that Je ne c'est quoi? Perhaps it was a combination of the personalities of Michael and Molly (the dog)! Michael Hatton continued to remain totally loyal to the school and his kindness was an example for all. He coped admirably with the changes going on around him although we never did manage to persuade him to update 'Moab', his private facilities.

It goes without saying the key linchpin throughout my time at St Michael's was my wife Liz who played a fairly key part in the arrival of our three beautiful children but managed somehow to combine this with the multifaceted roles of: full-time mum, bursar (until Chris Young came to the rescue), seamstress, interior designer, games coach, geographer, school cook (with babe on hip) and even ski-trip organiser.

The way tradition complements change is vital to the ethos of any school, especially a stand-alone prep school that surely has a unique old boys and girls association that has met annually since 1948. This is testament indeed to the sense of loyalty that those fortunate enough to have experienced the legacy of Arthur Tooth undoubtedly have.

Old boys and girls, after all is said and done, were 'The School'; pupils who seemed to genuinely appreciate and enjoy the environment in which they lived their formative school years. The pupils appeared to be living their dreams in the inspiring surroundings and it is this that remains most prominent in one's mind.

A combination of impressive academic results, a breadth of curriculum to match any school, the sports tours and family ski trips, the Sevenoaks Three Arts Festival, (three cheers for Isabelle Peacock!) school plays and the spiritual ethos all contributed to a truly holistic education for each pupil.

The '90s at St Michael's were certainly a time of change and growth and development but hopefully, innovation didn't destroy but added to its past greatness. Much was achieved within the six years we spent at Otford but the lasting memory is leaving a thriving, happy school where all members of the community were working together for the total fulfilment of each individual pupil.'

\* \* \*

The following postscript is added by Liz Cummins, Simon's wife.

*'Simon not only improved facilities and developed the site, he gave a buzz to the place that was infectious. Staff morale was very high and he always got the best out of them. He never asked a member of staff to do any work he wouldn't do himself. Parents were never aware he got up at 7am to mark out pitches and clean toilets in the pavilion if they hadn't been done. He would be the first person on the scene in any disaster such as flooding, gas leaks and burst*

*pipes. He spent hours in knee deep water saving the newly built Nursery classrooms! He was always hands-on and helped with everything. He helped wash up after all school events and always hoovered the carpets!*

*Despite having just had a hernia repair he still managed to walk the entire length of the Pilgrims Way to raise money for his beloved Sports Hall and Swimming Pool project.*

Taking a well-earned rest with teachers Anna Golding and Anna Godfrey (plus a friend) who joined him for part of the walk

St Michael's pupils held a mini sponsored walk of their own but their efforts were confined to the grounds on a misty weekend.

*'I could go on for pages listing his exploits but they are safe in our memories! It was hard work, tremendous fun and gave us a huge sense of achievement. It was a true family school and it was like giving our child up for adoption when we left!'*

**Liz Cummins – 1990/96**

*'As parents, we were wooed by Simon Cummins, the then new Headmaster when we first decided to visit the school as a possible choice for Tiffany's education. Of the schools we decided to visit, he was the only Headmaster to take the time to show us around personally.*

*The grounds were still heavily wooded and the Pre-Prep accommodation still little more than stable blocks. His belief in a positive future and a vision of better things swayed*

*us to place our precious daughter with the 50 or so boys currently at the school.*

*This hands-on partnership between the staff and the parents created the family atmosphere. Memories of cutting hedges, painting classrooms and finally building the sports pavilion in the freezing rain will be etched on our minds forever.*

*Fundraising with the summer fayre appeared to become more competitive each year. During Tiffany's final year, 93/94 I think, we even managed to persuade my business clients to support the event. An American holiday company supplied and manned a hot-air balloon for tethered rides. SAAB (GB) agreed to allow a local dealer to lend us a convertible car so we could raffle the chance to use it for a weekend. As part of the active Parents' & Friends' Committee, we needed little excuse to create fund-raising events, 60s evenings, Christmas parties, Valentine's Dinners and the Summer Balls were legendary.'*

*From the first day she attended the kindergarten at just 3 years 6 months old as one of the only 2 girls among the sea of boys' faces, Tiffany rose to the occasion.*

*She showed then a steely determination to hold her own in such competitive company. It was this competitive spirit and dogged determination learnt during these early years at St Michael's that we believe stood her in good stead for the battles ahead.'*

Tiffany died in May 2002 of a progressive, debilitating, and fatal brain disorder caused by an infection by a mutant virus. She had become something of a celebrity in Otford as the community rallied round to raise money for her treatment.

The Pre-Prep maintained its links with the family even after her death which occurred eight years after leaving St Michael's:

*'Following her death and funeral which coincided with the academic summer half-term, Vanda Marchetti expressed a desire to commemorate Tiffany's contribution to the school. (At the time, we now understand, our decision to send Tiffany to St Michael's was pivotal in the school's history as to whether it continued or failed). Vanda invited us to attend the Pre-Prep end of term concert and prize-giving ceremony. Here, to our amazement and delight, the whole event was dedicated to Tiffany's memory with words warmly spoken by the staff, many of whom had taught her, and finally the unveiling of a bench dedicated to her in the walled garden. A fitting location as Tiffany always considered this was her garden as her class occupied each of the new classrooms in turn as they were completed.'*

**Chris and Sherri Barnes Hannah, parents of Tiffany who attended 1991/94.**

The second ski trip to Les Collons in Switzerland. 1992.

# Simon Cummins 1990 - 1996

**1990** – Simon Cummins and his wife Liz arrive at St Michael's.

**1990** – Excavations commence to provide three new sports pitches. Floodlit tennis courts are created.

**1990** – The Pre-Prep is extended to incorporate a nursery.

**1991** – The first Parents' and Friends' ski trip is organised.

**1991** – The swimming pool is renovated and the cellars are turned into a music block. A new driveway is created so access to the school is now via Row Dow.

**1991** – Girls are allowed into the Main School for the first time.

**1991** – The Royal Philharmonic Orchestra perform an Open Air Concert in the grounds. It rains!

**1996** – Simon Cummins completes a 145 mile sponsored walk from Winchester to Canterbury along the Pilgrims Way. He raises more than £10,000 for the building of the new sports hall and swimming pool complex. The children enjoy a mini sponsored walk in the grounds.

**1996** – Boarding is no longer offered as an option.

**1996** – Simon Cummins leaves St Michael's to take up the Headship of the Millfield Preparatory School.

# ~ 18 ~

# Outdoors

*'There lies the world before me a beautiful world full of sunshine and promise – life everywhere a gallant struggle for the good, for the best.'*
**[Arthur Tooth]**

In 1925 St Michael's moved from the suburbs of Croydon to the unspoilt countryside of Otford. The effect of having 88 acres of grounds for the boys to enjoy was immediate.

---

**20 March 1925:** Now that the weather is becoming finer I find that the large extent of playing ground that the boys have is very beneficial. The exercise in running up and down the hills must be very conducive to good health.

---

The boys also enjoyed the wider countryside:

*'Fox hunting, though now frowned upon, was a regular 'extra mural study'. Several senior boys were allowed to attend meets of the West Kent Foxhounds and would often be seen duly arrayed in scarlet jerseys and white shorts, following the hunt on foot. This would involve us covering considerable distances - returning to school, sometimes after dark, footsore, weary and very hungry.*

*Rabbiting, too, was an enjoyable diversion. We kept several ferrets on the school premises and, with a certain Mr Card (a local gamekeeper) we would be let off lessons to go out and catch the rabbits.*

*During the summer other outdoor activities included pulling up ragwort (a noxious weed in abundance throughout the grounds) and, for my own part, as well as a few others, catching butterflies and moths. I left in 1931 with quite an impressive collection, including a few rare specimens such as Clouded Yellow, a migrant from southern Europe.'*

**Douglas Keddie 1923/31**

'The fox hunting season was a time we all looked forward to. It was the time that we would don our red jumpers, go to the meet wherever that may be and follow the hunt on foot. Before we left we were each given a couple of thick doorstep cheese sandwiches and strict instructions to follow the hunt.

The red jersey which no doubt could be spotted miles away was meant to be a deterrent for us to do otherwise but being a strong believer that rules are meant to be broken this was the opportunity to go hunting in a different way. In my book orchards were fair game and turnip fields also; anything edible was at risk if it came to that. Having done our foraging we would endeavour to locate the hunt and if possible get there for the kill and perhaps the dubious honour of being bloodied. This meant being swiped across the face with the brush of the poor fox that had already been cut off.

John White (Charles Blofeld's adopted son) helping to find supper.

We were frequently detailed for a day's rabbiting with three ferocious ferrets we had acquired. We were inundated with rabbits and the area known today as the warren was our favourite hunting ground. Many an evening was spent making the necessary nets for these expeditions which was a pleasant diversion from homework. On an average we would come back with a dozen rabbits much to Sister Hilda's delight and for us a week of rabbit pie. Eventually rabbits became so numerous we were compelled to bring in the men with guns. We got used to the odd pellet or two in our stew.'

**Gerry Winter 1924/30**

'Permission to go on the warren was another excitement. Perhaps a visit to the quarry (out of bounds of course) or a wonderful game of chase, sometimes in pick-up teams. We were never short of ideas from French Cricket in the summer, troglodytical activity in the grounds, gardening etc., to sledging in the winter. We often had snow, or so memory suggests.'

**Roy Haines 1932/38**

'On Sunday afternoons we were expected to take part in decorous walks. We didn't exactly hold hands, but we were reasonably decorous, mainly I suppose because it was the Sabbath.

*A fairly usual walk was up the hill behind the stables. At the top one came to a T-junction. In the triangular piece of spare ground within the junction was a wooden sign. On it carved out with (I imagine) a hot poker were the words:*

Resemble not the slimy snail

That with its filth records its trail.

Let it be said, where you have been,

You've left the face of nature clean.

*Wise words and I've never forgotten them.*

*Normally we would turn right at the junction, and a short distance further on take a left turn over a stile and along a footpath leading to a beautiful dell that rejoiced in the name of 'Magpie Bottom' - much smutty laughter from the boys of course.*

*The 'bottom' was also the venue for an annual picnic, much enjoyed by all - but how the logistics could have been arranged remains a mystery, especially at this distance.*

*Sunday walks also took us through neighbouring villages, those on the Southern Railway commuter system being especially enjoyable. We liked crossing the lines, showing off our deviltry by hop-scotching across the electric line. It was said that one could safely stand on the live rail, provided one did not at the same time put a foot on an ordinary rail. However, I do not remember anyone demonstrating the truth of this theorem.*

*Another pleasure was to place a ha'penny on the line and have it converted magically into a penny by the passage of a train. Shopkeepers weren't often fooled by ultra-thin irregularly shaped pennies, so not many of us made our fortunes in this venture.'*

**Eric Crabbe 1934/38**

*'One day at the Warren on the very extremity of the school grounds, we were invaded by a large number of young boys (evacuees). We managed to hold the line with our conkers but they did not ration their ammunition so ran out of missiles. They then used stones which was 'not cricket'. We withdrew but they decided not to push forward. We never had any trouble again.'*

**Tony Harrison 1937/42**

These local boys from Kemsing were named 'Gites' by the St Michael's boys as a derivative of 'Guttersnipes', switched round to 'Shuttergites'. During the battle, a cross was made by Julian

Beeching [1941/45] and a dignified withdrawal was made in a procession behind this symbol, held aloft.

*'One of our favourite 'outdoor' activities was 'Hares and Hounds'. Our normal 'outdoor' boundaries were set fairly close to the school buildings, but on Saturday afternoons we would seek permission to use the entire school acreage which included all the open spaces and large wooded areas of the 80-plus acre site, and split ourselves into 'Hares' and 'Hounds'. The Hares would be given time to go and 'hide', to be sought and 'captured' later by the 'Hounds'. The Hares would simply scatter to all four corners and virtually dig themselves out of sight, whilst the Hounds would group up to seek them out. Great fun and the game would last all afternoon.'*

**John Read (Read 1) 1946/49**

*'The vastness of the school grounds was a never-ending source of wonder for me. They seemed to me to be infinite and were a delight to the intrepid explorer. I was never happier than when I was able to wander through the woods.'*

**John Hutchinson 1949/50**

*'We were taught in the room immediately to the left of the front door, and I remember spending a lot of time looking out of the big windows at the birds, especially, the jays, finches, robins and magpies, which lived around the school in abundance. At that time the junior school had its own playground at the bottom of the hill to the south east of the school and we also had our own garden plots down there, where we tried to grow radishes and other vegetables with very limited success. As I recall the planting was fun and full of expectations, which were seldom fulfilled, because we neglected the poor things after we had planted them.*

*Most of my fondest recollections of St Michael's, other than playing sports, are of how we spent our free time. When the weather was reasonable we were allowed outside to roam the grounds and invent our own games. These involved the obvious ones like hide and seek, pick up games of rounders, conkers, trying to hit squirrels with our catapults, creating camps in the undergrowth, tobogganing on the path down to the cricket field, snowball fights etc, but we also had some quite elaborate games. These typically divided the school into two teams and were in effect battles.*

*The two types of battle I recall best were dust battles and 'regular' battles. Dust battles were fought for control of the evergreen copses, which had no greenery underneath their branches and were pockmarked with rabbit burrows. We used to collect dirt in our neckerchiefs and hurl the dirt using the neckerchief as a sling. Obviously, we tried to cover our mouths and noses either with our hands or a spare neckerchief but they were certainly very dirty affairs. Because we dusted ourselves off, it was quite a while before someone figured out what we were doing and banned them. The more normal battles were fought with bows and arrows and spears (made from saplings and dead shoots) and it was a miracle that nobody was seriously hurt!*

*Other times, I loved just climbing the trees and wandering about in the woods. Tree climbing was particularly fun in the old weeping beeches that used to be on the right of the driveway about opposite to the lane to the stables. In fact, my fondest memories of St Michaels are the times I spent in the woods. It was particularly fun to climb the trees that overhung the driveway and lanes, pretending to be Robin Hood and not be seen by the people passing underneath!*

*The man that looked after the grounds, Mr Sankey, died at the start of my last term and we, managed by Cormack, had to mow the grass and roll the cricket wicket etc. I was given the task of mowing the back edge of the field, which for some reason had been allowed to grow much longer than the rest of the field. Cormack was making a big performance out of watering the cricket wicket with a hose that ran from the fence, along which I was cutting the grass, out to the wicket. I had managed to negotiate the hose with my mower a couple of times and I suppose I got a little careless because, on the third pass, I managed to cut the hose. I will always remember, with a combination of horror and hilarity, the look on Cormack's face as the water suddenly stopped coming out of the end of his hose.*

**Kendall Carey 1949/56**

*'Was the weather different then? I have vivid winter memories of tobogganing and snow fights in good falls of snow and the occasional pea-souper, rolling down from London to envelop the school in acrid fog so thick that visibility was barely a yard or two. Summer in the memory is filled with warm sunny days, cricket and sports day; C.B. Fry presented the prizes one year, I still have his autograph.*

*The school grounds provided ample scope for the imagination of young boys, whiling away 'free time'. Myxomatosis afflicted the rabbits one year; boys formed 'mercy' squads, armed with iron bars, to put the poor creatures out of their misery.'*

**Paul Hoddinott 1950/55**

[Paul Hoddinott became the youngest man to be made a Royal Naval captain. He captained HMS Glasgow in the Falklands conflict which was the first ship into the war zone and first warship home. She had a miraculous escape on May 12 1982 when a bomb passed clear through her without exploding and without causing serious injury.]

*'Mr Sankey, the bearded art teacher and head gardener, shot himself – can this be true? – and for a time the pupils would have to maintain the green houses, pausing occasionally to terminate sick rabbits infected with myxomatosis. On one occasion in ignorance I pulled up the school's entire termly supply of young lettuces. I don't think head gardener*

*was a demanding job. The huge and exciting grounds were left untouched: the copses in which we learnt to smoke a pipe (not easy because impoverished anglo-catholic parents used to smoke cigarettes down to the last quarter-inch), the pathways along which we ambled at the head of the Corpus Christi procession (the strawberry walk), a day when other Anglican extremists used to descend on the school.'*

**Stephen Winkley 1954/57**

*'One of the positive aspects of the school for me was having 80 acres of rough ground to play in. Such play was generally unsupervised and staff were never seen in most places. But of course closer to the school one encountered them. There was a wide flattish grassy area on one of the tracks down to the cricket pitch (I can't remember what it was called but it will have had a name – every bit of the grounds did). I remember that on at least two occasions the Assistant Master, Michael Bond and his friend Mr (?Edward) Pugh went down there in their cars on summer evenings and drove around it as if it were a skid pan, chasing half-a-dozen or more senior boys. Amazingly no one was hurt. Michael had an MGB at the time I think. Mr Pugh drove a variety of cars as I recall but the only one I remember clearly was a Saab.'*

**Mark Bowden 1965/70**

*'On a cold and grey Sunday afternoon in October – after chapel, chores and lunch were done - we were ready for mufti. Jon Goodinson and I decided to explore the bomb crater, a little south of the badminton courts. Looking for nothing in particular we often played at being amateur archaeologists, poking at the soil with sticks. The most exciting find was*

*usually a flint or two and we'd try to make a fire with kindling, but we were to discover something far more interesting today.*

*As I scraped away at the crater wall with my stick, a small stone object fell to the ground. The archaeological dig was abruptly over as Jon and I inspected my find.*

*"What is it?" Jon asked, as I rubbed it between my fingers and thumb - my thumb doing most of the work. "I don't know, but I think we've got something," I replied.*

*Imagine an object about the size of half an avocado. The avocado 'stone hole' is in the right place but the stone is missing. As I rub and peel the mud and clay from the object, I discover a much smaller hole towards the thin end of the half avocado, raised about half an inch above where the stone should have been, and a small channel connecting the two. I really had found something!*

*Once we had cleaned it up, it was obvious this was something out of the ordinary. I recall asking a few seniors if they had seen anything like it. Andy Mullins suggested it might be a Stone Age or Bronze Age thing. (He seemed so smart to me. To this day I credit Andy with my remembering how to spell the word 'business'.)*

*Scouring the encyclopaedias, Jon and I are shocked to find a photograph of our find in a book. "That's it!" we exclaimed in unison. "It's a Stone Age lamp." Used to burn animal fat, it provided light to man thousands of years ago. The picture was so identical to the object I held in my hand, it was as if my lamp had been photographed for the book.*

*Mrs Macadam (Juniors Teacher) was suitably impressed and quite proud that one her boys had made such a great discovery – right there in the 90 acres of private grounds of the school. The exact timeline of events and memories are long faded now, but I recall a good deal of excitement and interest followed and then the lamp was forgotten for a while.*

*Some time later (perhaps a week, maybe a month) I am visited by a thin tall man in drab coloured clothes. Apart from my father, he was perhaps the most serious man I have ever met. It appears my Stone Age lamp discovery had piqued the curiosity of a museum and the man quizzed me about the find. Funny how at nine years old I was already 'over' the lamp discovery - looking forward to the next adventure, no doubt. As requested, I went back to my drawer to show him the lamp but discovered the lamp missing. He was unimpressed. A lecture followed about the seriousness of the loss. I remember thinking just how funny he sounded. "Why was he so mad at me? It was MY lamp, not his."*

*Perhaps someone reading this account will feel a tiny prick of guilt of theft, perhaps not. To this day I have no idea who might have taken it, and I have never disclosed the location of the find, but I can't help but occasionally wonder about the bomb crater. After all, if there was one lamp found there, it is quite possible there are many other discoveries waiting to be made. Happy hunting!'*

**David Humphreys 1974/79**

## The Great Storm – 16 October 1987

*'The night of the great storm of 1987 left the drive blocked but fortunately little damage to the school. Tony Good and I with some senior boys spent most of the day clearing the drive with the help of residents and parents. We were off electricity for three weeks. I bought a generator which gave us enough power to carry on in the day time (by juggling what equipment we used) but for safety boarders went to the homes of day boys. It gave some boys a Common Entrance Geography project to identify and plot the fallen trees (about 1000 in the grounds) on a map showing contours. Tony Good replaced thirty tiles on the roof by tying a rope around his waist to the chimneystack and hanging almost upside down. He said he did it when it was nearly dark so that he could not see the ground 70 feet below! He knew that the chimney stack was firm because that had had to be replaced when we found we had asbestos to the boilers and the old chimney was swaying precariously when the builders tried to fit a new lining.'*

**Revd Paul Cox, Headmaster 1981/90**

One of the casualties of the storm was the notorious Golden Oak which had been a hindrance to many a cricketer because of it's position at the edge of the boundary.

It was "a special and beautiful tree" as Old Michaelian Tony Rumm says and therefore efforts were made to nurse it back to life.

The Golden Oak was raised and then propped up. Unfortunately, despite best efforts, the Golden Oak failed to show any signs of life and it was eventually cut down completely.

## Changing Landscape

The grounds at St Michael's remained largely untouched from 1925 when the house was bought by Father Arthur Tooth until Revd Paul Cox became Headmaster in 1984. During his time at the helm, large areas of the grounds were opened up by cutting back the scrubland and by frequent mowing - mostly carried out by the Headmaster himself! Father Cox also cut the route out through the woods to create an interesting and demanding cross-country race.

It was Simon Cummins' vision and persuasive skills that resulted in the Governors agreeing to more radical landscaping of the grounds. Trees were felled, JCBs moved in and three new pitches and two tennis/netball courts were created.

Today the sporting facilities are frequently used to their fullest extent and St Michael's is able to host major sporting tournaments. The grounds are the envy of many of the school's sporting competitors!

Children enjoying the Pre-Prep garden

# ~ 19 ~

## Dr Peter Roots

### Headmaster – 1996 to 2002

Dr Peter Roots joined the school after the resignation of Simon Cummins. He had previously been a Franciscan monk, and had subsequently served as an assistant professor at Truman University (Missouri) as well as Head of Divinity at The King's School, Chester. His post prior to Headmaster at St Michael's was as Director of Studies at Port Regis School in Dorset.

***What were your aims for the school?***
I think my aim was essentially the same as that of my predecessors, that St Michael's was to be a place where all pupils should have maximum opportunity to be *happy*, *successful* and *good*. For the six years I was Headmaster I had on the wall by my computer a sheet of paper that stated, "Every decision and every process must have as its basis the welfare and education of the individual child."

More specifically, building on the success of my predecessors and responding to the school's rapid growth, I felt the tasks in hand were:

(i) to achieve the highest standards possible in 11+, Common Entrance and Scholarship exams, while not forgetting that we are a very inclusive, non-selective school (ii) to make St Michael's famous as a warm, Christian and caring environment, where high standards of behaviour are based on a positive, praise-focused culture, and where there is a balance between old-fashioned politeness and a friendly relationship between pupils and teachers; (iii) to improve the fabric of the school buildings and to develop the facilities and resources (iv) to continue the tradition of breadth as well as depth in the curricular and extra-curricular life of the school.

**How did you go about achieving your aims for the school?**

Achieving academic goals was obviously a long-term matter and came down to getting the best teachers possible, year by year. Equally important was getting the right *mix* of teachers, in terms of skills, interests, age and gender. One of the most important appointments we made in 1996 was that of Ruth Marx, our first Special Needs Coordinator, whose specialist skills complemented the increasing number of teachers who were able to challenge even the most able pupils. Vital appointments in this respect were Dr Gerda Frank-Gemmill as Head of Languages and Academic Deputy, Peter Nixon as Head of English and Drama, (and then Deputy), and Sarah Bridgman as Key Stage 2 Coordinator (and then Director of Studies).

Recognising that my own strengths lay on the academic side rather than the sporting, I sought to build the best possible team in Physical and Sports Education. As a consequence, I decided to take on a heavier teaching load than is normal for a Headmaster, in order to release these outstanding sports staff for Games. In relation to our second goal, the pastoral, this was a horse ready to be led. The school already had a culture of warmth and praise and it was easy to build on this culture, through assemblies, stars, prize-givings etc, and smiling a lot at the children! Increasingly, we developed a staff body that enjoyed a warm relationship with the children, people like Ray Willis, a real grandfather figure to the children, although he still thinks he is young. One of the great stars in the pastoral area is Vanda Marchetti, the wonderful Pre-Prep Head. Some of the best memories of hundreds of former pupils and parents will centre on the loving culture that Vanda Marchetti has created in the Pre-Prep.

Improving the fabric and facilities of the school was a real challenge to begin with, because of the school's tight financial situation. Chris Young, the Bursar, is one of the great unsung heroes of the success of St Michael's in its recent history. Faced with a cash-flow problem, Chris and I decided to get rid of most of the antique furniture and fireplaces which were cluttering the school, were hurting children's heads, and were detracting from the school's warm atmosphere. We got rapped over the knuckles by the governors for selling off school assets without their permission, but the money raised paid for a vital overhaul of the pupils' dining facilities and some fresh coats of paint, plus carpet to replace the broken "lino" that existed in various parts of the buildings.

As the years went on, and the school's financial situation improved, we were able to do more and more to the point where we able to start a building programme of nearly £2 million pounds in 2002.

Offering a breadth of curricular and extra-curricular opportunities for pupils has been a long-established tradition at St Michael's and Judith Yarnold's unbounded energy, enthusiasm, and a real commitment to the interests and needs of all pupils, have ensured that St Michael's has an extra-curricular programme which would shame most boarding schools. Similarly, the work of Glynis Dickinson, Jo Chapman, and the whole Music Department, has made St Michael's a name synonymous with high-quality music education and performance.

***What did you enjoy most during your time at St Michael's, what gave you the greatest pleasure while you were there and what are your fondest memories?***

These are the easiest questions to answer. Most of all I enjoyed working with the pupils, whether it was going down to Pre-Prep, teaching Year 4 History and Latin, senior Religious Studies, Latin and History, or playing chess or Lego during lunchtime or after school.

Making the Headmaster's Study a place where pupils went to have fun, rather than be in trouble, was not just an important part of what I wished to achieve in my time as head, it was a great joy. It was part of what I felt a prep school should be and part of why I became a teacher.

Other fond memories include the Archery activity, even when one of the pupils managed to hit our car with an arrow. I am still surprised that our cats survived six years of St Michael's archery. One of the highlights of the activity was senior pupils lighting the annual bonfire at the school with flaming arrows. Unlike Kevin Costner they did it for real!

A related pleasure was that of the camping activities and the overnight camps, which we ran several times. On occasions like this one sees a completely different side to pupils, and new strengths, as well as some interesting weaknesses. I shall never forget

the Year 8 pupil who tried to fry a boil-in-the bag curry over an open fire. He was most surprised when the plastic melted in the pan.

Walking up to the school from the house in the early hours of a frosty, sunny morning was a real delight which we experienced hundred of times. Similarly, when the pupils and I were all too tired to do Latin last thing in the afternoon, exploring the school grounds and climbing trees was great fun and, again, part of what prep school should be about. Achieving high teaching and learning standards is important but so also is the wider experience, the quality of daily life for pupils and teachers, the "Mr Chips" factor.

I have mentioned several memorable staff but I cannot finish without putting in writing the superb quality of the secretaries at St Michael's. Mrs Jan Ayton and Mrs Leigh Henderson are key figures in the pupils' and teachers' happiness and in the smooth flowing of the school's daily life. They do a wonderful job and their achievement deserves to be mentioned, as does that of Mrs Sally Mason, who preceded Leigh as School Secretary and did an equally superb job.

Most importantly of all, a great deal of the success of St Michael's School over the last six years has been due to the energy, efficiency, warmth and character of Mary Roots, Headmaster's wife and school registrar. Between 1996 and 2002 Mary was the lynch pin in the work and development of the school. The tributes to her that flowed in when we left in July were truly deserved. We shall both miss the school dearly.

**Dr Peter Roots. Headmaster 1996/2002**

\* \* \*

Dr Roots resigned his Headship in spectacular fashion at the annual prize-giving ceremony held in a marquee in 2002. As staff, governors, parents and children listened to the usual mix of citations and entertainment, little did they know that before the evening was out, the school would be left without a Head. Dr Roots' resignation, without notice, was as much a shock to the Chairman of the Governors as to everybody else. His reasoning for announcing it in such a fashion was that he wanted everybody to hear the news at the same time.

It was only later that everybody learned that his resignation had been prompted by serious health concerns.

Here are a few comments from pupils about Dr Roots which give a fuller picture of the man:

*'I really liked Dr Roots. When he stood in for absent teachers he used to read us stories like an old Grandpa would. They were mostly biblical stories like the story of Jonah and the Whale. We all listened.'*

*'I remember throwing wet sponges at Dr Roots at the Summer Fair. It felt strange but he encouraged us to do it! One year the fair was held indoors because of rain so he allowed us to do it to him the following week!'*

*'I was in the Ramblers after-school club which was taken by Dr Roots. He used to put face-paint on us so we were camouflaged like soldiers. He encouraged us to climb trees and leap out of branches on to an old mattress. Great fun!'*

*'One time I had to stay at school instead of going on the Year 6 two-day outward bound expedition because I had broken my arm. Dr Roots organized it so that me and a some other children could camp on the old pitch so that we had an adventure as well, and didn't feel as if we were missing out on the fun.'*

**Recipe for a Dr Roots**
Take a pair of green eyeballs,
And a bushy black beard,
A couple of bibles, and a Trojan House shield.

Mix together 3 knights and a king,
1 bow and arrow
And hum the school hymn.

Add a big happy smile,
In the Headmaster's room
2 cuddly pet cats
And a "Good Afternoon".

**Nicholas Bilsby, 5B. 2000**

# Dr Peter Roots 1996 - 2002

**1997** – The new Sports Centre is opened by Mike Denness (former England and Kent cricket captain). Douglas Keddie, the oldest Old Michaelian is a special guest.

**1995** – Parent Sue Isted leads a team of Mums in setting up a second-hand uniform shop named Déjà vu. Over £7000 has been raised for the school in this profit-sharing scheme. The money has been used by the school to buy books, play equipment and a host of other items.

**1998** – Michael Hatton, who had been with the school since the 1930s dies aged 79 and is buried in St Mary's Church, Kemsing.

**1998** – The Pre-Prep department receives a superb report from its OFSTED inspection and two full school inspections are also excellent.

**2002** – Building work commences for a major expansion at the school costing over £1.8 million. The new facilities will include a large art/craft/technology complex, two outstanding science labs, a new drama/assembly hall and staff accommodation.

**2002** – Peter Roots retires from St Michael's through ill health.

**2002** – Frank Skipwith takes the role of Interim Head for a year.

**2003** – Keith Crombie takes over as Headmaster.

# ~ 20 ~

# Fun & Games

Entertainment for the boys at Woodside (1878 to 1924) consisted of simple pleasures. Activities in the playground, exploring the grounds and sport were the main past-times. According to Edmund Thornton [1915/18] during the First World War 'hobbies' included: *'felling, sawing and chopping the large trees in the grounds, grafting, pruning and tending the fruit trees and collecting and storing the fruit.'*

Otherwise, to keep the boys amused, Father Tooth used to hang an old tin basin from a branch of the tree outside his study window. The boys then shot at it with an old gun which they were allowed to use. The pupils rarely left the grounds, and only then for very special reasons. A yearly pantomime at Shirley was one excursion they all looked forward to.

Boys relaxing in a classroom in the 1930s

Once lessons were finished for the day, boarders were often left to their own devices:

*'There was always plenty to do even on wet days; later on it was billiards (though I scarcely played that), bridge (which I played avidly), draughts (infuriatingly Derek Long*

*[1931/38] was a past master), chess, and every kind of card game. I never understood why we did not learn backgammon, since we had the boards, though admittedly not the counters.*

*After prep there was a mad dash to the end classroom where we 'bagged' the next game. Somehow we retained a great sense of justice and order. Our differences might be resolved in extreme cases by informal (quite unofficial) boxing rings, but these never to my knowledge went to extremes.'*

**Roy Haines 1932/38**

*'I have strong memories of our Dinky Toy collection, numbering several naval vessels in my collection. Where are they now? Also I had an elastic driven 'frog' aeroplane which once flew from the main drive almost down to the cricket field. I also recall being in Paul Barraclough's 'string telephone' which worked over a span of 150 yards or so.'*

**Jeffries Stratton 1937/41**

*'Hot Rice, French Cricket, chasing rabbits, poking and collecting wasps nests, looking for Roman snails, hide and seek, scouts and school walks on Sunday afternoons. Tobogganing down the warren over the ramp built rather like a V1 launch ram, or two on the sledge – one on top of the other.'*

**J. Martin Beech 1943/47**

Scouts and Cubs in 1946

Although the boys were often left to entertain themselves, Father Thomas Blofeld gave some structure to their 'free time' by encouraging them to take up scouting. Father Blofeld had been connected with the movement ever since its formation, and immediately on taking up the Wardenship of St Michael's in 1939, he set up a troop. In 1948 he became the official Group Scoutmaster of the 22nd Sevenoaks (St Michael's School). The boys participated in many scouting activities, strove to gain stars and even went on camp to Edinburgh.

Towards the end of his life Father Blofeld was awarded the Scouts' Medal of Merit and the Long Service Decoration. Thanking the County Commissioner for the awards, Father Blofeld emphasised that it was his aim to turn out "boys with character".

Scouting continued until 1972 when the troop was disbanded because of difficulties which had arisen over the double authority of the Headmaster and the Instructor so far as the boys were concerned.

Other hobbies provided the basis for clubs at school and stamp collecting and model making were two of the most popular.

*'When it rained we had a ping pong table and the billiards table on the landing on the second floor, making planes and other things out of balsa wood, marbles and lots of other games that we invented, most of which were battles of one kind or another.*

*The two I recall most clearly were naval battles fought with ships we built out of balsa wood, and land battles using toy soldiers, guns that shot matches with plasticine on the ends and all kinds of boxes that we used as forts. The rules for these games were very elaborate in terms of movement, how the enemy could be destroyed, what had to accompany what piece of equipment for it to be usable etc. They were probably what was most influential in teaching us fairness, the need for rules and how to be sociable.'*

**Kendall Carey 1949/56**

*'With virtually no radio or TV and a lot of free time to fill, books featured large in our lives. 'Classics Illustrated' comic books were read, re-read and swapped in the Junior School. In the Senior School I particularly remember large compilations were a prized possession. 'The Complete H G Wells', 'The Complete Sherlock Holmes' (I still have mine) and the book that tells you everything about St Michaels and every other boy's prep school, 'The Complete Molesworth'.*

*Anyone getting hold of a new Western would have it borrowed by Cormack before they had a chance to read it themselves but he would finish it and give it back to you the same day!*

*The only comic approved by the school was 'The Eagle' although I am not sure how we were supposed to be morally corrupted by the 'Beano' or the 'Dandy'. Cormack used to put the comic section of the Sunday Post on the senior classroom newspaper board so we were exposed to some D C Thomson material in "The Broons" and "Oor Wullie".*

*Cormack could often be found in the mornings at the newspapers with his favourite "piece", two huge doorsteps of white bread with a bar of chocolate in the middle! If you were lucky you might be offered a bite, whether or not you could get your teeth through it was another matter!*

*As far as television went, the number of hours broadcast was very limited and the programmes thought suitable for us, almost non-existent. We did get to watch something, probably a Dickens adaptation, around teatime and realized fairly quickly that it was followed by one of the early pop music programmes, 'Oh Boy' or 'The Six Five Special'. Cliff Richard when he was a moody James Dean-obsessed teenager, real subversive stuff in its day! As the television was on the billiards landing outside Father Blofeld's room, the trick was to turn down the volume and cluster around the set so that no one else could see what was on. Sometimes it worked.*

*In the summer of 1960 a few of us were surprised to get permission to have portable radios for limited use. It was severely limited anyway by the price of batteries necessary to power a portable valve radio but enough to listen on a Sunday to 'Uncle Mac', 'Two Way Family Favourites' and 'The Clitheroe Kid'. Prior to this several attempts at constructing crystal sets had all failed.'*

**Alec Stevenson 1954/60**

*'My father made a crystal set for me, to which I would listen clandestinely under the bedclothes after lights out. Even more excitingly, I discovered that, by holding the earphone terminals against two screws that secured a cable conduit in the changing room, I could listen in on Father Blofeld's telephone conversations; I had become a phone-tapper, not that anything very startling was revealed!*

*An avid reader, like many boys I devoured war stories that at that time were being published thick and fast. One day, in a book about the Japanese advance in Malaya, I came across a new word for which I did not understand the meaning – rape. I asked a member of staff and, immediately, the book was confiscated and I was questioned about how I came to have it in my possession. Clearly I had come across a very special word indeed but, even when I found its entry in the dictionary, I was none the wiser  an age of innocence for children of tender years which has long passed.'*

**Paul Hoddinott 1950/55**

*'I ran a railway club at school which was very popular. We created a large layout with track, hills and model people etc. and we had great fun at lunch-times with the locomotives. We would get our material and engines from the model shop at the top end of Sevenoaks High Street.'*

**John Jennings – Housemaster and Head of History 1990/93**

Today, the extensive activities programme for the children gives them the choice of extending their school day past the 4pm finish to either 4.40pm or 5.15pm. The programme changes from term to term but always includes a variety of sports, creative classes and even academic subjects (made fun).

A sample from the Michaelmas 2003 term includes: Design and Build Castles, Cookery, Roald Dahl Club, Fun French Club and Cross Country.

The Pre-Prep Department also offers extra-curricular activities such as Judo, Gardening, Country Dancing, Pottery (with Mrs Watson) and Ballet (with Miss Kim).

A Pre-Prep Judo Team

# Trips Home and Abroad

As orphans and children of impoverished one-parent families, often far from 'home', pupils at St Michael's in the early years rarely left the school, even for holidays. Trips out were few, though kindly benefactors would sometimes treat the boys to a visit to a circus or pantomime.

---

**4 February 1938:** Fr. Mills and Mr & Mrs Axtell invited the whole school to the Lyceum Pantomime as a mark of their appreciation of the school plays. This was a red letter day and will I am sure be long remembered by all who went.

---

There were occasional educational visits but very few compared to the number that pupils enjoy nowadays. It was during Father Cox's Headship that the frequency increased as he realised that it was only the team players, playing away, who ever managed to escape the confines of the grounds.

*'On Saturdays & Sundays I was in charge of the boarders, and we would often have outings to various local places. We went to Knole Park, Eynsford and sometimes up to London to have tea with my Mother in Earl's Court! There was no school transport, so we would walk down to the Railway Station and make our excursion from there.'*

**John Jennings – Housemaster and Head of History 1990/93**

Today, children are taken on theatre trips (the Polka Dot Theatre in Wimbledon is very popular); to art galleries, nature parks, museums, and even to theme parks. At the end of Year 6, all children participate in a two day outward-bound experience and spend a day in France.

*'The first St. Michael's Ski Trip took place in Easter 1991. Whole families came with us and this soon became an annual event in our school calendar. The group which soon grew to around a hundred, travelled to Italy, France, Austria Switzerland and Spain to ski. There were several families who attended all ten trips which we organised.'*

**Vanda Marchetti, Head of Pre-Prep 1990 –**

## House Competitions

In 1938, the school was divided into two houses – Greeks (green) and Trojans (blue) - for the purposes of competitions, both sporting and academic. A short time later as the school grew in size, a third House was introduced called Barbarians (red) though this House was renamed Celts during the 1990s. At the beginning of the academic year 2002, the Houses were changed again. As the weekly newsletter reports:

> The great 'House' debate is over. What would the names be? What about the colours? Who would lead the houses?

> Well, all is now revealed. In a sports hall, packed with children and staff, in a highly charged atmosphere of excitement and eager anticipation, each year group helped in the democratic process of selecting, first the colour, then the name, and finally a House Leader.

> The choice for House names followed a long debate behind closed doors and CASTLES were chosen to reflect an aspect of history that, over the years have enthused many a young mind.

> Each round of the selection process was greeted with cheers of support with the decibel level reaching new heights – up to castle in the air (!) until the final moment when the House Leaders were selected.

> DOVER: led by Mr D Sinclair, and has taken the colour Green

> LEEDS: led by Mrs A Lloyd, and has taken the colour Blue

> ROCHESTER: led by Miss Lovett, and has taken the colour Yellow

> WINDSOR: led by Mr G Arkley and has taken the colour Red

> The selection process ended with each house meeting together to celebrate the results and so, a new era with new houses begins at St Michael's.

House competitions include maths challenges, subject quizzes, chess competitions, music festivals, sporting matches, swimming galas, and of course Sports Day itself. Children can also earn points for their Houses by winning Headmaster's stars for good behaviour and academic success. St Michael's has always encouraged friendly competition amongst its pupils.

# ~ 21 ~

# Academic Work

*'Persevere, grow wise and give thanks'*
**[School Motto]**

The academic results at St Michael's have fluctuated during the years with the comings and goings of different staff, with the pressures of external forces (such as two world wars) and with the academic ability of the pupil intake. The school blossomed academically during the Headship of Dr Peter Roots when the average mark for Common Entrance results went up year on year and an impressive seventeen senior leavers gained scholarships to top schools in 2002. The school continues to build on the successes that he achieved.

There has never been an academic selection process for entry to the school. Continuing with Father Tooth's original selection criteria for the school, children were, for many years, accepted only if their parents were from 'the Professional or similar class'. The other criteria were:

> That the financial standing of the Parents is shown to be such as to warrant their taking advantage of the School's Endowments, which alone make it possible for the School to accept boys at such low fees

> That the parents are willing that their boy should be brought up in the doctrine of the Church of England according to the Catholic tradition and that they will encourage him to practise the same when at home.

> That it is the intention of the Parents that the boy should eventually proceed to a Public School, or other Higher Secondary Education to complete his education.

The criterion for entry nowadays depends purely on gaining a place on the waiting list (for some years this has been in double figures!). Dr Roots reported to the Board of Governors in 1997 that he had been offered his first bribe if he could find a place for two children by Christmas! 'They stayed at the end of the waiting list' he asserts.

## Life Skills

For many of the early years, the emphasis on schooling was just as much about 'life skills' as about academic work:

> As an educationalist, he [Father Tooth] speaks rather sadly of our present system. It is unfitting the people for their walk in life. They are growing up with no notion of tolerating anything, and they want everything, and do not want to earn it. They are losing sense of the duties in life……

**The Croydon Reporter 1912**

Many parents will agree with Father Tooth. With competitive league tables, a restrictive curriculum and fierce competition to get into good secondary schools there is nowadays less time to spend on other than academic subjects. However, children in the main school are currently given weekly lessons entitled 'Personal, Social and Health Education' which covers such subjects as health, relationships, environment, citizenship and safety.

A classroom in the 1930s

Some current staff members can remember the days where lessons could be recklessly abandoned in favour of a walk in the grounds on a sunny day. This option being no longer possible, teachers inject fun and novelty into the curriculum by arranging special events, outings and competitions.

## English

The English Department holds an annual poetry festival at which every child performs, an annual essay competition and riddle competitions. The Head of English, (who is also the Deputy

Head) Peter Nixon, regularly collects together samples of the children's creative work to produce an anthology with a series title 'Impressions'. This is his introduction to the latest edition:

> A number of the pieces included in these five anthologies have won prizes in local and national competitions. Kit Glennie and Catherine Gluckman were runners up in the Simon Elvin Young Poet of the Year Competition run by the Poetry Society, in 2000. In 2001 Bryony Nicholls was one of six winners, out of 7,000 entries in the 'Write Away' Competition run by the Times Educational Supplement in conjunction with the National Association for the Teaching of English.
>
> Several St Michael's pupils have gained prizes in the SATIPS Prep Schools Poetry Competition each year and in 2001 Imogen Crockford won the top prize in the Sevenoaks Schools Poetry Competition, as well as being the first winner in the newly inaugurated Old Michaelian's Essay Trophy.

The English Department arranges frequent visits to the theatre and to other venues in connection with the children's studies. Both the main school and the pre-prep have benefited from visits from authors and poets who keep children enthralled with their participative workshops. The children have participated in 'readathons' and 'spellathons' to raise money for charity and annually dress up as their favourite book character to celebrate World Book Day.

## Languages

The Languages Department also arranges outings and events to supplement the classroom learning. Year 6 enjoy a day trip to France and in Year 7 a five day trip is organised where the children stay in a chateau and visit a local bakery and goat farm as well as participating in other activities. The Department has held a French evening where the children and the staff performed songs, poems and plays and the catering staff have treated the children to various national food days where they have the opportunity to taste national specialities and learn the names of foreign food. There is even a 'Fun French Club' held weekly after school.

*'I encourage the children to speak to me in French whenever they see me around the school so that it becomes second nature to them.'*

**September Chappelle-Edwards (Head of Languages)**

Latin is still taught to the top sets in Years 7 and 8.

*'When I was a new boy aged 11 with no knowledge of Latin I was nevertheless asked to read a paragraph from Caesar's Gallic Wars in the original language. I did not understand the amusement caused by my pronunciation of "Titus" as "Tittus". I do now.*

**Paul Barraclough 1935/38**

## History and Geography

The history department keeps its pupils enthused with a variety of expeditions to local historical sites and even holds re-enactments of battles for the older children. One of the most popular

events is the annual Greek and Egyptian Party where children are encouraged to dress up appropriately and provide authentic food for the picnic.

The extensive grounds at St Michael's provide a wonderful learning environment for the children who study such topics as map-making and the weather; and geography field trips widen the children's understanding of the world we live in.

Year 5 making active volcanoes with Mrs Carol Bent

## Sciences

The founder of St Michael's took his degree in Science and possessed his own laboratory. He loved carrying out experiments and in his last years was injured by an explosion which he had inadvertently caused. He would no doubt have approved greatly of the new science laboratories,

which have recently been completed as part of a major expansion at the school. The Science Department now has the highest quality equipment and boasts interactive whiteboards, projectors, and flat screen computers.

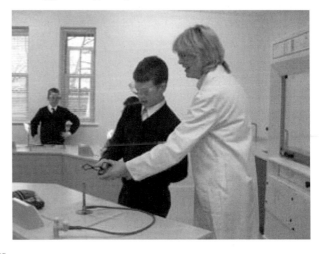

Mrs Jane Priestly (Head of Science) is very proud of the science facilities available to her pupils and makes full use of the new technology.

Competitions and challenges are regularly organised for the children and have included making the strongest bridge out of newspaper, designing a hot air balloon and devising mechanical toys.

Each year a Science Week is held and a variety of activities are organised for the children. Visitors to the school during these weeks have included 'The Bug Man' who not only encouraged children to hold creepy-crawlies but he persuaded a few brave souls to eat some!

## Maths

The emphasis on the teaching of maths at St Michael's is on mental agility and every lesson begins with exercises to improve these skills. House maths competitions are regularly held and the school has battled against others in inter-school maths challenges.

## Art and Design Technology

Trips to the art galleries in London are the highlight of the art year but the children also enjoy working towards an annual art exhibition. An advanced art after-school activity encourages enthusiasts to take their skills further. In 2001 Robert Malan won the school's first art scholarship to Sevenoaks School.

The subject of Technology is in its infancy at St Michael's but pupils are currently enjoying making models, using graphics and learning about robotics.

## Information and Communication Technology (ICT)

Children have regular access to computers by the age of four, weekly lessons in the main computers room from the age of six and learn to touch type by the age of eight.

Lessons for older pupils include word-processing, use of graphics, desk-top publishing, spreadsheets, mail merges, use of emails and, of course, the internet.

# School Prizes

The school rewards effort and achievement with termly and annual prizes. There are subject prizes, form prizes, sporting prizes and behaviour prizes. Dr Peter Roots was particularly keen to reward the children and offered several of his more unusual possessions as prizes to inspire the children including a Viking helmet and a Trojan shield.

This account in the logbooks [transcribed by Old Michaelian Paul Barraclough] so impressed past Headmaster Dr Peter Roots that he introduced a new annual prize to the pupil who showed the greatest achievement in the face of adversity:

**9 November 1918:** Philip Bayfield, I regret to say was today taken to the Hospital. It appears that a boy (R. Huskinson) threw a pen at one of the lockers as a target. Philip was doing his lessons at a table and the pen struck him in the eye. This took place on Sunday night. The boys have been constantly warned of the danger incurred by throwing things about. This accident has grieved me very much. Philip has been a most assiduous worker in preparation for the forthcoming exam. I do not yet know the extent of the injury but from the report I have received I am afraid it is very serious.

**22 November 1918:** Today I have learned that Philip Bayfield's right eye has had to be removed - a very sad and regrettable happening.

**29 November 1918:** I called up at the Hospital and saw Philip Bayfield who is making good progress.

**6 December 1918:** Philip Bayfield has returned to school. He will sit for his Exam: next week although influenza and the loss of an eye have severely handicapped him.

**3 February 1919:** Last week the result of the Camb: U. Local Prelim: Exam: was received. Philip Bayfield has obtained Honours and Allan Wakeford, Leslie Lorton, Henry Clifford & Noel Kennedy qualified for certificates - a very satisfactory result indeed. The Revd Mother gave a supper to the successful candidates at which I attended! A Holiday to the whole school was also given yesterday by the desire of the Revd Father. We had no failures.

# ~ 22 ~

## Unsung Hero - Michael Hatton

*'St Michael's School could not function without all the staff, both teaching and non-teaching, working together. The support of the ancillary staff, in the School Office, Canteen and Grounds, has been vitally important in helping to create a smoothly running, well-knit community.'*
**Keith Crombie, Headmaster from 2003**

There is, however, an unsung hero who stands out head and shoulders above all the rest and it is appropriate to finish the book with a chapter dedicated to this admirable character.

'**Michael Hatton** joined St Michael's as a boy in the early 1930s. As for many other boys at that time St Michael's provided a refuge from a difficult family situation. For more than 65 years the school community was his home. He soon became a special part of that community.

Michael was always a very humble man. He was most happy when serving quietly, especially when this involved preparation for Christian worship in the school's chapel. For most of his life he lived in a tiny room in the upper part of the school, walking down the corridor each morning to a Victorian washroom. His day then focussed on the Christian life of St Michael's.

The villages of Kemsing and Otford would hear the school's Angelus Bell sounding across the valley three times a day for over sixty years, rung dutifully and expertly by Michael Hatton.

The chapel was Michael's real home. Arriving at the school soon after the death of

Father Tooth, Michael made it his special responsibility to care for the chapel and help maintain its practices in the Anglo-Catholic tradition. However, Michael's was not a Christianity of chapel worship only. His service was both to God and to his fellow man. In particular, he was a friend to the hundreds of children who studied and, for many years, lived at the school. At first he was an older brother to pupils then an uncle, and then a favourite grandfather. It will be no surprise to anyone who knew Michael that he regularly received more post than the rest of the school put together, especially at Christmas.

In old age one thing worried Michael - that he might have to leave his beloved home and chapel if he was no longer able to live independently. When he went into hospital his stay was a brief one. There were only twelve days between when Michael was caring for the school normally and the day when he passed away. From hospital he wrote to a cousin: "I wish now either to go home or to go to eternity". God granted his wish and Michael passed away peacefully on the morning of Tuesday 27th January. He has gone home, to God.'

**Dr Peter Roots in the St Michael's News. Friday 30th January 1998**

## Extracts from the funeral address by Revd Paul Cox [Headmaster 1981-1990]

'My first visual memory of Michael was whilst I was having tea with Donald Cormack on my first visit to the School. I have the picture of a blue cardigan shuffling with a tea pot towards what was then called "Piggy Table" and then retiring until later that evening when he came into what is now the Headmaster's study with a saucepan of soup. It may well have been that an early job description for Michael was a 'kitchen porter' but we all know that his heart and soul were in the very central place of the school — the chapel.

Through Michael I would be introduced to former boys when they came to visit. No one came to St Michael's without making sure they saw Michael. There was always a welcome, a cup of tea, a friendly wry smile, a laugh and a joke and a concern about how the other person was doing. And not just the old boy, but also his family and other siblings.

There are so many things that were special about Michael which we all could see in him and which he never saw in himself. It is a comment on his openness, warmth and loving involvement with those he met and came to know that I am sure that many of you, if not all, feel that he is special to you personally; that your particular relationship with him was extra.'

*'Plenty can be said about Michael Hatton. Seemingly he had the intention of becoming a priest, but for reasons I don't know this came to nothing. When I was very small I remember his covertly dispensing a few sweets to grateful recipients. He was away for the war (as, of course, was Donald Cormack), but for most of his working life he kept the place clean and gave all sorts of assistance. It was a dedicated existence. He knew all the boys; most went to see him when they came back. For very many years he sent a card for my birthday and Beccles, Bungay, Dunmow and the Essex churches were always close to his heart.'*

**Roy Haines 1932/38**

*'Michael was always singing and sliding along the corridors rushing from one place to another putting something right. He had a grand sense of humour. He never seemed to complain about all the work he had to do. He was good company if ever you were helping him. He used that "pull & push" heavy floor polisher and the chapel always looked immaculately clean. The chairs would slide forward with ease! Michael did the flowers around the school, many of which came from the grounds.'*

**David Sharpless 1951-57**

*'Michael Hatton was a good friend to me while I was at St Michael's. We would always cook each other a late night meal in the kitchens after our evening's off-duty. Michael told me many tales of times with the nuns, and he would describe the kitchen garden in days gone by, when it grew all the vegetables for the school's use and the tunnels of flowering roses growing over the pathways.'*

**John Jennings – Housemaster and Head of History 1990/93**

Dear Michael

Please, Please,

Be Happy in Heaven.

May God be kind and look after you

As you were kind and looked after us.

We love you Michael

And we shall miss you.

**Year 3 children 1998**

Daily, the school reminds the pupils of the unique contribution Michael Hatton made to St Michael's as they sit on the terrace benches inscribed with his dedication. On an even more poignant note, the Michael Hatton prize is awarded annually to the pupil who has given the greatest service to the school through the year. The worthy recipient in 2003 was thirteen year old Yasmin St Clair-Pearce.

No-one better epitomises the spirit of St Michael's School. Michael Hatton was passionately interested in people and places with a real love of learning things new. He saw the beauty in everything and everybody and judged no one. He was dedicated to the school – its spirit and its faith and was always willing to put himself out for others. He was happy and comfortable in his surroundings, was loath to leave but excited about the place he was moving on to.

St Michael's School today strives to instil the same values and strengths in all its pupils – and is, by all accounts, succeeding.

# Appendices

## Wardens and Headmasters

| Warden | Headmaster |
|---|---|
| **Father Arthur Tooth**<br><br>1872 - 1931 | **Frederick N Wareham**<br><br>1872 - 1916 |
| | **Charles Manning Jaggard**<br><br>1916 - 1932 |
| **Father Charles Harcourt Blofeld**<br><br>1931 - 1938 | **Michael Cork**<br><br>1932 - 1941 |
| **Father Thomas Guest Blofeld**<br><br>1939 – 1964 ||
| **Donald Hope Cormack**<br><br>1964 - 1981 ||
| **Revd Paul Cox** 1981 - 1990 ||
| **Simon Cummins** 1990 - 1996 ||
| **Dr Peter Roots** 1996 - 2002 ||
| **Frank Skipwith** 2002 – 2003 (Interim Headmaster) ||
| **Keith Crombie** 2003 - ||

# St Michael's Governors 2003

Gordon Owen – Chairman of the Governors

Sue Cooper
J Martin Hammond
Alex Glennister
Gillian Swaine
John Underwood

# St Michael's Staff List September 2003

**Headmaster**
Keith Crombie
**Deputy Head**
Peter Nixon – Head of English
**Head of Pre-Prep**
Vanda Marchetti
**Director of Studies**
Sarah Bridgman
**Senior Mistress**
Jane Priestley – Head of Science & Technology
**Director of Pupil Development**
Judith Yarnold
**Director of Physical and Sports Development/Senior Master**
Guy Drayton

**Main School Department**
Graham Arkley – Head of PE
Tabitha Barratt – Art
Carol Bent – Year 5
September Chapelle-Edwards – Head of Languages
Claire Dumper – Year 4
Darryl Edwards – Head of Art and Design Technology
Abby Lloyd – Year 3

Laura Comber – Head of History and Religious Education

Gaynor Bennion-Pedley – Head of Music

Fiona Drayton – Mathematics and Games

Revd Richard Freeman – Chaplain and Religious Education

Elaine Heath, Cert Ed – Year 3

Winn Inkson – Head of Latin

Gillian Long – Science

Saskia Lovett – Head of Girls' Games

Ruth Marx – Additional Educational Needs Co-ordinator

Karen McLaren – Year 4

Lyn Nixon – Lower School Co-ordinator

Catriona Pearson – Drama

Sheila Read – Year 6

Sue Rivett – Head of ICT

Duncan Sinclair – Head of Geography and PSHE

Louise Skelly – Year 6

Stephen Wade – Head of Mathematics

Antonia Watson – Pottery

Ray Willis – Games

**Peripatetic Special Needs**
Maureen Birkett

**Peripatetic Music**
Jo Chapman
Robert Connell
Peter De Croos
Sally Hitchcock
Adrian Petitclerc
Colin McCann
Rachael Laing
Janet Story
John Summers
Linda Payne

**Teaching Assistants and Learning Support Assistants**
Pat Davies
Sarah Godwin-Brown
Diana Gordon
Alex Jenkins
Louise Farrelly
Tegon Baines
Greg Scott

## Pre-Prep Department

### Nursery

Jocelyn Barton – Head of Nursery

Janet Clark

Annie Scarsi

Patricia Taylor

### Kindergarten

Theresa Hawkins

Elaine Martin – Head of Kindergarten

Sue Rowlands

Mary Webb

### Reception

Alex Jenkins – Classroom Assistant and SENCO Support

Vanda Marchetti – Class Teacher and Head of Pre-Prep

Paula Pallett – Class Teacher and Maths Co-ordinator

Eve Showell – Class Teacher and Science Co-ordinator

Rebecca Williams – Classroom Assistant and Trainee Teacher

### Year 1

Karen David – Class Teacher and Maths Co-ordinator

Amanda Farmer – Class Teacher and English Co-ordinator

Emma Sanderson – Teaching Assistant

Felicity Shipton – Class Teacher and Library

### Year 2

Andrea Kirkpatrick – Class Teacher, Director of Studies and Additional Needs Co-ordinator

Dorothy Clough – Class Teacher and Science Co-ordinator

### Music

Sally Beesley

### Physical Education

Liz Taplin

### Office

Pat Whiting

### Support Staff

### Bursar

Chris Young

### Registrar / Headmaster's Secretary

Jan Ayton

### Academic Secretary

Leigh Henderson

### Catering Manager

Wendy Halford

### Estate Staff

Tony Bailey

Tim Barber

Rob Webster

# School Hymns Ancient and Modern

Holy Michael, great Archangel,
Nerve thine arm and bare thy sword,
Lead us with thy dazzling legions,
In the battle for the Lord:
Sure defence and trusty safeguard,
Let thy mighty strength afford.

Not with flesh and blood we wrestle,
Not as man with man contend,
But against the powers of darkness,
Who on craft and lies depend:
Treachery and shame and violence,
All the cause of Hell befriend.

Through GOD'S threefold fair creation,
Through the earth, the sea, the sky,
Wander Satan's loathly spirits,
Luring souls of men to die:
Cast them down, O Prince of Angels,
By the Power of GOD most high.

All who pouring out their life blood,
More than conquer in the fight,
All who in the unequal combat,
Fall beneath the oppressor's might:
CHRIST the King's great Standard-bearer
Lead into the Holy Light.

**(Tune: Lights Abode Celestial Salem)**

**Father Richard Masheder**
**(reproduced by kind permission of Charles Masheder)**

Let there be love shared among us
Let there be love in our eyes
May now your love sweep this nation,
Cause us O Lord to arise,
Give us a fresh understanding
Of brotherly love that is real,
Let there be love shared among us,
Let there be love.

Extract taken from the song
"Let There Be Love Shared Among Us"
by Dave Bilbrough.
Copyright © 1979 Thankyou Music*

Let us be friends to the friendless,
Care for each one great and small,
Nourish the starved, help the homeless,
Pick up the weak when they fall,
Teach us to value you each other
And show everyone that we care
Let there be love shared among us,
Let there be love.

Let us see God in each other,
Show us the way we should live,
Seeking to help those in trouble,
Rather than take, let us give.
So that the earth may be radiant,
Reflecting His care everywhere,
Let there be love shared among us
Let there be love.

**Bridgit James (reproduced by kind permission)**